FOUR MAIN LINES

The Old Caley: West Coast express near Abington, Caledonian Railway, in 1882, headed by Benjamin Conner's 8 ft. 2 in. single No. 87

FOUR MAIN LINES

HAMILTON ELLIS

LONDON
GEORGE ALLEN AND UNWIN LTD
RUSKIN HOUSE MUSEUM STREET

PRINTED IN GREAT BRITAIN
in 11 point Baskerville type
AT THE UNIVERSITY PRESS
ABERDEEN

625

A PROPER historian, or author of technical and educational works, begins by stating why he wrote such a book, and for whom. But should one ? In the old Classical Fourth we had a little book of stories in Latin—all about Balbus and his wall, and Arion and the dolphin, and someone who was found without his head in Rameses' treasury. They were jolly, chatty stories, and made Latin translation almost tolerable. Then one day, when I was supposed to be preparing the story of Damocles, I read instead the reverend and learned author's preface. He fondly believed, poor man, that his book would suit the middle forms of preparatory schools. It was a horrid shock. I knew that the Classical Fourth was not quite the same as the History Sixth, but were we really the intellectual equals of nasty little kids in short pants ? So let me be careful about making the same mistake as did the author of *Fabulae Faciles*!

Since the British railways became BRITISH RAILWAYS, necessity has compelled us to consider their components separately. To say that you are travelling to Scotland by British Railways is simply to say that you are not going by road, sea or air. To say that you are travelling thither in the London Midland Region is ambiguous and still inadequate. You must specify West Coast or Midland. The Western Region now contains the Southern lines west of Exeter ; and the Wilts, Somerset and Weymouth, *inter alia*, has gone into the Southern Region. A murrain on your Regions ! So we come, once again, as in the days of yore, to think of the different main lines and branches as entities, and to call them by their old names. Further, we might perpetuate older, more particular names, such as Shrewsbury and Hereford, Somerset and Dorset, and Portsmouth Direct. How perfectly self-explanatory they are ! So are East Coast, West Coast, Great Western and South Western. So in all respect to our Railway Executive, let these concise and often very beautiful names survive !

The parts of the book that follows do not compose a standard text. I have tried rather to give miniature portraits of the lines concerned and of the trains that ran on them. With the third and fourth, the Great Western and the South Western, you may notice a more intimate approach, in places, than that given to the two giants preceding. They are not such long lines, and in each case, at least in later history, only one company was concerned at a time. I could therefore give less space to them than to the others. But would I ? Oh no, reader ! How could anyone do so, who had grown up on one of them with the other for a neighbour ? One seemed beautiful, in far-off days, and the other one funny, both endearing qualities. So if the dehydrated history of Great Northern, North Eastern, North British, and London and North Eastern be sometimes indigestible, if the pudding of West Coast constituents wax heavy, turn to the Great Western, and with it, your author's own *ghost train ;* turn to the South Western, and meet the baby who loved a T 9 ! For (let me risk it after all) this book has been written for those who love such things.

Many people have helped me in the making of it, and with illustrations. In particular, let me mention the interest and generosity of Messrs. A. R. Bell, Frank Box, C. R. Clinker, George Dow, and E. W. Twining. To Mr. D. MacAulay, late C.M.E. of the Bengal Assam and the Eastern Bengal Railways, I owe the certain knowledge that once there was a tartan engine on the North British Railway. Mr. Dow had suggested it, in *The First Railway over the Border.* In *Some Classic Locomotives*, I expressed doubts unworthy of a romantic. In token of my recantation, I have, with loving care, made this prodigy the subject of Plate III, *The Royal Crampton*, in the book now presented.

CONTENTS

ILLUSTRATIONS

IN COLOUR FROM THE AUTHOR'S OIL PAINTINGS

and 70 half-tone reproductions
of photographs
as insets between pages
60 and 61, 108 and 109, 172 and 173

A GOOD many years ago, the Publicity Department of the Crown Colony of Bermuda, in showing reason why people should make holiday or retire there, proudly claimed that the isle was *untrammelled by railways*. One could settle down there (given indispensable private means) with a pony and a nice little equipage, contemplate the coral strand, keep a pet iguana, and live happily ever after without seeing anything remotely resembling a train.

But why? Places fairly remote from a railway were one proposition. One could be very happy for a while in further Sutherland or Wester Ross, where a ride of forty odd miles, in a motor van that always made the girls very sick, was yet rewarded by the glorious spectacle of the night mail from the south rolling into Lairg, perhaps a couple of hours or so behind time, headed by *Ben Clebrig* and *Skibo Castle* in superb tandem. But quite another thing was an island home where the nearest railway was, apparently, the Norfolk and Western in Virginia, about 800 miles away across a desert of blue water and drifting Sargasso weed. In the end, even Bermuda thought twice about being untrammelled, and built a dainty little line worked by motor trains.

What a lovely thing is a railway! Just as there is beauty in the Pool and the docks of London; in the tamed and disciplined Clyde with its great shipyards; yea, in the sadly filthy Tyne, so is there a grim splendour in even the gloomiest railway station. It is hard to imagine less promising spots than the stations of Crewe, or Willesden Junction, or Glasgow Queen Street, yet how grand are these places in their smoke-shrouded life! It is almost physically impossible to build a really ugly ship*—the tanker *Delphinula*, if she is still afloat under another name, might come near qualifying —and so it is with the most gaunt and uncouth locomotives (really frightful ones such as one sees loafing across the Hungarian Plain or creaking southwards through the Vale of Tempe). They remain creations most superb.

A century and more ago, those who loved their England were often desolated at the searing wounds which the new railway companies were inflicting on her fair face. Where once had been pleasant prospects, now stood gigantic viaducts; where formerly

---

* Always excepting aircraft-carriers.

had been gracious curves, now stretched an abominable straight line in all its outrageous newness. Though the beholders knew it not, it was the novelty and the rawness of the great new railways that chiefly offended.

A day-old baby is beautiful only to its mother ; a house just finished, unfurnished, untenanted, standing straight up and down in its arid plot, is a desert place ; and Corfe Castle, on the day when the robber baron first tested the portcullis, must have been the biggest abomination in the south of England. Being suddenly confronted, today, with a new airfield, or an arterial road in all the bald indecency of its imperishable white concrete, gives us some idea of the impact of the rail on the eye of the early Victorian aesthete.

But the country, the great mother country, gentled the condition of her gawky new child. The filth and the squalor of the navvy towns became part of the earth that had suffered them ; wild things came to riot over the great embankments and cuttings which had lately seemed such incurable wounds ; Reynard the Fox contemplated the rushing engine and quickly invented a new and wonderful way of defeating his pursuers and also killing half the pack. A century later, in rural Sussex, he was likewise to discover the glorious defensive possibilities of the electric conductor rail. Then, slowly, men perceived that there was a grand beauty in such things as the Royal Border Bridge and the Ouse Valley Viaduct, and that it was not really necessary to disguise them with towers and battlements, as at Conway, or to hide the shining rail altogether beneath a needless tunnel, as at Patcham and some other places.

Trouble was taken with the trains themselves. Charles Beyer,* an immigrant Saxon engineer, did more than any to instil a tradition of beauty in British locomotive engineering; his pioneer standard designs for Sharp, Roberts and Company in the late 'thirties and 'forties of last century were works of great art. Beyer was the Bach of locomotive engineering. Such successive designers as Alexander Allan, Patrick Stirling and William Stroudley, as William Dean, G. J. Churchward and Nigel Gresley, carried on that tradition. The spectacle of their engines, racing across country, proudly plumed in white, was one that few could resist.

So it came about that what had seemed scars on the country's face strengthened that same face, giving it a new splendour and dignity. It was the most important thing of its kind since the great abbeys and churches had come to dominate the squalid towns and unkempt English landscape of the Middle Ages.

* Founder, with Richard Peacock, of the famous Manchester firm.

It was natural that those steeped in one set of traditions could not always see this new beauty. To Ruskin, the railway remained an abomination to the end, and he described it as such, in picturesque language.* William Morris perceived little if any of the magic of a night journey from King's Cross to Edinburgh,† though he enjoyed the views afforded by the North British Railway between Berwick and Dunbar, where Ruskin would have been too busy grumbling about the smoke.

Dickens seems to have been the first eminent English author to have marked the grandeur of the railway, though to him its beauty was always rather overseasoned by terror. The rail came in very usefully for killing Mr. Carker at the end of *Dombey and Son* (the scene is guessed to have been Paddock Wood on the South Eastern, and I like to imagine a Crampton engine doing the job). That same South Eastern Railway came very near to killing Dickens himself when he was in the Staplehurst smash of June 9, 1865. The accident profoundly disturbed his nerves, and five years after it, to the day, he died. Dickens loved travel, but he had not that love for the railway which he would have enjoyed had he known it from childhood. Even so, he knew the delights of going down to Dover on a locomotive, of his own headlong advance on Abbot's Cliff Tunnel, with the great wall of chalk towering above the tall chimney and brass dome before him.

Later authors dealt more sympathetically with the rail, yet still they touched but lightly on its intrinsic beauty, and only in our own times, when the Almighty Motor has bred monstrous spawn,‡ when the railway itself is in the toils of change, is that beauty coming to be acknowledged by those whose fathers saw only what it spoiled. They, the turgid, Philistine *They*, who *said* things in Lear's limericks, thought Whistler eccentric when he painted London River. Yet when Brangwyn immortalised Cannon Street Station, most Plutonian of London terminals, *they* began to admire. Long ago Wordsworth, who had written a good poem deploring the very modest advent of the rail in his beloved Lake Country, forgave the new industry and wrote a new poem, not so good, welcoming it to the lands of Furness. It was left to W. H. Auden to give us the glorious rant of *This is the Night Mail crossing the Border*.

* " There was never more flagrant nor impertinent folly than the smallest portion of ornament in anything concerned with railways or near them . . . the whole system of railway travelling is addressed to people who, being in a hurry, are therefore, for the time being, miserable."

† *Journal of Travel in Iceland*, 1871.

‡ Your author humbly believes that he knows just how Ruskin felt.

Yes, the railway, ignored in the days of its monopoly save as a mere conveyance, hated by poets as a disturber of immemorial solitudes, has come to be loved at last, not only by children and the faithful few, but by many who have an eye for that which is noble and beautiful to behold. Neither the levelling of State monopoly, nor the dead hand of standardisation, nor the clay feet of popularity, nor even the disgusting dirt and neglect which belong to modern economy, can take away that nobility.

A thing worthy of remark, before closing this introduction, is the influence of the railway on social distribution. Migrant families during the past hundred years flocked into the cities along the new lines of railway. The southward surge came first along the lines of the London and North Western and the Midland, so that one finds the speech and the manners of North and Midlands well south of the Trent. Luton is about the same distance out of London as Tunbridge Wells, yet Luton is a peculiarly Midland town; the two places might be a couple of hundred miles apart. The thing invades the very London suburbs. There are scarcely subtle differences between Muswell Hill and Sydenham Hill, between Hornsey and New Cross, and for these differences we may thank, respectively, the Great Northern and the London, Brighton and South Coast.

This is a brief story of four main lines. Of these, the West Coast, the Great Western and the South Western were the first main lines out of London, and the fourth, the East Coast, was the challenger of the first-named. The original and succeeding companies have gone, now, but the four main lines remain among many others, individual as four great rivers, having made as household words the names of Euston, Paddington, Waterloo and King's Cross.

PART ONE

CHAPTER ONE

Euston

SUPERB in its grime, Euston's Doric portico challenges the London skies, proudly now as when it gave entry to the first and only main-line railway out of London. It has been praised by its contemporary post-Regency admirers, decried by Victorian Goths, condemned by Neo-Georgian Vandals, praised again by the Georgian Group, and reprieved by that very London Midland and Scottish Railway which had sentenced it to oblivion between the wars. No thanks to the L.M.S. for that, either. Someone said that when the L.M.S. was formed in 1923, it didn't deserve to get Euston.

One can construe that either way, of course. By reason of its having grown up haphazard, in confined spaces, in the course of the nineteenth century, Euston became, from the passengers' point of view, one of the most inconvenient and bewildering terminal stations in London, a rival of London Bridge, beating Liverpool Street hollow, and exceeded in chaotics only by the old Waterloo. Nor is it a station likely to be loved by either the traffic or the locomotive departments. It is a station tumbled all over a narrow place like a drunk in a gutter, lying appropriately over against a bottleneck at the foot of a steep hill. One can take more time getting from Chalk Farm to Euston than one has previously taken to get from Watford Junction to Chalk Farm.

At intervals down the years, trains have charged the buffer-stops after a too-optimistic descent of the Camden Bank, and once in a while they have violently hit each other in the cramped and dreary tunnel outside. But against these things there has been much to admire. Philip Hardwick's portico and pavilions are among the architectural gems of England, and the Great Hall is without peer. It is less terrific than the upper concourse of the Grand Central Terminal in New York, with its golden clock and its celestial ceiling with the stars all in reverse. It is less absolutely magnificent than the marble clerestoried hall of the Pennsylvania Station there. It is cold and severe beside the chandeliered hall of Copenhagen. Yet architecturally it soars above even the last-named. Not least of its merits is the element of surprise in its approach through those unobtrusive swing doors.

Have its heirs ever been worthy of it? The London and North Western at one time put in one corner the meanest type of Victorian railway bar, all lavatory-marble and puffing-billy tea urns, but that was nothing to what the L.M.S. did, when, in 1930, an inquiry booth was stuck up in the middle, blotting out the view down the hall to the great staircase, giving at one dastardly swoop the impression of a Brobdingnagian funeral parlour, with George Stephenson's great statue meditating before the catafalque.

Your present author once suggested the enthroning of the historic locomotive *Hardwicke* in the middle of Euston Great Hall, a notion which he now publicly regrets as an offence against the fitness of things, but even that would have been a sight better than actuality. If our Railway Executive, of which we are so proud, reprieves the Great Hall as well as the Doric portico, that will be one up to it, and against that private enterprise which it has succeeded.

Euston Station is very much a part of London, indeed, it is in some ways a microcosm of London, with its shapelessness and its business, its squalor and its grandeur, its beauty and its ugliness; even the treatment of the Great Hall has a close affinity to the sort of things that happen, when patriotism and political expediency demand, to Trafalgar Square. Yet at the same time it is characteristic of that which it serves, and of which it is also a part, the great West Coast Route to the north and to Scotland, with, too, the Royal Mail Route to Ireland via Holyhead. In the most normal of times, its halls and platforms and passages have always been filled, not only with the pungent speech of Cockaigne, not only with the tongues of Lancashire and Cheshire and the Midlands, but with the braid Scots of Carrick and Clydesdale, the clipped Scots of Glasgow, the burr of the far north-east, and the soft English of the Highlands; with the beautiful brogue of Dublin and the less beautiful brogue of Belfast; with both the English and the Welsh of Wild Wales, the Gaelic in its several kinds, and the Polish and Ukrainian of immigrants from Eastern Europe to Canada.

Euston is old; older than most other railway stations of the world. A century ago, Waterloo had recently been opened and Paddington did not yet exist on its present site. But Euston was there. It had been there for more than a decade, and was junior only to London Bridge, down in the Borough. For all that, it was not at first intended that the London and Birmingham Railway, as it was in the beginning, should penetrate as far into London as Euston Square. Chalk Farm had been one of the city's duelling grounds, safely beyond the suburbs, and there, as first planned, the railway terminus was to be kept—in its place.

The London and Birmingham Railway Company and the Grand Junction Railway, the latter linking Birmingham with the Liverpool and Manchester Railway at Warrington, were both incorporated on May 6, 1833. The extension of the L. and B. to Euston Square was not authorised until July 3, 1835. The Grand Junction was opened throughout, across quite easy country, on July 4, 1837. The London and Birmingham, as we shall see, was a tougher job, and was not completed until September 17, 1838, having been open in parts since June 27, 1837.*

Euston, as it was then, contained four roads, covered by a two-span roof of iron and glass. The departure platform or " stage " was on the west side, and the arrival on the east. Both had cab drives, that for departures leading straight in through the portico. The four tracks were connected by turnplates, each sufficient for one of the small four-wheel carriages of the period; there was a set at each end of the station, and one intermediate set. The northern set of turnplates led to a carriage shed on the east side.

This was the Euston of Mr. Osborne of the descriptive railway guides, the gentleman whose zoology was not as good as his garrulity, for he likened the puffing locomotive to a sea-horse. This was also the Euston of Dickens, for while the South Eastern Railway may have provided that fine bloody scene in the end of *Dombey and Son*, it was Euston that, in the earlier chapters, exemplified the coming of the railway with all its changes to the great, self-satisfied metropolis. First there was the upheaval, the digging and piling up of great cuttings and embankments, the propping up of tottering houses, the " Babel towers of chimneys, wanting half their height " which belonged to the stationary engines at the top of Camden Bank. Then came Euston in all its magnificence: " Where the old rotten summer-houses once had stood, palaces now reared their heads, and granite columns of gigantic girth opened a vista to the railway world beyond." So the scene was set for Mr. Dombey and Major Bagstock to make their journey to Leamington (apparently the cable system was not yet in operation when they made it, or Fireman Toodles would not have been on the platform). Euston was ready for all the other Dombeys and Bagstocks, and the Forsytes and the Herries who would come after

* Public opening, July 20.

them. It was the greatest new landmark to come to London since the city had risen out of its ashes and Wren had given it St. Paul's, more significant than Buckingham Palace, more in people's minds than Somerset House.

The two platforms which are now Nos. 9 and 10 were added on the west side, on land already owned by the company, to handle traffic brought to Euston by the opening, in 1840, of the Midland Counties Railway to a junction with the London and Birmingham at Rugby (Dickens' *Mugby Junction*). To this day, No. 9 is known as the York. In 1846, when the L.N.W.R. was formed by amalgamation of the London and Birmingham and Manchester and Birmingham with the Grand Junction (which had already absorbed the Liverpool and Manchester), the central block of offices was begun and with it the Great Hall, completed in the following year, again by Hardwick. The Hall's flat panelled ceiling, based on that of St. Paul Without the Walls in Rome, was, and still is, the largest of its kind in the world; the only one comparable to it in England is in Buckingham Palace. A later intention to decorate the great walls with frescoes by G. F. Watts was not carried out—perhaps fortunately. Euston Great Hall is 128 ft. long by 62 ft. wide, and the ceiling is 64 ft. above the pavement. Above and beyond the grand staircase are the boardroom and the shareholders' room, the latter a noble apartment where, in later days, the London, Midland and Scottish Railway held its annual general meetings. Writing a little wistfully, as one who reported many of those merry gatherings (though it was at a London and North Eastern meeting that a lady called the chairman an old kangaroo), let me recall that the lighting of the L.M.S. shareholders' room was very much to the advantage of the directors and officers. If the shareholders looked too long at their Board, they were very properly dazzled by the dayspring from on high. In earlier years, the meetings were held in the Great Hall, where, if they felt inclined, the assembly could relieve their feelings by hurling their copies of the London and North Western Annual Report at the impassive figure of George Stephenson. The erection of the Thing in the middle of the hall made this no longer possible.

Other milestones in the history of Euston: In the winter of 1839-40 were completed the original block of the Euston Hotel, south-east of the portico, and a dormitory block, known at the time as Victoria, to the south-west. The former was one of the first railway-owned hotels in the world. In July, 1881, the two blocks were joined, with an arch below for road traffic, greatly increasing the capacity of the hotel, but spoiling the very fine view of the portico from the Euston Road. In 1941 the part which had once been the Victoria dormitories was severely damaged by enemy bombing. The station was originally named, in the Act authorising the extension of the line from Chalk Farm, " Euston Grove ", but " Euston Square " was the title generally employed in Mid-Victorian years. In 1870 the simple name " Euston " was cut, and gilded, on the portico.

During 1871-3 the present arrival platforms were built, with the cab bridge from Seymour Street (renamed Eversholt Street in 1933), and the original roofing was raised 6 feet. This drastic operation was carried out within a week, every pillar being jacked up and a new pedestal put in underneath. The long departure platforms on the west side were built during 1887-92, and during this time the wooden island platform, now serving electric suburban trains, was put in below the ancient roof on the east side.

As is well known, the steep incline from Euston to Camden Town, the gradient of which was aggravated by the need for crossing over the Regent's Canal at the top, was regarded for some years as unsuitable for locomotive traction, and it was arranged for working by two Maudslay 60 h.p. stationary steam engines (one to be held in reserve), working an endless rope 4,780 yd. long and 3 in. thick. This installation was not ready until October 14, 1837, and in the meantime the trains were locomotive-hauled, being banked up the incline by a " powerful engine " hired from Robert Stephenson and Company. It was probably a 0-6-0 variety of the Patentee type, of that firm's standard design of the period. The bank would have been beyond the unassisted powers of the little engines built by Edward Bury for the London and Birmingham line in its earlier days.

Nearly a mile long, with a ruling gradient of 1 in 70, the *inclined plane* from Euston to Camden was a fearsome thing in those days, though it seems to have caused much less alarm amongst the general public than such bogeys as Primrose Hill and other tunnels, which many expected to be lethal, or at least liable to shorten one's life. It had quadruple track from its opening, as it was originally intended that the Great Western Railway also should terminate at " Euston Grove ". Down trains were shunted out by horse and hand, and attached to the rope. Incoming trains tobogganed solemnly down at an absolute maximum of 10 m.p.h., in the charge of special brakesmen. Their advent was announced by a siren, connected by an air pipe with the top of the incline, and producing, in action, " a low, melancholic moaning ". On July 25, 1837, an attempt was made to replace this cheerful appliance with Cooke and Wheatstone's new electric telegraph, but the latter, in its infancy, failed to function efficiently, and Wailing Willie was reprieved.

On June 27, 1837, the day of formal opening, fortunately before the public was admitted, the first up train ran away on the incline. The brakesman in charge, Kirkup, who had come from the Stockton and Darlington Railway, turned his brake-handle the wrong way (which would have been the right way on the S. and D.), and the train went through the buffers at Euston and " crashed into the wall of the ' receiving house ' which thus lived up to its name in an unexpected way ".* Cable operation lasted on the Camden Bank until July, 1844.

Over on the up side at Camden Town was the old locomotive shed where Edward Bury's little four-wheel engines with their bar frames and haycock fireboxes were stabled for many years, challenged only by such occasional prodigies as Crampton's magnificently troublesome *London* and *Liverpool*, which came, conquered, and then mysteriously vanished into the limbo of all machinery that is before its time. Mr. Bury provided motive power by contract, and saw no reason why a locomotive should be bigger than it ought to be. This led to double-heading, and, eventually, a chronic unpunctuality. At last the exasperated company requested Bury to provide something competent to deal with the rapidly increasing weight of the trains, or else go. He went.

The roundhouse of 1847 still exists, being used as a warehouse, and the tradition of " Camden Loco." has remained unbroken from earliest times to the present, that of the oldest locomotive depot in London. For many years the sheds have been on the down side. They have known many locomotives—Problems, Jumbos, Cauliflowers, Webb compounds, Precursors, Georges, Experiments, Princes and Claughtons, good engines and bad, but all characteristic of the London and North Western's great and usually noisy family. The din of a Jumbo coming up Camden Bank on a hot summer night with a heavy train, spouting her cinders high into the still air, was unforgettable.

We seem to be getting in advance of our story. It is not possible to chronicle the vast changes that have come over Euston in modern times, for they haven't, yet. The station remains much as it was in the 'seventies, and I, for one, am glad, though nobody would be sorry if some of the lavatories looked a little less like the interior of the Parkes Museum. At the functional other-side the dining-

* Supplement to *The Railway Gazette*, September 16, 1938.

room has somehow a greater dignity and a more complete tranquillity than any other railway restaurant in the country; its good dinners will be fondly remembered for long years to come.

The station has been under sentence more than once. Late in 1899, it was planned to bring the frontage forward to Euston Square, with a vast and entirely new station behind it. Before the outbreak of war in 1939, the London, Midland and Scottish was well away with a generally similar plan, and on July 12, 1938, the late Lord Stamp, sitting in the shareholders' room, turned a switch which closed a circuit and blasted out some 100,000 tons of limestone far away in the Caldon Low Quarries, providing raw material for the new station. Sir Francis Joseph, one of the L.M.S. directors, selected a choice block, which was to be made into the foundation stone. The war came, the bombs came; Lord Stamp, who had said he would never forsake his Victorian house in Beckenham until he was blown out of it, was fatefully taken at his word. But old Euston stood fast as Craigellachie.

CHAPTER TWO

The Road to Merrie Carlisle

WHEN Robert Stephenson undertook the survey and planning of the London and Birmingham Railway, he designed a line that was to be and to remain second to none in the world. Magnificent grading, easy curves, and everything in the grand manner—it was a bulldog among railways, but, as with the bulldog, its whelping was not easy. Its superb profile was at the expense of very heavy earthworks, and of tunnelling on a scale that daunted. London's own metropolitan prodigy on the new railway was the tunnel under Primrose Hill, originally a single bore for two tracks, with a length of 1,164 yd. The spoil dug out of the hill was used for the embankment at Camden Town, and, in order that the beauty and dignity beginning with Euston's portico should be perpetuated, the southern end was embellished with an Italian style portal by W. H. Budden. All proud and white it rose, in the freshness of unsullied stone, and thither, to the adjoining slopes, young Harry brought his Selina of a Saturday evening, and Mamma would bring her numerous children, to watch the noble progress of the Birmingham trains in the intervals of dalliance or picnic. They are gone, and nobody would select such a spot for a picnic as this is today, but Budden's portal is still there, under the honourable grime of a century and more.

How quickly the line reached the open country, even the deep country, in the old days ! Far out was Harrow Hill with its school, lapped in rural calm, and to this day the green fields stretch from hill to railway by Harrow. To this day, also, we see in passing the two old weather vanes at Bushey and Watford, the one in the form of a Stephenson locomotive, and the other a Bury. At Watford there was the chalk to be pierced, treacherous chalk split by veins of sand and gravel, one of which came pouring through a fissure during excavation and killed ten men in the workings. But the tunnel was built on time, and the trains which had previously plunged into the Italianesque front of Primrose Hill now hurled themselves into the northern chalk under a severely classical pediment.

Beyond were heavy earthworks: Tring Cutting—the great embankment, the longest on the line, with its viaduct across the Ouse Valley near Wolverton—Roade Cutting through hard rock, 1½ miles long, 65 ft. deep. The Ouse Viaduct is scarcely a peer of its great namesake on the Brighton main line, but it is a fine, handsome piece of work, for many years now widened for quadruple track, with six main elliptical arches of 60 ft. each and 46 ft. high to the crown. From Roade Cutting, a million cubic yards of rock and earth were removed, and the work cost £220,000, about double the estimate. On the great embankments, and in the earth cuttings such as that at Tring, horse-runs were used, whereby a horse trotting on level ground at the top towed each barrow, with the navvy holding on to it, up the steep plankway. It was a dangerously acrobatic performance, and there were numerous accidents, but a substitute in the form of a barrow lift was promptly wrecked by the irate navvies, who regarded it as part of a conspiracy to save time and wages.

Kilsby Tunnel was the great terror, and with its origin is associated that deathless tradition that the people of Northampton would not have the railway near them at any price, with the result that it had to be taken through the hills on its way to Rugby, a tradition later vehemently denied by Northampton patriots. Work was begun on Kilsby Tunnel. Two hundred yards from the southern entry, the optimistic contractor who had tendered for £99,000, encountered, under a blanket of clay 40 ft. thick, a quicksand which, it was estimated, stretched for 400 yd. along the course of the proposed tunnel. The contractor suffered a violent nervous breakdown. The London and Birmingham company relieved him of his obligation to complete the tunnel at that price, but the contractor was broken. He died.

Robert Stephenson undertook to finish the job for the company by direct labour, after several eminent engineers, called into consultation, had advised its abandonment. He installed engines and started pumping. After a while, several springs dried up, and wells went down in the vicinity, which, if it showed that the pumping had some effect, showed also that the quicksand extended over several square miles of underground country. The workings were being carried forward from the ends and from the intermediate shafts, and the brick lining was being put in, by twelve-foot lengths, as the excavation went on. A party working from one of the shafts, under Charles Lean, a junior assistant engineer, tapped the quicksand near the roof, and a deluge burst in on them. With the pumping engines going full speed, a gang of volunteers raced against the rising water to complete that section of the arch, working on a raft. They did so, crouching below the tunnel roof at the end, and Mr. Lean then jumped overboard with a tow rope, and swam with the raft to the working shaft, where the party was hoisted to grass overhead. The water rose up the shaft to its own level and the working was drowned out.

Kilsby now seemed such a hopeless proposition that the L. and B. directors were reluctantly inclined to abandonment. Stephenson implored more time, even a fortnight, and it was granted. With thirteen engines going, and delivering what then seemed the in-credible volume of 1,800 gallons a minute, the workings were cleared and kept clear of accumulating water. Kilsby Tunnel was completed in two years and a half from the laying of the first brick. There were 1,250 men and 200 horses on the job, and thirty-six million bricks were used, enough, as delighted con-temporary statisticians remarked, to make a yard-wide garden path from London to Aberdeen. Be it remembered that the job was done with primitive tools and slow reciprocating pumps, and that nothing like it had been encountered before.

So came Kilsby Tunnel, and so came the railway from London to Rugby, where Dr. Arnold welcomed it with a liberal enthusiasm unusual among headmasters of the eighteen-thirties. " I rejoice to see it ", he said, " and think that feudality is gone for ever. It is so great a blessing to think that any one evil is really extinct." Whether he would have rejoiced at a later practice of Rugbeians, that of walking through the tunnel without getting killed—or, more important, caught—is open to doubt. What a pity Tom Brown did not go to Rugby even five years later than he did ! With what gusto might he and Harry East have carved their names in two-foot capitals on the brickwork of the 130 ft. shaft ! But by that time, with the awful example of Master Flashman, and the sweet influence of the wretched Arthur, poor Tom had grown up into a rather goody-goody young man. He was in-sufferable at Oxford, and the British public then gave him the reception he deserved. Very sad, after that promising beginning with the school clock !

With the opening of Kilsby Tunnel there was ended that pre-posterous gap in the London and Birmingham main line, over which passengers had to be ferried by Chaplin and Horne's coaches between Denbigh Hall and Rugby. But the Denbigh Hall Inn is still there, over against the old railway bridge, providing rest and refreshment for those who drive by night the great motor lorries on Watling Street.

Summary: London to Boxmoor, opened July 20, 1837; Boxmoor to Tring, October 16, 1837; Tring to Denbigh Hall, and Birmingham, Curzon Street, to Rugby, April 9, 1838; Denbigh Hall to Rugby, September 17, 1838. The old Curzon Street station, a stately piece of late Georgian classical design, still stands, together with the hotel block subsequently added, though it has been the district goods manager's office for many years. The Grand Junction, be it noted, had been opened throughout since July 4, 1837. On the L. and B., Wolverton was chosen as a central station (" grand intermediate " would have been more properly descriptive). There engines were changed. There massive pork pies were consumed with brandy-and-water. When the L. and B.R. and the G.J.R.W.,* together with the Manchester and Birmingham Railway, were amalgamated to form the London and North Western, what had been the L. and B. became the L.N.W.R. Southern Division, and Wolverton went on just as before. Locomotives were built there until John Ramsbottom centralised all locomotive construction and heavy repair at Crewe in 1862.

It was in 1840 that the London and Birmingham and the Grand Junction first ran a direct Scottish service, and if it were not yet an all-rail route, it was at least all steam, taking $26\frac{1}{2}$ hours under good weather conditions, with 14 hours at sea. It was via Liverpool and Ardrossan, and was maintained by a steamer with the ominous name of *Fire King*. Glasgow was connected by rail to Ardrossan on August 12, and thus, what was to become the Glasgow and South Western Railway provided the West Coast Route with its first entry into Glasgow. The *Fire King* connected with the day mail trains between Euston and Liverpool.

But in May, 1841, the regular port of embarkation was shifted to Fleetwood, a new harbour established and named after Sir Hesketh Fleetwood. Its railway connections had been completed in the previous summer. Of these, the Wigan Branch Railway had been opened from Parkside, on the Liverpool and Manchester Railway, as far back as 1832. The Wigan and Preston Railway, amalgamated with the former as the North Union Railway, was opened on October 21, 1838, and on July 16, 1840, there had followed the Preston and Wyre Railway, providing the last link in a continuous line from London to Fleetwood via Birmingham and the L. and M. Junctions at Earlestown and Parkside. The direct cut-off between the old G.J. main line at Winwick Junction,

---

* These were officially the company's initials, for " Grand Junction Rail Way," and in old engravings of Grand Junction trains they appear on the engine tenders, one of the first examples of this afterwards widespread practice.

and Golborne Junction on the Wigan Branch, avoiding encroachment upon the Liverpool and Manchester line by passing under it, was not brought into operation until August 1, 1864, by which time through railway traffic from London to Edinburgh, Glasgow and Aberdeen had long been established.

Chronologically next comes the extension of the growing West Coast Route to Carlisle, but it is convenient first to deal with a very important cut-off which was made farther south, and that was the Trent Valley Line. Such a route was projected as far back as 1838, though the Grand Junction company, with an eye to its through traffic via Birmingham, regarded it sourly. It was not until 1845 that the Trent Valley Railway was incorporated, its line to run from Rugby, via Nuneaton, Tamworth and Rugeley to Stafford, enabling the main route to the North to avoid the congestion of the Black Country. The first sod was cut by Sir Robert Peel on November 13. Secretary to the new railway was Edward Watkin, later to become a formidable power in railway politics, full of jugglings with the Manchester, Sheffield and Lincolnshire, the Metropolitan and the South Eastern. The later history of this august rascal is no concern of the present book, but he showed promise even then, by negotiating the sale of the Trent Valley, in 1846, to the London and Birmingham Railway, just before the latter and the Grand Junction amalgamated to form the London and North Western. The L.N.W.R. opened the Trent Valley line on December 1, 1847.

To this day it remains a strongly individual line, for all the successive ownership of the North Western, the L.M.S. and the State. It takes you through some of the most gracious country in the Midlands, a country of stately views; far, far it seems from the smoky crescent embracing Birmingham, Dudley and Wolverhampton; a place of great seats, woods and parklands. Even the stations assumed a pseudo-Elizabethan guise, far removed from the severely classical Euston and Curzon Street, though akin to Bletchley. Where the line crossed part of Shugborough Park, south of Stafford, the Earl of Lichfield required that it should suitably harmonise. So the startled wanderer of today is confronted there with an underbridge carrying the West Coast main line over an inconsiderable road, yet embellished as the architect of a century ago thought fit for a nobleman's park, armorial bearings included, and Shugborough Tunnel's gloomy condition was enlivened at the northern end with towers, and battlements, and crenellations, and a Norman arch. Generations of enginemen have called the place the Gates of Jerusalem.

Much was made of tunnel portals when railways were new. Having noticed those of Primrose Hill, Watford and Shugborough, all different, let us recall that of Kilsby. As if to reassure people who had heard stories of quicksands, of broken-hearted contractors, and of young engineers swimming with ropes, Kilsby was given a particularly solid outside appearance. A feudal-looking crenellated top, in conjunction with a pronounced batter each side, produced an outline something between a Norman keep and an Egyptian pylon. Not one passenger in ten thousand notices these things today, but when they were built, the honest fellows and respectable females in the open third-class carriages had a good view of them as, perhaps quaking somewhat, they approached each Stygian cave, and so, too, did the observant Mr. Osborne who sat, goggled and caped and muffled on the old-fashioned box seat.

Then there is the story of Crewe. About the beginning of the eighteen-thirties, a lawyer bought Oak Farm, near Crewe Hall, in the Cheshire parish of Coppenhall. To the original 6c acres, he then added 140. In time, the Grand Junction Railway came and required some of Oak Farm for its line from Birmingham to the North. The Chester and Crewe Railway, authorised in 1837, took another slice, and the Manchester and Birmingham, which might have been more accurately named the " Manchester and Grand-Junction Junction ", and was opened in 1842, scooped in some more. As there was already a Coppenhall station on the Grand Junction, the station where these three lines converged was named Crewe, after the local seat. In 1843, the Grand Junction Railway moved its locomotive works from Edge Hill to Crewe, taking 30 acres more out of Oak Farm for its purpose. So our learned friend's estate grew into a great industrial town, together with the largest railway-owned engineering works in the world. Our more recent ancestors liked to point a moral and declare unto their sons the foresight of the legal gentleman who had bought and added to, Oak Farm. But it seems unlikely that he could have foreseen Crewe as it was to become. Rather, this is one of those entirely amoral success stories, like that of Hilaire Belloc's Ned, who was knocked down by two people on a tandem, then run over by a motor car:—

> *The damages that he obtained from these*
> *Maintained him all his life in cultured ease.*

The Fleetwood route to Scotland, though much esteemed at the time, was not to last for long. *The Railway Times* had said of it: " What more can any reasonable man want ? If he were to travel the whole way by rail at 20 miles an hour, he could but arrive two or three hours earlier, before breakfast was ready or anyone up to bid him welcome." But men are unreasonable, and in regard to night journeys sufficiently so to point out that they might start later and arrive at the same comfortable breakfast time as before. Moreover, the East Coast Route was emerging out of chaos, albeit with its lower half provided by the West Coast and long stretches of the rest filled in by the 10 m.p.h. stage coach.

As suggested, once Camden Bank was cleared, the North Western main line from London to West Lancashire was a dream, alike for locomotive man and traffic man. The most formidable thing south of Crewe was the Madeley Bank, which included just over three miles at 1 in 177, falling towards Crewe. Just south of Warrington there was the little hump of 1 in 135 up and down, with Acton Grange Junction at the summit, and the bigger one between Wigan and the present milepost 202, or just south of it, with a rise at 1 in 104 to Boar's Head and a fall at 1 in 114 at the end, with very short and slightly steeper sections near the summit.

But when the all-rail route to Scotland came into being, things were far otherwise, both south and north of the Border. Lancaster was reached in 1840, the same year as Fleetwood, and the mails were carried thence by coach over Shap Fell. But before this, plans for a through West Coast line to Scotland had been afoot. Influenced by Lord Lonsdale, George Stephenson put forward a plan, in 1836, for a Great West Coast Railway which should join Lancaster to Carlisle via Ulverstone, Millom and Whitehaven, thus avoiding heavy gradients but involving a great embankment across Morecambe Bay between Hest Bank and Kents Bank. It was probably the magnitude of this task that killed the plan.

The Lancaster and Carlisle Railway was incorporated on June 7, 1844, much of the capital having been subscribed by the London and Birmingham and the Grand Junction, and some by the North Union and the Lancaster and Preston Junction companies. Locke and Errington were appointed engineers, and the contractors were Stephenson, Mackenzie and Brassey. By the middle 'forties, steam locomotion had advanced sufficiently for Robert Stephenson to contemplate taking trains over Shap Fell, since George Stephenson, less than ten years before, had favoured a roundabout but flat route. The days of the great mountain railway were not yet; the Semmering and Mont Cenis passes were untried. But past already was the time when such easy race-tracks as London to Bristol and London to Birmingham were considered the only thing possible for fast steam conveyance. The Lancaster and Carlisle Railway was completed as far as Oxenholme, and the Kendal and Windermere Railway (Wordsworth's aversion) in September, 1846. The West Coast expresses now ran to Kendal, where the coaches were picked up for Scotland. This was not for long. Carlisle was reached on December 17 of the same year, and for a short time again, the train-coach transfer was made at London Road Station, Carlisle. Carlisle Citadel Station was opened on September 1, 1847.

To those accustomed to the London and Birmingham, and the Grand Junction, the Lancaster and Carlisle was a startler indeed. Following a little hump north of Carnforth, the first big climb came at a point just south of the present 243rd milepost, near Milnthorpe, and went on continuously through Oxenholme to Grayrigg. South of Oxenholme the ruling gradient was 1 in 111; north of this place it stiffened for a short stretch to 1 in 104, and with little easing went on to the top, at 1 in 124, 1 in 131 for over two miles, and two miles at 1 in 106 reaching almost to the summit—thirteen miles of continuous climbing. Then came a breathing space, following a drop at 1 in 204, with two level stretches near Low Gill and south of Tebay. Thence came the final rise; about a mile and three-quarters at 1 in 146 and a final climb of four miles at 1 in 75 to the summit level. Thereafter came the long toboggan ride down to Carlisle, 31 miles, almost continuously downhill, with seven miles at 1 in 125, and a maximum gradient of 1 in 114 near Calthwaite.

Such was the Lancaster and Carlisle, and such, of course, it is; a famous section today, and a century ago, a prodigy. Many lines more formidable have been built since then. English lines outclimbed its summit level of 914 ft.; in Scotland the Caledonian did so very soon; beside the Andean lines it is but a hillock, and beside the Alpine, North American and Norwegian lines also, but its peculiar grandeur has survived, with its steady upward march from near sea level at both Carnforth and Carlisle, some 30 miles each way from a mountain in the middle, and this on one of the fastest and busiest railways in the world. Who, in days past, could watch *Courier* or *Merrie Carlisle* shouting her way up the Lune Valley with the Corridor without a quickening of the blood? Who, today, can look out of the Night Scot in a chilly summer dawn, amid the driving spray of Dillicar Troughs, without a thrill of delight?

CHAPTER THREE

The Caley

IN their later, greater years, the London and North Western and the Caledonian companies had little in common, outwardly, however closely they might be associated in origins and operation. Both companies painted the upper panels of their carriages white —at least, the Caledonian did on all but its suburban and workmen's trains. Both companies showed more than proper pride in their armorial bearings; the North Western appropriated Britannia from the coinage of the realm, sat her up the other way round and added a lion for company and Sankey Viaduct for scenery;* the Caledonian calmly lifted the Scottish royal arms, unicorns, crowned helmet and all. There, resemblances seemed to end. The blue engines of the Caledonian, from Drummond's time onwards, bore no family likeness to the volcanic black ones of the North Western. The Caledonian used the characteristic Scottish signal—board and spectacle glass fixed to a circular boss on the pivot, iron lattice-work post, ball and spike finial. The North Western signal was a severe, rectangular thing; the post solid with a flat-cap finial, the board corrugated, squarely fixed to the spectacle glass, and as near the top of the post as possible. The North Western station was a puritanical looking establishment painted in severe black and white and buff, scrubbed but not adorned. But in puritan Scotland, the stations of the Caledonain Railway blossomed; gardens grew on the platforms, fountains played where water was plenteous, moss-lined baskets of exuberant geraniums hung in rows under glazed iron roofs. On the North Western stations, an idle boy could get chocolate out of a slot machine, and if he had twopence there was nothing to stop him buying a smoke and the matches to light it. But on the Caledonian, by putting pennies in slots, he could play a football match between two lonely goal-keepers, make a figure like unto W. G. Grace slog at underhand lobs, try his grip, shoot his penny out of a brass

* Doubtless inspired by the Grand Junction Railway, whose seal bore a similarly massive and militant lady, backed by a ship and a Braithwaite and Ericsson locomotive, and accompanied by a huge shield, a bale of cotton, a cornucopia, a marble bust and other luggage.

pistol at an inviting target, and heaven knows what besides. Such *trivia* emphasised great differences.

The Caledonian system to-be, unlike the North Western, had purely local beginnings, or at any rate its oldest constituents had. Scotland's first permanent steam railway, the Monkland and Kirkintilloch, eventually absorbed into the North British, was opened in 1826, and a very short stretch of this line, between Gartsherrie and Garnqueen South Junctions (52 chains) came eventually to provide a link in the West Coast Route, for the Caledonian, and the L.M.S. after it, exercised running powers thereover for all the traffic between Carlisle and Stirling. This section indeed, belonging to rival interests throughout the long years of company ownership, is the oldest part of the West Coast Route.

The oldest line which was to belong to the Caledonian Railway was the Glasgow and Garnkirk Railway, incorporated in 1826 to connect a terminus at Glebe Street, St. Rollox, Glasgow, with the Monkland and Kirkintilloch at Gartgill Colliery, by way of Robroyston, Garnkirk and Cardowan, a distance of 8¼ miles. It was not exactly an imposing effort, apart from the great embankment across Robroyston Moss. It was not an inter-city railway on the scale, even, of the Liverpool and Manchester, but it came with grand fanfares, feasting and oratory. Mineral traffic began in May, 1831, but the general public opening, for passenger traffic also, took place *en fête* on September 27, with George Stephenson driving one of the first trains. A dinner was held in Glasgow that evening, and a prophecy made, in one of the speeches, that it would soon be possible to travel by rail from Glasgow to Edinburgh in 2 hours, and to London in 20 hours. The Garnkirk and Glasgow lines became part of the Caledonian in 1846, following which it was extended to Buchanan Street (1849), thus forming what was to be the Glasgow terminal connection to the West Coast Route for purely Scottish traffic to Aberdeen.

Some more old Scottish local lines deserve our attention. Between 1838 and 1842, the Wishaw and Coltness line was built and opened as an extension of the Monkland and Kirkintilloch to tap the collieries in the Motherwell area, its original purpose being solely the carriage of minerals. In 1845 the Garnkirk and Glasgow Railway put in a junction with this at Whifflet, thus gaining a southerly access without recourse to the Monkland and Kirkintilloch. This was destined to provide the Caledonian company, which leased the Wishaw and Coltness in 1846 and absorbed it shortly after, with its first access to Glasgow. The first line in

Scotland north of the Tay, although not a part of the main West Coast Route, also merits notice. This was the Dundee and Newtyle Railway, 10½ miles long, and opened in 1831. It began with a steep inclined plane out of Dundee, and there were several other inclines, all worked by stationary engines and cables. Horses worked the flatter sections until 1834, when locomotives—Carmichael's celebrated side-lever 0-2-4 bogie engines, made their appearance.

A digression: Scotland's first native locomotives were so different from England's that one may guess that, but for contiguity, the later Scottish school of locomotive design might have developed along lines as original as those of North America. As things were, the two schools collaborated so closely that national differences were mostly minor ones, and those of one country would turn up in the other. Alexander Allan, a Scot, first rose to eminence in England. William Stroudley and Samuel W. Johnson, both Englishmen, did their first noteworthy work on Scottish railways. Another point: Carmichael's old engines, and those on the early lines around Glasgow, were so phenomenally ugly that one may wonder whether uninfluenced Scottish locomotive design might have gone forward along those lines of ostentatious inelegance which have so long characterised the railways of Eastern Europe. No, hardly likely! Unless, perhaps, Allan and Patrick Stirling had never lived. All the same, I have an idea that Dugald Drummond would never have produced the beautiful engines he did, but for his coming under the influence of Stroudley. When he did break right away from Stroudley's traditions, lo, he produced a Caliban among locomotives! But that belongs to the South Western part of our story.

As we have seen already, the earliest West Coast Route to Scotland, incorporating the Liverpool and Fleetwood to Ardrossan steamer services, was completed by a constituent of the later Glasgow and South Western Railway, and at one time it seemed as if the first all-rail route to Scotland would do likewise. Peculiarly Scottish though the Caledonian came to be, there was much of English influence in its origin. The Grand Junction Railway in particular was anxious to extend its connections north of the Border to Edinburgh, Glasgow and beyond, and the company's engineer, Joseph Locke, reported on alternative routes from Carlisle. He considered one through Annandale and Clydesdale, but shied at the heavy climbing necessary over the watershed north of Beattock, and favoured rather a line through Annan, Dumfries, Nithsdale and Kilmarnock, giving a total distance of 417 miles between London and Glasgow. The original Preston-Carlisle survey was part of the same project, but the fulfilment of this has already been described.

The then M.P. for Dumfriesshire, J. J. Hope Johnstone, sent a copy of Locke's report to Charles Stewart, factor of the Annandale Estates, who saw greater advantages in the route which Locke had provisionally discarded. Not only would it benefit the country along Annan and Clyde, but Edinburgh could be directly served by a line diverging at Biggar. The distances from London to Edinburgh and Glasgow would be shortened by 50 and 20 miles respectively, compared with those involved by the Nithsdale line, which could only offer rail communication with the Scottish capital through a separate line from Glasgow, then in contemplation. Stewart met Locke, who agreed that the Annandale line was possible, subject to the building of inclined planes north of Beattock.

Locke, however, was in an awkward position. Glasgow interests strongly favoured the Nithsdale route. Promotion of a line from Glasgow to Kilmarnock was getting going, and Locke feared that its sponsors would claim to have furthered it in direct response to his report on the Nithsdale route to Glasgow. He emphasised that if the Annandale line were to be favoured, the scheme should go forward as quickly as possible, before things should get too far advanced in the Kilmarnock direction. He agreed to undertake the survey as soon as his own line, the Grand Junction, should have reached Warrington.

So Locke carried out his survey in the late summer and autumn of 1837. Unfortunately, money being short, it only covered the route Carlisle-Biggar-Edinburgh, which was playing into the hands of the Glasgow party with their Nithsdale scheme. In his report to the Annandale Committee, which had been formed under the influence of Stewart and Hope Johnstone, Locke soft-pedalled the difficulties of the inclined plane north of Beattock, though adding a word of caution on the possible hazards of *descending* traffic. Things hung fire until, in March, 1839, a resolution was passed at a meeting in Glasgow, that two distinguished engineers, one English and one Scottish, should arbitrate and report on the merits of the rival schemes. The two chosen were Locke and John Millar. As might be expected, each reported in favour of his employers' route, Locke for the Annandale and Millar for the Nithsdale. Meanwhile, the Government had appointed a Royal Commission to investigate and report on railway services to Scotland and Ireland. The Commissioners, Colonel Sir Frederic Smith and Professor Peter Barlow, issued a massive report on March 15, 1841, in which they asserted that potential traffic would support only one railway from England to both Edinburgh and Glasgow. They therefore recommended the carrying out of the Annandale scheme, provided that security be given of *bona fide* intentions to complete the Lancaster and Carlisle line.

This provision obliged the Annandale Committee (no company had as yet been formed) into closer collaboration with the Grand Junction and the North Union companies; moreover, support was not yet forthcoming from the Clyde party. So far the Annandale Committee had shouldered the burden alone. One reason for canniness on the part of the Lanarkshire people, apart from their original favour of the Kilmarnock, was the idea, then widely current and comparable with a more recent attitude in regard to airlines, that great main-line railways could not be made to function adequately without Government subsidy.

The progress of the Caledonian Railway-to-be owed much to the energy of Mr. Stewart, who was in correspondence on the subject of the railway with the Town Clerk of Lanark, Mr. Marr. Following the report of the Royal Commission, Stewart wrote in a letter to Marr: " Now, we think that you Lanarkshire people, landed proprietors, and burghers along the Vale of the Clyde, have shown a strange coolness and indifference in not supporting us in what is of great importance to you. For 50 miles the proposed railroad passes along the Clyde, opening it to all the world in the most efficient manner."

This seems to have produced some belated enthusiasm. Late in 1841 a large body of Clydesdale people, at a meeting in Lanark, moved in support of the new railway, and just previously the Glasgow Chamber of Commerce had also come out in favour of it. There was a very marked improvement in the financial side. But the Nithsdale Party was by no means moribund. It still had the support of a large section of Glasgow business interests, and the Edinburgh and Glasgow Railway (opened since February, 1841), with an eye to through traffic to England via the West Coast, gave its strongest support. Not only was the Nithsdale line to be built, the Beattock and Annandale route was to be *discountenanced* and scotched. There followed a tremendous hurly-burly, at the end of which, at a cost of some £75,000, the Caledonian Railway Act, 1845, became law. Hope Johnstone was elected chairman of the new company, which office he held until 1850, and Locke and Errington were engineers. The Act authorised the construction of a main line from Carlisle to Carstairs, 72¾ miles; the Edinburgh branch, 27½ miles; branch from Carstairs to a junction with the

Wishaw and Coltness Railway at Garriongill, 12 miles; junction line from Gartsherrie on the Monkland and Kirkintilloch Railway to Castlecary, 10 miles; spur at Castlecary to the Edinburgh and Glasgow Railway, and Strawfrank Junctions at Carstairs, ¾ mile each.

In the same year, there had been authorised the Clydesdale Junction Railway, involving 15¼ miles of connections in the Glasgow, Hamilton and Motherwell area, giving access to the Paisley Junction line, all of which the Caledonian took in during the following year, and the three railways which were to complete the West Coast route to Aberdeen in the far north-east, namely, the Scottish Central from Greenhill, on the Edinburgh and Glasgow, to Stirling and Perth; the Scottish Midland Junction from Perth to Forfar; and the Aberdeen Railway from Aberdeen to Guthrie via Montrose. Guthrie was already joined to Forfar by the old Arbroath and Forfar Railway (opened in 1839) which shared with the Dundee and Arbroath Railway, a year older, a gauge of their own, 5 ft. 6 in. Of these northern lines, more later.

Immediately on the passing of the Act, a start was made with the works. Lady Jane Johnstone Douglas duly put her little foot to an ornate spade to cut the first sod near Lockerbie House on October 11, 1845, and less than two years later, the Carlisle-Beattock section was passed by the Board of Trade inspecting officer. On September 9, the directors made a trial trip from Beattock to Carlisle and back. South of Beattock they overtook the Carlisle mail coach on the adjacent road, making its last trip. The mail guard sounded a long, mournful note on his horn, to which the engine, one of the first of Robert Sinclair's Crewe type, replied with a triumphant scream. Carlisle was reached inside two hours. The train then returned, and the usual *sumptuous collation*, with its attendant binge, took place in Beattock Station, which had been suitably decorated with the flags of the friendly powers of the period. It seems an unlikely event for Beattock's sober Presbyterian surroundings, but such was the invariable custom. The new Caledonian stations were the work of the notorious Mr. Tite, F.R.S., who built them in what he described as the " Early English " style. They bore no possible resemblance to Westminster Abbey, but, redubbed " Victorian-Scottish-Railway ", they were quite likeable, even without the geraniums.

Although the heaviest stretch of line was that north of Beattock, this original section of the Caledonian Railway had not been an easy one. Mossband—the old, bloodstained Solway Moss—produced the usual problems of a railway to be laid over a bog, and

35

north of Lockerbie was a two-mile rock cutting. No very fearsome gradients had been involved; though the rise was naturally towards Beattock, the line still tended to be gently undulating, topping its cols at and near Kirtlebridge, between Ecclefechan and Lockerbie just south of the present Castlemilk Siding, between Dinwoodie and Wamphray, with a final four-mile rise towards Beattock, mostly at 1 in 202, but stiffening at the northern end to 1 in 174.

North of Beattock began the big business, with a ten-mile climb to a summit level of 1,014 ft. Just beyond the station the gradient stiffened to 1 in 88, extending for over two miles, then, successively, to 1 in 81, 1 in 79, 1 in 74 over the next three miles. Thence to a point less than half a mile from the summit, the rise was mostly at 1 in 74-77, with a short stretch at 1 in 69. It was the toughest proposition yet imposed on a British main-line railway, but the idea of cable haulage had already been abandoned. Locke, though not a locomotive man, was closely associated with the engineers of the Allan-Buddicom-Trevithick school, and believed in the abilities of the Crewe type of locomotive, even making a vague claim to have had more than a mere something to do with its origin. Anyway, before the line was built, he had confidently asserted that " the impediments which inclined planes were at one time supposed to create will, in the continued improvement of the locomotive engine, be still further removed ".

Locke's influence in the locomotive world is seen to have been scarcely negligible. Where that influence was, there appeared the Crewe type of locomotive, with its outside cylinders, double frames, and inside bearings for the driving wheels. It was on the London and North Western Northern Division; it worked on the Lancaster and Carlisle line and on the Caledonian from the first; it worked on the other Scottish lines under Caledonian influence; Locke went to France, Locke went to Spain, so the Crewe locomotive distinguished the Ouest and the Barcelona-Mataro lines.

The northern incline to the summit was less severe where the line traversed upper Clydesdale. The sharpest gradient was 1 in 99 for some $2\frac{1}{4}$ miles between the summit and a point near Elvanfoot. North of Lamington came two undulations, including a northward fall at 1 in 100 to Thankerton. Strawfrank Junction and Carstairs were on a northward rise, and on the Edinburgh line came a stiff climb to Cobbinshaw summit, the steepest gradient being 1 in 97 for a little under a mile, close to the top. Thence the line was taken down to the Scottish capital with a steady fall for 16 miles, ranging from 1 in 100 to 1 in 220. The final short approach to Edinburgh was an almost unbroken level.

In 1848 the Caledonian Station in Edinburgh was in the Lothian Road, and was a shoddy little barn of a place (someone, doing his best, called it a " striking object "), falling far short of the stately terminus in the Italian style that had been fondly visualised. Twenty-two years later, a short extension brought the line to the west end of Princes Street, 101 miles from Carlisle, but this station again was scarcely worthy of its position and importance. It was fortunately much damaged by fire in 1890, though by that time the Caledonian company had already let the contract for a new station to replace it. This, the present Princes Street Station, occupying a triangular site, was completed four years later, and the superimposed hotel was opened in December, 1903. Boys, homeward bound from Fettes at the end of term, had a noble custom of stuffing themselves with an enormous ceremonial breakfast here before taking the train.

The history of terminal connections in Glasgow is more complicated. First access, as we have seen, was to St. Rollox via the Glasgow, Garnkirk and Coatbridge line, which was absorbed in 1846. In 1849, the opening of the Clydesdale Junction line gave entry to a station in Gushetfaulds, called South Side. For a little while, all south traffic was handled here, but on November 1 of the same year, Buchanan Street Station was opened in the north of the city and thither went the through trains, via Robroyston as before. As early as 1846 it was proposed to bridge the Clyde and build a central terminus in Dunlop Street, but the Admiralty interfered. Not until the early 'seventies was the Caledonian authorised to build a bridge between Gushetfaulds and Glasgow proper. The new Glasgow Central Station was opened on August 1, 1879, and thereafter the south traffic was handled here, trains to and from the north remained at Buchanan Street, while through traffic avoided the city by running, as it has done ever since, from Law Junction through Coatbridge. The present Glasgow Central Station, the largest in the city and the second largest in Scotland, was completed, with a new, parallel bridge over the river, in 1906.

On the northern route, the Scottish Central Railway was opened from Stirling to Greenhill on the Edinburgh and Glasgow line in March, and from Stirling to Perth on May 23, 1848. The Caledonian had been completed and opened to both Edinburgh and Glasgow on February 15, but it was not possible to run through on to the Scottish Central until the completion of the Gartsherrie-Greenhill line on August 7. Meanwhile, the southern section of the Aberdeen Railway had been completed between Montrose and Guthrie, on the Arbroath and Forfar Railway, the gauge of which had been narrowed, and on August 2 the Scottish Midland Junction was completed and opened between Perth and Forfar—a section later destined to see one of the fastest short-distance runs in the world. With the opening of the Gartsherrie link, the route from London to Aberdeen was now complete as far as Dubton Junction, a distance of 500¼ miles from "Euston Grove", making by far the longest continuous line of railway in the country.

Right at the beginning, the new West Coast Route earned a first-rate piece of publicity. In that year of 1848, Queen Victoria had leased Balmoral House, and made her first stay in what was to become the royal Highland seat. The outward journey was made in the royal yacht, but on the afternoon of the intended return there was a sea fog. An urgent message was received at Montrose, on the Aberdeen Railway, that a special train be kept in readiness to convey the royal party south. About half an hour later it was already on its way with the Queen, who spent the night at Perth and went forward next day to Crewe, taking from 10.30 a.m. to 7 p.m. The journey was completed on the third day, leaving at 7 a.m. and reaching Euston about eleven. The Queen is recorded as having expressed her pleasant surprise at the comfort of the carriage in which she travelled throughout, and to have conveyed her congratulations to the Caledonian officers. The carriage in question, however, belonged to the Aberdeen Railway; not that it signified much either way, for it would be a four-wheel, three-compartment, ordinary first class, 6 feet high inside, with six massive stuffed seats to each compartment.

North of Dubton Junction (the Montrose terminal became a branch of the main line) the Aberdeen Railway was extended by three stages until it reached Aberdeen, and was opened to Guild Street, on the site of the present goods station, on April 1, 1850. The first Joint Station, used also by the Great North of Scotland, and, later, through running powers, by the North British, was opened in 1867. The present station was completed early in the 1914-18 war. Sharply undulating, the Aberdeen line skirted for many miles the ironfast North Sea coast, and travel in early days, in the teeth of a winter north-easter, was a fitting preparation for the cold smile of the Granite City.

While the old Caledonian Railway throve on heavy traffic in coal and ore, as well as the long-distance passenger and mail traffic between the great cities of England and Scotland, the original companies of the north-east had a leaner time. They soon came to a working agreement, with a joint managing committee and a locomotive pool. It was, however, a creaking arrangement, and was dissolved in 1854. Two years later, the Scottish Midland Junction and the Aberdeen companies amalgamated to form the Scottish North Eastern Railway. In 1863 the Scottish Central took in the Dundee, Perth and Aberdeen Junction Railway, whose system comprised the Dundee and Perth and the ancient Dundee and Newtyle. In 1865 it was absorbed by the Caledonian, and in the following year the Scottish North Eastern also.

Joseph Locke has had his panegyrists; among biographies of Victorian worthies, Devey's life of Locke is unusually readable. The London and South Western Railway, construction of which he took over from Giles, a nincompoop, named successive engines after him. He was to the Caledonian what Robert Stephenson was to the London and North Western. A genial, clubable man and a great raconteur, as well as an engineer of prodigious energy, he seems to have been rather coolly remembered, after his early death at fifty-five, in the country for which he had done so much. The Unco Guid never forgave him for making, as Liberal member for Honiton, a fierce attack on the Scottish Sabbath. To have criticised the Scottish Central, and other railways, for refusing to add coaches to the Sunday mail trains,* which pagan Westminster obliged them to run, was outrageous. To have dragged up the story of the Duchess of Sutherland, racing to her father's death bed, and standing in tears on the platform at Perth while the Sunday mail train steamed away without her, was unpardonable.

The first public train on the Caledonian main line left Beattock for Carlisle at 6.30 a.m. on September 10, 1847, the day after the formal opening. Prior to completion of the lines northwards, the 10 a.m. express out of Euston reached Beattock at 11.16 p.m., and the connecting stages were due to arrive in Glasgow and Edinburgh at 5.4 a.m. and 6.6 a.m. respectively. It was not an inviting journey, least of all in winter. The first through trains, following completion of the lines to Glasgow and Edinburgh, left Euston as before at 10 a.m. and reached Glasgow at 1.40 a.m. and Edinburgh at 1.30 a.m. next day. Desperate as these times may seem to us, the time of the fastest stage-coach service in 1837, when the railway challenge first arose, was 45½ hours from London to Glasgow via Rugby, Stafford, Lancaster, Carlisle and Beattock. On March 1, 1848, the railway departure time was altered to 9 a.m. and the arrival

---

* " A circular recently issued, in relation to the Scottish Central Railway, called upon the religious to purchase shares in the company, and to use their influence with other supporters of the Sabbath to do the same without loss of time, in order to defeat a proposal about to be made in the directory to run mail trains with passengers on Sunday. A guaranteed dividend of 7 per cent., or 35s. per £23 share, was held out as a bait."—Locke's speech in the Commons.

time became 10 p.m. During the summer of the same year the down train made Glasgow in 12 hours 10 minutes and Edinburgh in 12 hours exactly, but it was difficult to keep time, and the revised schedules of the autumn of 1849 gave a standard time of 12½ hours, which continued for some years.

Such was the building up of the Caledonian Railway insofar as it formed part of the West Coast Route. It will be understood that much other expansion and extension took place in the succeeding years, and that competitors arose in the company's own territory. The Nithsdale line was of course built, and the Glasgow and South Western Railway formed, though it was not until the Midland linked up with this in 1876, and with the North British at Carlisle also, that there was a serious challenge to the Caley's Anglo-Scottish traffic on that side. East Coast competition, of course, was another matter, to be dealt with in another place. It may be remarked in closing the chapter that the little Dundee and Newtyle and the Arbroath and Forfar companies, the latter having a brief part of the through route to Aberdeen between Forfar and Guthrie, continued to exist until the formation of the London, Midland and Scottish Railway in 1923, though the Caledonian had worked them for years.

CHAPTER FOUR

Buries, Bloomers and Dunalastairs

TO cram the subject of West Coast trains into two chapters, covering more than eleven decades of history, is a daunting prospect. To cover it all one cannot pretend, and that which follows must be regarded as a sketch of sketches. To the sad story of Edward Bury, F.R.S., who quitted the London and Birmingham service rather than build, against his conscience, anything bigger than a four-wheel locomotive, I have previously referred. Ahrons has recorded that in 1841, the London and Birmingham had 58 2-2-0 and 30 0-4-0 Buries, that not infrequently quadruple-heading was necessary on goods trains, and that Bury himself admitted, before the Gauge Commissioners, that it had been necessary to employ seven at once to move a 45-wagon goods train during a gale. In the same situation he remarked with pride that broken crank axles had prevented none of his engines from getting home, and that some had taken their trains on in this condition. Altogether, the London and Birmingham was singularly lucky that worse did not befall. There was a bad accident on the Brighton Railway in 1841, and a really frightful one near Versailles in the following year, both due to Bury locomotives breaking axles and leaving the road.

Anyway, Bury departed to vegetate abroad, and after his death Mrs. Bury wrote a little pamphlet eulogising him and his work, and incidentally showing an intelligence and interest in steam locomotive matters rare in women. It is easy to decry Bury and his funny little engines, but he was not a fool, nor was his influence unlasting. He was the first locomotive man to build practical locomotives with the cylinders inside, under the smokebox. He used bar frames, and the early export of Bury locomotives to the United States initiated the universal employment of this type, ever since, on North American railways. His little D-shaped firebox was a poor thing for raising steam, but in the spacious dome-shaped steam space over it lay the genesis of large, dry steam space over the Belpaire firebox. Bury's Birmingham locomotives lasted long enough to be used, in pairs and trios, on the excursion trains to London at the time of the 1851 Great Exhibition, and some

larger Bury goods engines survived for a very long time on the
Furness Railway, one of them, the old *Coppernob*, having been
preserved.

In the quest for something more puissant than the Buries, the
L.N.W.R. Southern Division, as the L. and B.R. became, tried
T. R. Crampton's patent locomotives with large driving wheels set
in rear of the firebox, and two magnificent eight-footers, *London*
and *Liverpool*, were built by Tulk and Ley, and by Bury, Curtis
and Kennedy, in 1847 and 1848 respectively. It is quaint that the
second-named, which at the time was one of the largest locomotives
in the world, should have been built by Bury's firm. The Cramptons
were rough on the road, especially *Liverpool*, an eight-wheeler with
a very long rigid wheelbase (18 ft.), which had a habit of causing
the derailment of the next train following. Prior to 1862, iron
rails were in use, and before 1853, when *Liverpool* was in full career,
there were no fish-joints, the rail-ends being brought together in
joint chairs. The best of the old rails were 75 lb. to the yard.
Much of the original permanent way was mounted on stone blocks,
and some of it consisted of 50 lb. fishbelly rail.

Crampton's locomotives were on the whole a failure on British
railways, largely owing to inadequate boiler power, while *Liverpool*,
as we have seen, though adequately provided in this respect, was
otherwise unfortunate. The only other Cramptons used on constituent lines of the West Coast Route were *Courier* on the L.N.W.R.
Northern Division, two on the Aberdeen Railway, and one, of the
earliest, most archaic type, on the Dundee and Perth. Later
experience in France showed that the Crampton had excellent
qualities on fast trains of limited weight. The white elephant
Liverpool, incidentally, could manage the heaviest trains at high
speeds between London and Wolverton, and with better permanent
way should have done well in her time. As it was, she made an
imposing exhibit at the Crystal Palace in 1851 without being too
sorely missed on the main line.* She was scrapped in 1858.

J. E. McConnell came to the rescue of the Southern Division
locomotive department by building some of the finest and most
powerful locomotives of their day. He built an odd engine at
Wolverton in 1849, a 2-2-2 with outside cylinders, outside frames
and outside cranks, similar to Hall's arrangement on South German
and Austrian railways. The consequent width of its motive anatomy
had unfortunate results with station platforms and other lineside

* More detailed notes on the original type of Crampton express engine form the first
chapter of my book *Some Classic Locomotives*, which contains a coloured reconstruction
of *Liverpool*.

structures, and the men called the engine " Mac's Mangle ". Crampton's *London* had previously collected such a rake-off during trials on another line.

Apart from the awkward Mangle, McConnell's locomotives were admirable and very advanced for their time. In those days, low centre of gravity was still a fetish with most locomotive engineers. In his first express engines of 1851-2, the boiler centre line was 7 ft. 1 in. above rail level—equal to the diameter of the driving wheels, and the pressure was 150 lb., though the company was nervous of the latter and it was later reduced to 120 lb. These were the first of the famous Bloomers, 2-2-2's with inside cylinders and inside frames throughout. The men gave them this name because they coincided in advent with Amelia Bloomer's attempted dress reform. The new engines, showing so much of their " legs ", were regarded as being in sympathy with the two unhappy panta-looned girls whom a righteous London crowd had lately hunted with lewd cries through the streets. McConnell's 5 ft. 6 in. heavy goods engines, also, were most advanced compared with general design in the 'fifties. His practice included some use of rubber springs and the celebrated McConnell double firebox for burning coal instead of coke, and he was an early experimenter in super-heating, or at least steam drying.

McConnell's Bloomers did excellent work on the L.N.W.R. Southern Division from the early 'fifties to the 'seventies. Their striking appearance, too—tall red engines with great wheels un-encumbered by visible bearing, rod or crank, and handsome corniced brass domes—tickled the public fancy. There were 29 6 ft. 6 in. " Small Bloomers ", used for ordinary and semi-fast trains, 20 7 ft. " Large Bloomers " for express trains, and three superb " Extra Large Bloomers "* with 7 ft. 6 in. drivers. One of the last-mentioned, No. 372, built at Wolverton in May, 1861, achieved fame at the time of the *Trent* affair during the American Civil War, when tension was high and dispatches were being rushed from Holyhead. Some remarkable running was achieved by the London and North Western Railway with the Queen's Messenger and the American mail. No. 372 came on for the Stafford-Euston run, which was made non-stop. Water troughs were yet unknown south of the Trent, so an extra tank was added to the tender. Times included 46 minutes for the 49½ miles of the Trent Valley line, and 29 minutes for the 32 miles from Tring to Euston, with a traditional minimum pass-to-pass timing, south of Tring, of six minutes for 8 miles. It must be allowed that the

---

* The term " outsize " was not yet in general use.

timing of the train was checked by very simple means; 80 miles an hour for 8 miles, even with a very light load of three old four-wheel carriages, sounds somewhat tall for 1861, but it is possible, and there is no doubt that there was some very fast running. For Crampton's *Liverpool*, by the way, a top speed of 79 miles an hour was claimed during trials.

On the Northern Division, locomotive development followed entirely different lines. The original Grand Junction locomotive stock was of the same heterogeneous order as those of many other early railways. Its reform and the standardisation of types was carried out by Alexander Allan and Francis Trevithick during the late 'forties and 'fifties, they using Allan's celebrated Crewe type outside cylinder engine with outside cylinder and frames, and inside bearings only for the driving and coupled wheels, the origin of which is described in another book.* Crewe's first locomotive, the famous *Columbine*, built early in 1845, has survived, together with the more freakish 8 ft. 6 in. single *Cornwall*. The locomotive practices of Crewe and Wolverton at this time were so different that, from a mechanical engineering point of view, the formation of the North Western by amalgamation might not have taken place. The only oddities built during the Allan-Trevithick regime were the *Cornwall*, already mentioned, the *Courier*, a small Crampton 4-2-0 with several Allan peculiarities, and the *Velocipede*, a large Crewe-type engine with Crampton's patent excentrics.

But having once encountered the Crewe-type engine at Stafford, on your supposed mid-nineteenth-century journey north, you went on seeing it. Robert Sinclair, who became general manager of the Caledonian as well as locomotive superintendent, built it from the beginning, and Benjamin Conner, who came after him, enlarged it into his fine 8 ft. 2 in. singles built between 1859 and 1876, which worked nearly all the best trains up to the early 'eighties, and various 2-4-0's, some with 7 ft. coupled wheels. Alexander Allan himself had gone from the North Western to the Scottish Central, taking his Crewe-type with him, and Thomas Yarrow built it for the Scottish North Eastern. In the middle ' sixties, therefore, a journey from Euston to Aberdeen would be made with Bloomers as far as Stafford, and the Crewe-type, in one avatar or another, for the rest of the way.

One type, however, which the Caledonian and its constituents used extensively but which was almost unknown in England was the 0-4-2 heavy goods engine with outside cylinders. Many examples and varieties were built, and they lasted for many years. Two were

* *Some Classic Locomotives*, Chapter Two, " Allan's Crewe Type."

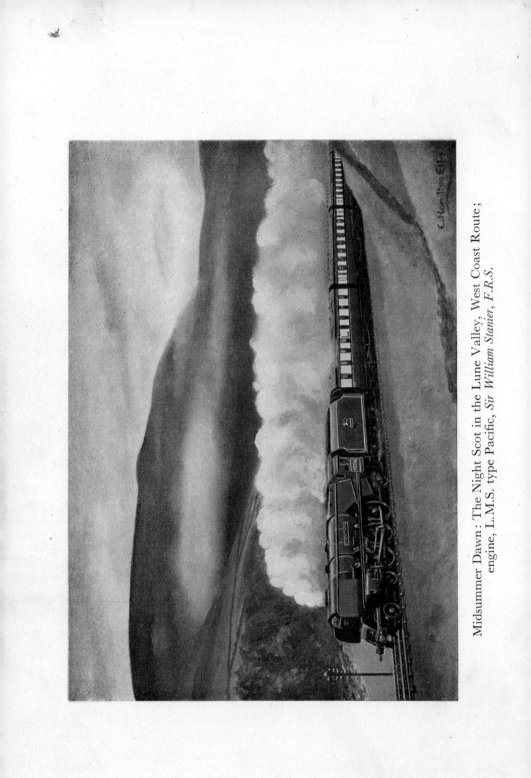

Midsummer Dawn : The Night Scot in the Lune Valley, West Coast Route ; engine, L.M.S. type Pacific, *Sir William Stanier, F.R.S.*

at Hamilton in 1930, and another engine, identical with the older Caledonian design and unaltered, though not belonging to that company, was working mineral trains into Calder Ironworks at the same time.

The passive part of a West Coast express during these years was rather less interesting than the locomotive, even to the keenest student of coach-building. The first-class carriages were of the unimaginative three-compartment type used for many years by all the standard-gauge main line railways. Second and third class were likewise small box-like four-wheelers. A sort of sleeping accommodation was provided, chiefly for invalids, by the " bed carriage," an arrangement originally installed in the mail train coaches of 1838. The carriage had a boot, like an old stage coach, but opening into the end compartment through hinged flaps. By night, a stretcher and a flat cushion, rigged across the foot-space, enabled the sleeper to lie down with his feet in the boot. The mails were carried in an oblong box on the roof. In later years, the compartments having got larger fore and aft, the stretcher or " twin sticks " and cushion were sufficient. In 1838 the travelling post office made its appearance, with the mail exchange apparatus for picking up and dropping the pouches at full speed, the invention of John Ramsay. The apparatus, with its folding net on the side of the carriage, differed little from that used today. A chute, however, was used for dropping the pouch into the lineside net.

In 1861, McConnell retired, Wolverton was given over to carriage-building, and all mechanical construction for the London and North Western Railway was concentrated at Crewe under John Ramsbottom. He was one of the great figures of the London and North Western in Victorian years, standing, as chief mechanical engineer, in the same rank with that great succession of general managers, Captain Mark Huish, whose coercive methods with smaller companies would have done credit to the head of any great military power, William Cawkwell and Sir George Findlay. The latter had belonged to the Shrewsbury and Hereford Railway, and remarked, once, that when the North Western jointly leased it in 1862, he was " taken over with the rest of the rolling stock ". Cawkwell and Findlay both served under the great and terrible chairman, Sir Richard Moon (1861-91), and I believe that on at least one occasion, Findlay shortly intimated to Moon that he was busy, and might be bothered some other time.

So with Ramsbottom. In his own sphere he was absolute. He *was* Crewe. Before the centralisation of locomotive construction,

4   45

he had already made his mark. He was the inventor of track water-troughs (first laid in 1860 on the Chester and Holyhead line near Conway). Ramsbottom must have made a neat fortune out of his safety-valve alone, which largely superseded the old spring-balance type. When yet in charge only of the Northern Division locomotives, he produced two most outstanding locomotive classes, the Problem class 7 ft. 6 in. singles with 16 by 24 in. outside cylinders, and the class DX 5 ft. 0-6-0 goods. Of the former, 60 were built, including the famous *Lady of the Lake*, awarded a gold medal at the London exhibition of 1862. They were fast and efficient engines, and though the first of them appeared in 1858, some survived into the present century. The DX class also made its first appearance in 1858, and eventually numbered 943 engines, the first example of large-scale mass-production in the world. One of them, built at the end of 1866, was Crewe's thousandth locomotive. Some of the class lasted long enough to belong to the London, Midland and Scottish Railway; others found their way, at second-hand, to various places. The Lancashire and Yorkshire bought 86; others turned up in Belgium, Sweden and elsewhere. The Swedish engine, Swedish State Railways No. 48, *Finn*, was delivered in 1862, and must have been almost, if not quite new. Later, Ramsbottom got into trouble for supplying engines new to the Lancashire and Yorkshire, the locomotive-building firms successfully contending that it was no part of a railway company's business to set up as a general manufacturer. *Finn*, by the way, came to a sad end at Malmö in 1883, when she crashed through the station on to the quay beyond.* In their day, the DX 0-6-0's handled successfully every possible sort of London and North Western train, from a heavy coal train to a Scotch tourist express.

Under the Allan-Trevithick regime, and under Ramsbottom, Crewe locomotives were painted a rich bluish-green, and Ramsbottom used also a steel chimney cap of ornamental complexity. With this and the brass safety-valve columns brightly polished, and the buffer-beam painted vermilion, with the carriages finished in chocolate and white, a West Coast express of the 'sixties must have been a very beautiful sight. Both the Problems, and the seven-foot " Large Crewe " type, were very graceful designs indeed. Ramsbottom followed the Problems with successive types of 2-4-0 express engines, and of these the " Newtons " were the forerunners of F. W. Webb's first and best passenger type, the " Precedent " or " Jumbo " 2-4-0 with 6 ft. 6 in. coupled wheels and 17 by 24 in. cylinders, first built in 1874. Just as the Jumbos derived to some extent from the

* Nils Ahlberg in *The Locomotive*, Vol. LIV. No. 673.

Newtons, so did Webb's 5 ft. goods, the Cauliflowers,* owe some of their origin to Ramsbottom's DX class, though in detail there were marked differences. Between them, they handled much of the North Western's heaviest traffic, passenger and goods, for the next thirty years and more.

Francis W. Webb was yet another of those severe autocrats particular to the London and North Western Railway, indeed, his reputation is that of the severest autocrat of them all. His gifts were those of a great original designer and inventor; his weaknesses those of a man who took offence at the mildest suggestion, who counted as nothing the experience of mechanics under him, and who fostered the illusion of his own perfection by a rigid censorship of all views other than his own. Webb was attracted to compound expansion by the experiments of Mallet in France in the 'seventies, and his first essay was the conversion of a Crewe-type single, used on the Ashby and Nuneaton branch, to a compound on Mallet's system in 1878. He brought out his first three-cylinder compound, No. 66, *Experiment*, in 1882, employing the system which he perpetuated thereafter through the 'eighties, and until the late 'nineties, two high-pressure cylinders driving the trailing wheels, and a single large low-pressure cylinder driving the middle pair, the two driving axles being uncoupled. There was a single carrying axle at the front end, making the wheel arrangement 2-2-2-0. The Greater Britain and John Hick classes of 1891 and 1894, with very long boilers having combustion chambers, were 2-2-2-2. Webb's system of compounding certainly economised in fuel and water, but there was a heavy debit balance on maintenance. Moreover, the engines were often laborious and erratic. This is where Webb's censorship came in. Only the good points were noted, and then with loud fanfares. It is not impossible that he himself knew little of the worst features of his engines. Nobody dared tell him.

The earlier three-cylinder compounds were also insufficiently powerful for such heavy traffic as that of the West Coast Route and the Holyhead line to Ireland. The best were the Teutonic class of 1889, with 7 ft. driving wheels, 175 lb. pressure, high-pressure cylinders—14 by 24 in., low-pressure cylinder 30 by 24 in. With the drivers coupled, the Teutonics might have made really satisfactory engines. As it was, the simple and compound departments were supposed to synchronise by mutual sympathy, and frequently did not, imparting a vicious surging motion, especially on starting. Then there was the queer arrangement of valve gear,

* A name supposed to spring from the appearance, at a distance, of the coat of arms on the driving-wheel splasher.

with a slip-excentric motion inside and, on the earlier engines, outside Joy gear for the high-pressure cylinders. The slip excentric frequently failed to slip, with the result that on attempting to start, the exasperated driver found his trailing driving wheels frantically spinning on the wet rail, while their fellows in front slowly turned in reverse. On the eight-coupled compound goods engines, of course, this fortunately could not happen, and high speeds not being involved, these were altogether more reliable engines.

All the same, the Teutonics could do very good work sometimes. In the celebrated race to Aberdeen in 1895, arising out of retaliatory time-cutting between East and West Coast, the *Adriatic* averaged 64.3 m.p.h. from Euston to Crewe. But still better work was done over the more difficult stretch from Crewe to Carlisle, where the simple Jumbo *Hardwicke* averaged 67.2 m.p.h. Earlier, in the races of 1888, there were really admirable performances, not by Webb engines at all, but by the two old Ramsbottom Problems *Marmion* and *Waverley*.

Yet the Webb three-cylinder compounds greatly stirred the imagination of the uninformed. Boys, watching them coming up Camden Bank, spouting fire like Roman candles, could not resist them. Only when Webb had gone, and the compounds were massacred as fast as Crewe could cut them up, was the awful truth fully known. Their appearance was imposing with its glossy black adorned by elaborate lining details, brass name-plates and Britannia ruling the waves; there was a mysterious magnificence, in the eyes of youth, about the enormous cover of the low-pressure cylinder behind the buffer-beam, and long ago a little boy stuffed an empty shotgun cartridge over the leading axle of his German tinplate *Jupiter* with admirable effect.

Jeanie Deans, of the Teutonics, was much admired at the Edinburgh Exhibition in 1890. *Queen Empress*, of the Greater Britain class, went farther afield, for she was sent to the Chicago World Fair of 1893, with a coach and a sleeping car, afterwards making an exhibition run to New York, perhaps fortunately by the water-level route. Yet still the Jumbos stole the show. *Charles Dickens*, built in 1882, covered two million miles by the summer of 1902. This was on the Manchester-Euston run, not on the West Coast expresses. *Hardwicke*, of the 'ninety-five race, was scheduled for preservation in 1932.

Webb finally turned to four-cylinder compounding and coupled wheels for all engines. His four-cylinder locomotives, all of which carried 200 lb. pressure, were less unreliable than the three-cylinder varieties, and the best were undoubtedly the Alfred the Great class of 1901. These and the previous Black Prince class were four-coupled with a leading four-wheel radial truck instead of a bogie. Of the 4-6-0 fast goods, which were optimistically intended to supersede the " Cauliflowers ", especially on the heavy task of lifting the Scotch tourist trains over Shap, the less said the better. They came and they went, and the " Cauliflowers " went on unto this last.

Francis Webb's locomotive policy became more than ever a liability on the London and North Western, and efforts were made to dislodge him. Announcements of his impending retirement kept appearing in the papers, to be emphatically denied. But he was ageing and ill. When George Whale was announced as his successor elect, it was the last straw. He walked into the Euston Hotel one morning, had breakfast, told the head waiter that he had no money and was looking for another job, and stalked out. Soon after making this cold, solitary joke, he retired to Bournemouth, where, after a few years, he died, leaving a great fortune to good works and worthy causes in the town of Crewe.

Turning to the Caledonian during the later years of last century, we see an increasing deviation from that Crewe practice which it followed so closely in early days. Even Conner's last engines, which were completed by George Brittain, were 7 ft. four-coupled with outside cylinders and leading bogies. They appeared in 1877, the first bogie express engines on the Caley, but there was not a standard-type bogie engine on the London and North Western until 1904. Conner designed, at the same time, a 0-6-0 goods with outside cylinders and long boiler, resembling the French " Bourbonnais " type, a very rare bird on British railways, though common all over the Continent.

Then came Dugald Drummond, with the large inside cylinder 6 ft. 6 in. 4-4-0 express engine which he had used so successfully on the North British Railway since 1876. Apart from the bogie, there was much Stroudley influence in the design, as there was in the standard Drummond 18 in. goods with 5 ft. wheels. Drummond's bogie engines, and John Lambie's, which came after but were very similar, did famous work in the 1895 races, the classic run being that of Lambie's No. 17, which, from Perth to Aberdeen, repeated Hardwicke's 67.2 average.

A unique engine was No. 123, built by Neilson and Company and shown at the Edinburgh Exhibition of 1886, a 7 ft. bogie single driver entirely based on Drummond's and Stroudley's previous practice, although the design was prepared at Neilson's Hyde Park Works in Glasgow. Purchased by the Caledonian after the exhibition, No. 123 did fine work in the 1888 race to Edinburgh. Scheduled for preservation at the same time as the North Western *Hardwicke*, this engine finished her career on the light Perth-Dundee trains and occasional piloting on the main line, being withdrawn in 1935 and thereafter kept at St. Rollox, restored as far as possible to her old Caledonian appearance.

But the finest and most famous of the Caledonian 6 ft. 6 in. bogie engines of last century were undoubtedly John F. McIntosh's original and enlarged Dunalastair classes, the first of which appeared in 1896. McIntosh, it may be remarked, was in many ways an opposite of Francis Webb down at Crewe. As an engineer he favoured simplicity; his attitude to locomotives was more that of a skilled workman than of a scientist, and whether in consequence or not, he produced much better engines. In character he was a sharp-eyed old Scotsman with a pungent tongue and only one hand. He found his stump-arm useful in driving home a technical argument or emphasising some Rabelaisian story. (Webb suffered no such thing as argument, and it is unthinkable that he ever discoursed in the style of the merry Vicar of Meudon).

Whether there was much originality about McIntosh may be disputed. But, putting it broadly, he took the basic Drummond express engine, put on a much larger boiler, so greatly improving the ratio of boiler power to cylinder capacity, and thereby produced some of the best engines, of their time, in the world. The first Dunalastair class had telescopic boilers with a minimum outside diameter of 4 ft. 8⅛ in. and a total heating surface of 1,403·28 sq. ft. compared with 1,210·7 sq. ft. in the Drummond engines. The pressure was 160 lb. Drummond, it may be remarked, had tried 200 lb. pressure in 1889. First Dunalastair cylinders were 18¼ by 26 in., a quarter-inch on the Drummond diameter. As well as great interest in the engineering world, considerable public enthusiasm was aroused by the new Caledonian express engines; quite a little crowd used to collect to watch the " Corridor " draw into Glasgow Central Station each evening.

The performance of these and following Caledonian locomotives has often been praised. In that same year of 1896 Irvine Kempt, the Caledonian traffic superintendent, initiated a startling timing of 32 minutes, start to stop, over the 32½ miles from Forfar to Perth, without consulting Mr. McIntosh. The latter's comment to the late Rev. W. J. Scott, was: " Och ay, juist like that beggar Kempt ! Ay weel, we'll have tae do it somehow." The Dunalastairs kept exemplary time on this exacting schedule. Kempt was the antithesis of McIntosh; cravatted and corseted, he resembled a Regency buck. One of the toughest turns of the Caledonian engines was with the up Corridor (the 2 p.m. out of Glasgow), which sometimes exceeded 300 tons, on the 23·8 mile climb from Carstairs to Beattock Summit, at an average of 42 m.p.h. Northbound, there was banking assistance from Beattock to Summit; even so, 125 minutes for the 117·8 miles from Carlisle to Stirling, with the heavy tourist expresses, was an exacting schedule, and the engines kept time. In the second Dunalastair class of 1897, the cylinders were increased to 19 in. and the total heating surface to 1,500 sq. ft. The pressure was 175 lb., while the grate area remained the same. Unfortunately, their appearance coincided with a falling off in schedules. Thanks to the derailment of the down tourist train on Preston curve, London and North Western Railway, in the previous year, enthusiasm for high speeds was waning.

The West Coast companies made the same gradual concessions to travelling comfort and convenience as did other British railways, which means that there were precious few until about the middle 'eighties. Lavatory provision in particular provides a story of slow, even inhibited adoption compared with that on many foreign railways. In the late 'fifties, Lord Dalhousie returned from India, old and broken in health, and Richard Bore, the then North Western carriage superintendent, rigged up some sort of *necessaria* for him in a first-class compartment, without which he could not have made the long journey to Scotland without mortal discomfort. Family saloons were more permanently provided in the 'sixties, and so were the new sleeping cars, from their introduction in 1873.

Only in the 'eighties did lavatories appear in ordinary coaches, and originally for first class only. (It was the Midland Railway that, in England, first acknowledged that third-class passengers also were human.) The new lavatories, both North Western and Caledonian, adjoined the compartments, which was convenient, but they often had the doors padded on the outside and access provisionally barred by a folding passenger seat, which was idiotic. Brave men who had faced the yelling Matabele or the wild Afghan, dared not importune Aunt Jane when she had planted herself down in the way of salvation, and were no better off than Cardinal La Balue at the celebrated supper party given by Louis XI.

The original West Coast sleeping cars of 1873 were divided into three compartments, with a central passage, an off-central vestibule, and end lavatories. The day seats were like sofas, changed into beds at night. Upper berths came down from the ceiling. A fuller history of old sleeping cars will be found in my *Nineteenth Century Railway Carriages*. North Western, and West Coast Joint vehicles remained short in the body for many years, owing to a short traverser which the Engineer's Department had thoughtfully installed at Euston, and which would take nothing larger than 42-foot carriages. These last were unpleasant vehicles, with Webb's patent radial trucks, which their designer enthusiastically described as being steadier than bogies. Their particular foible seemed to be an alarming lurch at irregular intervals.

Gradually the old oil pots were replaced by gas, the first experiment being with Julius Pintsch's system in 1875, though Pope's gaslight was afterwards standardised. For daytime lighting in tunnels, Bore tried luminous paint on the ceilings in 1880. It was not a success. In the same year, Webb introduced footwarmers containing acetate of soda instead of hot water. Four years later, Dugald Drummond tried steam heating on the Caledonian, but the thing was cannily done, using worn-out hosepipe for transmission between carriages. The first North Western diners appeared in 1889, but not on the Scotch expresses until July, 1891. Exactly two years later, the 2 p.m. West Coast expresses were given corridor coaches and dining cars for first and third class. The original diners had been first class only and without corridor access from the rest of the train.

CHAPTER FIVE

Coming and Passing of the L.M.S.

THE first half of the twentieth century brings our West Coast narrative into the realms of the familiar, and yet to changes which, of their kind, equalled those of the previous sixty-two years. In locomotive design, George Whale threw Webb's compounding overboard on the London and North Western, and followed McIntosh's policy of simple locomotives with large boilers. There were many who welcomed his Precursor class 4-4-0's in 1904, not so much with cheers as with deep sighs of relief. Moreover, *Precursor*, when she appeared, was not so very unfamiliar. In both outward and constructional detail, she was broadly describable as an enormous Jumbo with a leading bogie. In nearly all superficial details, the London and North Western engine remained the same from 1874 to the end of the company's separate existence—shape of chimney, dome, safety-valve, cab, nameplates, numberplates, smokebox doors, buffer-beams, colour scheme were invariable. The long, continuous splasher first appeared in Webb's 4-6-0 compound goods and became general with the appearance of Whale's 4-6-0 Experiment class. Observe how even class names were repeated. The original Precursors were small Webb 2-4-0's of 1874, and the original *Experiment* was Webb's first three-cylinder compound. One feature disappeared with Webb, the timber-framed tender, which was supposed to provide a shock absorber in case of trouble.

That North Western cab! There was nothing quite like it, perpetuating as it did the oblong panel-plate of very early days, changing only in the lengthening of the roof and deepening of the side-sheets. It had its kindred cabs, Adams's on the South Western, Johnson's on the Midland, McDonnell's on the Great Southern and Western, but they were by comparison ephemeral, and the Adams variety, indeed, was made only during the years 1879-87. The North Western cab, like the massive, square-based chimney, was a hallmark. A Bavarian mechanical toy manufacturer might make a gauge-nought 2-2-0 steam locomotive, with a brass dome and oscillating cylinders, that looked like nothing else on earth, but when he put the North Western cab on it, the effect was magical.

53

George Whale's other important contributions to North Western locomotives were his Precursor tank engines—the express engine with coupled wheels reduced from 6 ft. 9 in. to 6 ft. 3 in., the same as the Experiments, and with side tanks and a radial axle under the bunker, and his initiation of conversion of the four-cylinder Webb compounds to two-cylinder simples. He died in 1909, and was succeeded by C. J. Bowen-Cooke who, partly influenced by the excellent performance of a London, Brighton and South Coast 4-4-2 express tank engine working through between Brighton and Rugby, generally introduced superheating on the London and North Western.

Bowen-Cooke's most imposing design was the Sir Gilbert Claughton class four-cylinder 4-6-0 of 1913—again partly due to foreign influence, in this case trial runs on the North Western of a Great Western Star class four-cylinder 4-6-0. The Claughtons, though capable at times of outstanding work, were in some ways disappointing engines. Current limitations at Crewe prevented the putting on of an adequate boiler, and undoubtedly the most reliable designs of the Bowen-Cooke period, even of all North Western locomotive history, were the George the Fifth class 4-4-0 express engines with 6 ft. 9 in. drivers, and the Prince of Wales class 6 ft. 3 in. 4-6-0's (1911). They were superheated developments of the Precursors and Experiments, and both were extraordinarily efficient designs in their day. Ninety Georges were built from 1910 onwards, and 246 Princes, the last of these in the early days of the L.M.S.R. Both had 20½ by 26 in. cylinders and a working pressure of 175 lb. per sq. in. One of the Georges, *Coronation*, built in 1911, was Crewe's five thousandth locomotive. In this and later examples were revived the large bosses to the coupled wheels, extending over the crankpins, which first appeared in Webb's Alfred the Great class compounds and were to be a feature of the Claughtons. For goods traffic, Bowen-Cooke perpetuated the inside cylinder 0-8-0, initiated in its oldest and smallest form by Webb—strong, trustworthy, rather rough engines, not unknown to afflict new young firemen with travel sickness. A variety on this theme (the engine, not the malaise) was the 0-8-2 shunting tank, which finally developed into the 0-8-4 on the L.M.S.R. under H. P. M. Beames in 1924.

On the Caledonian Railway during the nineteen hundreds, J. F. McIntosh continued on his solid way, building engines that grew larger and yet larger, but all of the familiar Drummond stamp—even the prodigious 4-6-0 *Cardean* and her sisters. There was a legend about a projected super-Cardean Pacific, but this never materialised; nor did a de Glehn compound Atlantic with four cylinders. But the Great Reliables were the large 140 class 4-4-0's of 1904 and after, which were of the well-tried Dunalastair type, with the heating surface up to 1,615 sq. ft. An experience of Charles Rous-Marten, several times quoted, concerned No. 140 on the 10.5 a.m. train out of Edinburgh, 404 tons behind the tender. On the northern ascent to Beattock Summit, with Driver Stavert, speed dropped to 36 m.p.h. on the final ascent of 1 in 99 and remained at that level. " Each quarter mile was done regularly in exactly 25 seconds, and when we passed the summit the speed was exactly the same."

William Pickersgill, previously of the Great North of Scotland Railway, succeeded old Mr. McIntosh in 1914. His first, and most generally successful engines were somewhat similar to the large McIntosh 4-4-0's in their superheated form, and they have done good work for many years. In 1915, an odd thing happened. F. G. Smith had designed, and Hawthorn Leslie had built six large 4-6-0 locomotives with outside cylinders for the Highland Railway. Two duly went to the Highland, and there was the deuce to pay with that company's chief engineer, who had been left in the dark about axle-loads too heavy for various underline bridges. The Caledonian heard the row afar off, and charitably bought the offending engines, including the four awaiting delivery. They were the first new outside cylinder main-line engines to appear on the the Caledonian since George Brittain's time.

In the following year, Pickersgill brought out his own first 4-6-0 design (the 60 class), and here again were outside cylinders. He held to this practice to the end in his large six-coupled designs, which included the massive three-cylinder 956 class of 1921, which outwardly had a peculiar family resemblance to the ex-Highland engines. They were the largest locomotives ever built for the Caledonian Railway, with 2,640 sq. ft. of combined heating surface and a grate area of 28 sq. ft. The pressure was 180 lb., the three cylinders 18½ by 26 in., and the coupled wheels 6 ft. in diameter. They worked for some years on the Glasgow-Aberdeen expresses, but suffered the rather early disappearance to which small classes are fated, for there were only four of them, four drops in the ocean of 10,316 engines taken over from its constituents by the London, Midland and Scottish Railway in 1923. The old McIntosh 140 class continued to handle much of the West Coast through traffic northwards from Carlisle.

On both the North Western and the Caledonian, carriage design underwent very considerable improvement from the 'nineties onwards. Eight- and twelve-wheeled carriages were built by both companies, their respective noteworthy contributions being the North Western's superb end-door corridor coaches built for the 2 p.m. Scotch expresses,* and the Caledonian's famous Grampian corridor stock for the Glasgow-Aberdeen trains. They were most comfortable, and in full accord with the fashion of Edwardian times were decorated in a richly pompous style for both first and third class. Internal features of the new Caledonian coaches were the arched false roofs to the compartments, hiding the ugly broken ellipse peculiar to side-corridor stock, and cromets or slings on each side of the doors in the third class, hitherto regarded as a first-class perquisite. From the early nineteen hundreds onwards, all new stock for the North Western, Caledonian, or the West Coast Joint Stock was electrically lit and steam-heated. Many of the older North Western corridor coaches, all the same, retained their Pope's gas lighting to the end.

Modernisation of the North Western coaching stock had been progressive after C. A. Park succeeded the veteran Richard Bore in the 'eighties. Special vehicles were more numerous than on most other railways, the nature of the seasonal traffic between England and Scotland having much to do with this. In addition to handsome sleeping and dining cars there were several varieties of special saloons, more elaborate in arrangement than the usual family saloon of Victorian days, with sleeping berths installed. Queen Victoria's royal train, in which she made so many journeys to and from Deeside, was a sight to behold with its wild variety of saloons, coaches, sleeping cars and vans, all different shapes and sizes. The train built for Edward VII and Queen Alexandra, which succeeded it, was a model to the world. The royal saloons proper were supplemented by very fine " semi-royal " carriages, which, incidentally, anyone could hire at a price. In 1900, too, the North Western company built a private coach for the Duke of Sutherland, which was in some ways the guinea-pig design for the Edwardian royal saloons that followed.

No fashion is more derided than one recently outmoded, though, as it gets more remote, it recovers popular estimation. Fashion-plates of 1926 are ghastly; of 1901, funny; of 1879, delicious. Crinoline can almost save a bad film. So with furniture, with a rather longer time-lag, and consequently, with vehicle interiors. Though we are surrounded today by trains that are sometimes decorated in tolerably poor taste, and road motor coaches of loudly screaming vulgarity, your modern traveller will approve, and even enthusiastically admire. If the same person gets into an old North

* The prototype coaches were built for the American boat expresses in 1907.

Western or Caledonian carriage that has survived in something of its primeval state, it will be sniffed at, and condemned as a stodgy, stuffy old thing, and a disgrace to British Railways. Probably it *is* stodgy and stuffy in its old age, faded, none too clean, worn, and damaged by the yahoo. Yet in its heyday, with its fresh blue plush or that famous green " saladin ", with its gilt-edged lincrusta panels and its door squab padded and buttoned in red morocco —yea, even with its electric lamp brackets frilled like a Victorian young person's trouserines—it had a rich dignity, and a measure of comfort lacking in many a more modern conveyance. Those were the things one could appreciate in the Corridor and the Grampian forty years ago: warmth, comfort, cleanliness, *and dignity*. How smoothly they ran, too, above all on the North Western's superb permanent way of 95 lb. sixty-foot rails laid on what was then the best roadbed in the world ! In the races to Aberdeen during the summer of 1895, the time taken for the $539\frac{1}{2}$ miles from Euston on that final exhibition run (when *Hardwicke* and Caledonian No. 17 achieved immortality) was 512 minutes for just under 540 miles. Of course, this was not expected to be transferred to the timetable as a standard schedule in future, and, moreover, the North Western lost its nerve after the Preston smash in the following year. In 1914, the fastest West Coast regular booking was 11 hours 15 minutes (down), which was 10 minutes longer than the fastest (up) on the East Coast. Edinburgh and Glasgow were both 8 hours from Euston.

The outbreak of war in 1914, and the very severe restrictions which came into force in 1917, removed any spectacular elements from West Coast passenger running, as from the fast services of all other British railways, but this first world war period brought compensating features such as the operation of the famous Jellicoe specials, which carried naval traffic—passenger and coal—between Euston and Invergordon and Thurso. It also brought to the West Coast Route the most terrible accident in British railway history, when, on May 22, 1915, through a combination of bungling and irregularities, two signalmen at Quintinshill Box, Gretna, allowed an up troop special to collide head-on, at full speed, with a stationary down local from Carlisle. This had been shunted on to the up road to let the two sections of a night Scotch express (running late) to overtake it. One of these had already gone through before the collision took place. The troop train engine (McIntosh 4-4-0 No. 121) and the local train engine (McIntosh Cardean class No. 907) broke each other's backs on impact. The troop train was of Great Central stock, chiefly old gaslit six-wheelers, which were crushed into a mountain of rubbish between the overturned engines and a few heavier bogie vehicles at the rear. Immediately after, the wreckage was run into at full speed by the second part of the night express from Euston, double-headed by the original No. 140 and sister engine No. 148. Fire broke out in the jumbled mass of engines and demolished vehicles, burning all that day and through the following night, and 227 persons, chiefly soldiers, were killed or died of their injuries. The presence of the local train on the up road was due to the fact that both the long sidings at this place were occupied or about to be occupied by coal trains. Every accident has its freaks. In this one, although engines 121 and 907 were damaged beyond repair; although the fire engulfed not only the troop train and the express, but the standing coal trains also; the carriages of the local, pushed back along the up road by the original shock, survived with but slight damage.

In 1923, the London and North Western Railway, having just previously taken its ally and partner of many years, the Lancashire and Yorkshire, to its ample bosom, was itself engulfed in the new London Midland and Scottish Railway under the Railways Act, 1921. Many optimistic admirers of the North Western had a rosy idea that, at least where locomotive practice was concerned, this meant simply that Crewe had gained a vast new empire, and that in due course Claughtons and such-like would be running to Aberdeen. (A few did, indeed, get on to the Midland main line, where one was destroyed in the Doe Hill smash of 1929.) A few fanatical amateurs refused to believe that there was no longer a North Western company. I remember a lunatic who used to send many close-written pages of ferocious abuse to a well-known railway journal because (in the nineteen-thirties) it continued to give information regarding the Great Western Railway while ignoring the London and North Western.

At first, there was little apparent change. George Hughes of the Lancashire and Yorkshire was C.M.E. of the new company, but H. P. M. Beames at Crewe, Sir Henry Fowler at Derby on the Midland, and W. Pickersgill at St. Rollox on the Caledonian, carried on very much as before. Mr. Hughes did indeed put some of his L. and Y. type 4-6-0 express engines on the West Coast expresses, and made some praiseworthy experiments with one of them in the form of a four-cylinder compound.

In 1925, he retired, was succeeded by Sir Henry Fowler, and Derby was let loose with a vengeance. Fowler was a metallurgist; Fowler was an organiser; Fowler was not a designer of locomotives. But he set about standardising the L.M.S. locomotive stock, and it was on Midland lines and with Midland methods that he did so. The first obvious attempts to impose the customs of Derby elsewhere often had funny results. One night a transferred inspector, on the North Western side of Birmingham New Street, made a fuss about the weight of a train being dispatched for Euston behind one engine. " What the bloody hell d'you think this is ? " roared the driver. " The Midland ? "

It looked like it, anyway. Midland compounds (Fowler's drawing-office variation on an original theme by R. M. Deeley) blossomed like Dorothy Perkins* at Camden, and all the way up the West Coast Route, amid a dissonant chorus of adulation and abuse. Later, there was something like the ancient Bury ultimatum, resulting this time in the Royal Scots. Midland coach-building methods were standardised, and R. W. Reid introduced at Derby in 1923 a very admirable mass-production scheme in carriage shops. Nobody could quarrel with this; Midland carriages had been famous for their excellence since the 'seventies, and much of the North Western corridor stock was getting decidedly antiquated. Many of the veterans were sent north to the Highland main line, which had very few indigenous corridor carriages.

The ten o'clock day Scotch express out of Euston was named the Royal Scot, and names were given to other well-established trains. The 1.30 p.m. to Glasgow and Edinburgh, successor to the old 2 p.m., became the Midday Scot, though people went on calling it the Corridor, and the principal night expresses to Glasgow and Edinburgh, and to Inverness, became the Night Scot and the Royal Highlander respectively. No very startling speeds were attempted; the L.M.S. aimed first at regaining something of that reputation for punctuality which the North Western had enjoyed before 1914, and made a new feature of very lengthy non-stop running. Many years ago, the Great Western had started running non-stop from Paddington to Plymouth, $225\frac{1}{4}$ miles via Langport and Castle Cary. In the summer of 1926, the L.M.S. decided to trump this with a non-stop run from Euston to Carnforth. The schedule was not a brilliant one: 265 minutes for the 236 miles. Carnforth to Symington, 130 miles, including Shap and Beattock summits, was allowed 167 minutes, and the remaining 35·4 miles into Glasgow, 50 minutes. The thing went off with a burst of trumpets, and the inaugural train was proudly headed by two old North Western engines: 5299 (old No. 1137) *Vesuvius*, a rebuilt superheated Precursor, equal to a George, and 5934 (old No. 186), a Claughton. North of Carnforth, the train was taken on by new

* The compounds were sometimes called " Crimson Ramblers ".

Midland compounds Nos. 907 and 908. The North Western engines gained 5¾ minutes on schedule, and the compounds gained 8¾ minutes to Symington, where the Edinburgh and Glasgow sections divided.

This non-stop stunting was soon extended. On September 26, using the new and magnificent three-cylinder 4-6-0 express engine *Royal Scot*, the first stop was made at Carlisle, 299¼ miles, at an average speed of 52 m.p.h. with a load of 420 tons. The public liked it, loads increased, sometimes in excess of 500 tons, and time was kept very well on the whole. Of course, the L.M.S. had to run non-stop to Carlisle, because the London and North Eastern had started running non-stop to Newcastle, 268·3 miles. There was a glimmer of the old racing spirit, though no more. When, in the first half of 1928, it became known that the L.N.E.R. was going to run the Flying Scotsman non-stop to Edinburgh, the L.M.S. stole its neighbour's thunder on April 27 by treating the Edinburgh portion of the Royal Scot as a separate train and running it non-stop from Euston to Princes Street behind compound No. 1054. It was not a permanent arrangement, but a giddy jest, undoubtedly a good one.

Still, there was more than a drop of decadence in the L.M.S. Locomotive Department under Fowler's standardisation programme. Hundreds of obsolescent Midland type locomotives were built for service all over the system. The only really bold new design brought out for express passenger service was the Royal Scot, and that was a very creditable piece of collusion between the North British Locomotive Company and the late R. E. L. Maunsell of the Southern Railway, who most handsomely lent full working drawings of his *Lord Nelson*.

The nineteen-thirties saw a renaissance. When Mr. Stanier, afterwards Sir William Stanier, F.R.S.,* came from Swindon, the impact of Great Western practice on L.M.S. locomotive design was scarcely unexpected. Save that it lacked the Great Western's baroque embellishments in bright copper and brass, the first Stanier express engine, *Princess Royal*, of 1933, was just what one might have expected had the Great Western decided, a second time, to try the Pacific-type locomotive. There were the domeless taper boiler, with top feed,† the outside cylinders set in rear of the bogie and inside cylinders, the low degree of superheat—Swindon had surely come to Crewe !

* The first F.R.S. to hold office as head of a locomotive department since Edward Bury.
† A few of Stanier's earliest mixed traffic engines had the safety-valves mounted between the top feed clacks, as on the Great Western.

1. Euston Great Hall in the
   nineteen twenties

(*British Railways Photograph*)

2. The Corridor climbing
   Camden Bank;
London and North Western
Claughton class engines
JOHN O' GAUNT and
COYOTTE

(*Photograph by H. M. Moore*)

NSET
ONE

3. Castlethorpe Station, London and North Western Railway, about 1910; a study in carriage roofs

4. The old water tower and London and Birmingham bridge over the Grand Union Canal, near Blisworth; a recent view

5. Kilsby Tunnel about sixty years ago

(All from Locomotive and General Railway Photographs)

6. Old No. 1 Gantry at
Rugby,
London and North Western
Railway

7. The " Gates of Jerusalem "
(northern portal of
Shugborough Tunnel)
near Stafford
Trent Valley line

8. Rugeley station,
Trent Valley line,
in the 'seventies

(All from
Locomotive and General
Railway Photographs)

9. Sunny South Express passing Kenton, about 1914;
L.N.W.R. 2-4-0 PUCK piloting Webb four-cylinder compound LA FRANCE;
South Eastern and Chatham tricomposite brake carriage leading

10. Webb four-cylinder compound No. 1017 on goods train passing Tamworth,
Trent Valley line, in the early nineteen-twenties

11. L.N.W.R.
Problem class
MARMION piloting
a Webb three-cylinder
compound

12. L.M.S. local train leaving Carstairs, headed by ex-Caledonian superheated
Dunalastair IV class engine No. 14445

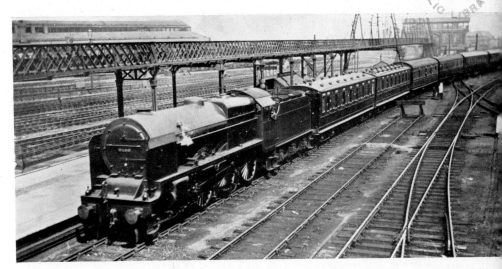

13. Up West Coast express entering Crewe, with L.M.S. Royal Scot class engine A J A X,
two old L.N.W.R. corridor coaches leading ; beyond is the old suspension bridge
which connected Crewe Works with the station

Up Royal Scot
ar Rugeley ;
-2 engine No.
6227
J C H E S S O F
V O N S H I R E
h Caledonian
" Grampian "
welve-wheel
ach leading

(All from
ocomotive and
eneral Railway
Photographs)

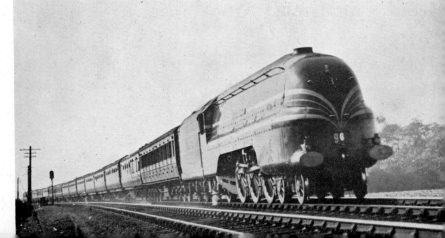

6. Up Caledonian
local goods train
near Stirling;
Drummond
standard goods
engine No. 371

(*Photograph by
Henry L. Salmon*)

17. Caledonian Dunalastair
class engine No. 735 at
Carlisle in the 'nineties

(*Photograph by C. M. Doncaster*)

Newcastle Central Station, York, Newcastle and Berwick Railway in the 'fifties, with some specimen first-class carriages ; on left, the old Milepost Zero at York

(*Locomotive and General Railway Photographs*)

19. York Station, looking north

(Photo : *Yorkshire Post*)

20. The famous High Level Bridge at Newcastle-upon-Tyne

(*Photograph by the Author*)

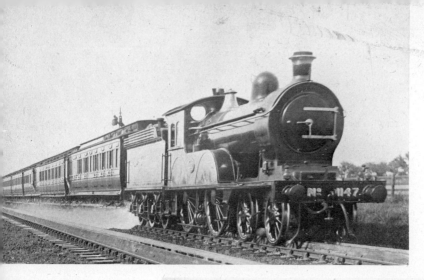

21. Newcastle-Sheff
Express on Wisk
Moor troughs ;
N.E.R. class R engi
No. 1147

(Photo : *Locomotiv*
Publishing Co. Ltd.

22. Bridge No. 126 between
Grantshouse and Reston
after the great washout
of August, 1948

(*British Railways Photograph*)

23. Traffic during the gre
washout ; East Coast fast
goods at Kelso,
Tweedmouth-St. Boswell
line, headed by
British Railways No. 6198
from Heaton shed

(*Photograph by the Author*)

Many of these features were modified in later engines. Domes appeared on the after rings of new Stanier boilers, superheating elements increased in number, and the Great Western influence became less obvious, though still there. The Pacific became the standard large L.M.S. express locomotive, supported by hundreds of express and mixed-traffic 4-6-0's. On main-line goods traffic, 2-8-0's of a type adopted by the Government after the outbreak of war in 1939, and heavy moguls, appeared where once London and North Western 0-8-0 coal engines had shunted and bucked on their way. The Midland compounds, which had done valiant work in both England and Scotland, especially for engines so relatively small, began at last to play second fiddle on lighter passenger trains, and there began a ruthless massacre of the old London and North Western types. Nearly all the Claughtons had gone already, some nominally rebuilt as three-cylinder 4-6-0's (Patriots *alias* Baby Scots).

Modern L.M.S. locomotive practice is too recently and too fully publicised to require detailed description here. In the public eye, the high spot of the nineteen-thirties was the appearance of the Coronation Scot service in the summer of 1937, with the first streamlined trains to run on the West Coast Route. The new express locomotives, of the Pacific type, had 6 ft. 9 in. coupled wheels and four 16½ by 28 in. cylinders, combined heating surface of 3,663 sq. ft., 50 sq. ft. grate area, and a working pressure of 250 lb. per sq. in. Certainly nothing so imposing, so puissant, had been seen on the West Coast heretofore.

With these Princess Coronations, and a light standard make-up of 297 tons tare, it seemed that a dashing field-day was assured. It was. On June 29 the first engine of the class, No. 6220 *Coronation*, made a trial run from Euston to Crewe and back, with the load reduced by one kitchen car to 270 tons. Driver and fireman were T. J. Clarke and J. Lewis, both of Crewe, and the train was timed independently by Cecil J. Allen,* D. S. M. Barrie, and S. P. W. Corbett. From the Euston start to the Norton Bridge pass, 138·9 miles, the train ran in 115 minutes 45 seconds, or just over 14 minutes inside its schedule. So far, maximum speed had been restricted to below 90 m.p.h. The fun took place on the final 19·2 miles from Norton Bridge to Crewe. They were covered in 14 minutes 1 second pass-to-stop. Speed was at or above 100 m.p.h. for 4½ miles, averaged 100 m.p.h. for 10 miles, and touched 113 m.p.h. about Milepost 156, two miles south of Crewe. The three able observers agreed on this peak speed, while the Hasler

* Mr. Allen's account appeared in *The Railway Magazine* of August, 1937.

speed recorder optimistically registered an absolute maximum of
114 m.p.h. The headlong approach to Crewe was viewed by the
authorities there with some alarm, and when the train came
roaring in over the reverse curves of the crossover, the ambulance
department was standing by. This incident was not publicly recorded at the time, and nought worse befell than some crockery
smashing* and some unrehearsed embraces between passengers.†

On the return journey, with the same 135 minute schedule,
Euston was reached in 119 minutes. The first 10½ miles uphill to
Whitmore troughs took 10 minutes 42 seconds, a remarkable time,
and the maximum speed was a steady 100 m.p.h. from Roade to
Castlethorpe troughs. There was no question then about the
feasibility of the regular 6½ hour schedule for the new trains between
Euston and Glasgow Central. The Coronation Scot, in spite of
the challenge of the Coronation train to Edinburgh on the East
Coast Route, became the most widely publicised express, for a
while, in the world. The daily papers wrote the usual rubbish
about it; even a contributor to the *New Statesman and Nation* con-
descended to remark on the discomfort of its carriages, and, as was
the Royal Scot in 1933, and Webb's *Queen Empress* with her little bit
of a train in 1893, this train was sent to America for exhibition.
There it was caught by the outbreak of war in 1939. The engine
was brought safely back through Hitler's submarine pack, but the
carriages, which as usual on these trips included a sleeping car,
remained in the United States for the duration, and were used as
an officers' club. In both the later tours, the engines used were
not the supposed originals. The *Royal Scot* locomotive which went
to America was previously No. 6151, *The Royal Horse Guardsman;*
likewise, the touring *Coronation* was really No. 6229 *Duchess of
Hamilton.* The names and numbers remained permanently swapped
thereafter.

The crack in the *New Statesman* about the Coronation Scot
carriages was somewhat jaundiced. Now that the days of hard
seats on British trains are so far away, the comfort or otherwise
of train seating is dependent on one's own development *a posteriori.*
The former Furness Railway, in spite of heavy upholstery and considerable springing, contrived to provide third-class carriages of
quite refined discomfort for all who had anything other than very
short thighs and concave backs. But the worst that could be said
about the standard L.M.S. third-class seating of the nineteen-
thirties was that it was not always quite so comfortable as it looked.

* Acknowledgement to R. A. Riddles.
† Acknowledgement to C. J. Allen.

On the whole, the West Coast standard of comfort was well maintained, and up to the war old carriages were scrapped on a regular
schedule. This was not a faultless arrangement; it meant that
comfortable Midland and North Western stock might disappear
some years before the less praiseworthy legacies of the Lancashire
and Yorkshire and the Highland, because the latter had been more
recently built. On the other hand, one soon sought in vain for
such antiques as the neighbouring L.N.E.R. mustered in such
large quantities to the end of its independent existence.

In the autumn of 1928, the L.M.S., in common with the L.N.E.
and the Great Western companies, brought in the long-awaited
third-class sleeping car, which in general arrangement resembled
the French first-class *couchette*. It was high time, too. Several road
motor-coach companies had provided sleeping berths previously;
the Swedish State Railways had had third-class sleepers since
1910, while the " hard " sleepers of Russia and the colonist cars
of Canada were of ancient lineage. A praiseworthy contribution
to passenger comfort was the installation, on sleeping cars and in
the Coronation Scot coaches, of power-driven ventilation, which
saved the passengers from the old, unpleasant choice between fug
and draught.

The imposing blue and silver livery originally used on the
Coronation Scot did not last very long. It weathered extraordinarily
badly, and was replaced by crimson and gold. Later locomotives
of the Princess Coronation class were without the streamlined
casings, and these last have been removed from the original engines
also. Sir William Stanier left the L.M.S. to serve the Government,
but his influence in steam locomotive design was lasting. C. E.
Fairburn, who succeeded him, found that steam was getting along
very well as it was for the present, and will be best remembered for
his work on the development of diesel shunters. The beautiful
lines of the Princess Coronations are still apparent in Mr. H. G.
Ivatt's big Pacifics.

And so we come to modern times, and British Railways, and
the first large main-line diesel locomotives in Great Britain. That
these are destined to revolutionise British railway transport (on
imported fuel) I am not prepared to suggest.

PART TWO

CHAPTER SIX

East Coast Build-Up

TO a boy, one of the most favoured spots of all the indoor world
was a third-floor landing window on the backstairs of the
Royal Station Hotel, York. Passing bootses and chambermaids
were sympathetic, or at any rate left one alone, to sit there for an
hour, or two, or more, gazing at the magnificent panorama of the
North Eastern Railway, of beautiful green engines with gleaming
brass casings to their safety-valves, of stately plum-coloured carriages, proudly clerestoried, of immense mineral trains, seldom
loading less than ninety wagons. The glittering, brown-varnished
down Scotsman would go out in the early afternoon, behind what
seemed then an enormous Atlantic-type engine, and soon after that,
the up Scotsman would be coming in round the great curve from
Poppleton Junction, between the twin bastions of Leeman Road
and Waterworks signal-boxes. Then there was the Scarborough
line, with all manner of engines: Fletchers with their rounded cabs,
Tennants, Waterburies, and with reasonable luck a beautiful bogie
single. They are gone, now, and their successors are not lined-out
with gold, nor deviced with a handsome coat of arms, nor crowned
with glittering brass, nor have the majority what Mr. O. V. S.
Bulleid once called " nice real chimneys ". But the fire that swept
York Station in the war spared the hotel; the backstairs seem to be
still there, and thither your author would automatically slink away
if presently he had the chance.

The East Coast, in its entirety, is the youngest of our four main
lines, now considered, though part of it was carrying traffic between
London and Scotland before the West Coast was completed. As
we have seen, there was a time when one's journey from Euston
led one nevertheless to the north-east. Perhaps, in the days of
the old companies, the North Eastern Railway was most rightly
entitled to the status of senior partner, for although it was formed,
as a company, as late as 1854, its constituents included some of the
oldest railways in the country. From the passengers' point of view,
it was a much better railway than either the Great Northern or
the North British. The Great Northern's reputation was largely

based on such showy services as the East Coast and Leeds expresses; a North British ordinary train was a grim sort of conveyance; but on the North Eastern there were excellent local expresses at really smart timings—Leeds to Northallerton, Newcastle to Carlisle—and even the local from Pilmoor to Pickering, with its old Fletcher tank engine, was made up of carriages which one would have welcomed with delighted surprise on any average express between Edinburgh and Glasgow. To grey old towns by moor and wold, they brought a flash of urbane elegance.

Behind a kiosk on York Station there used to be a sort of North Eastern family tree in the shape of Milepost Zero, bearing the initials of all the old railways that once had York for their starting point, and, in most cases, George Hudson for a parent. Hudson—the *Railway King*,* the Draper of York who bestrode with his massive corporation the war-horse of railway speculation in the eighteen-forties, an incarnation of the Southern Englishman's idea of uncouth Northern Plutocracy, who bowed Queen Victoria into her carriage when she went a-railroading, this *big swollen gambler*† fell as far as he rose, but undoubtedly he was responsible for the building of many of the country's most important main-line railways. Milepost Zero would have served him well as a tombstone. It had a sad end in the " Baedeker " raid on York in 1942.

To go into the detailed history of the main lines that are Hudson's monument—a worthier one than his own reputation—would occupy far too much of what must be regarded as a sympathetic survey rather than any sort of a learned book. For that one must turn to the late Mr. H. G. Lewin's masterly *Railway Mania and its Aftermath.*

Forerunner of the East Coast Route was that known as " Midland and Eastern ", which had nothing whatever to do with the later Great Northern Railway, but a great deal to do with Hudson. From Euston to Rugby it was concurrent with the old London and Birmingham line, which provided the southernmost part of the West Coast Route. North of Rugby, the Midland Counties Railway was opened thence to Derby in stages, the first being the Derby to Trent Junction section of the Derby-Nottingham line (June 4, 1839), followed by Trent Junction to Leicester on May 5, 1840, and Leicester to Rugby on June 1, 1840. North of Derby, there was the North Midland Railway to Normanton, whereof the Derby-Masborough section had been opened on May 1, 1840, and the continuation to Normanton (and incidentally Leeds) on June 30. So far, these were constituents of what was to become

---

* Sydney Smith.   † Thomas Carlyle.

the Midland Railway, and over part of this route, long years ahead, Scotch expresses would be running from London without touching the East Coast Route, or the West Coast except at Carlisle.

Hudson's York and North Midland Railway, which was destined in great part to upset him some years later, was opened from York to a junction on the Leeds and Selby Railway at South Milford on May 29, 1839, and reached Burton Salmon on May 11, 1840. Between this place and Masborough, a coach service was put on, and a regular service begun between Euston and York; the railway journey, with its stage-coach interlude, occupied 14 hours. On June 30, 1840, the York and North Midland had closed the gap, York was in direct communication with London.

The flat Plain of York was a railway promoter's dream, and lay in the heart of Hudson's kingdom. Between York and Darlington came the Great North of England Railway (gorgeous title !), 45 miles long, flat and straight, made for speeding and serving the standard gauge interests as a demonstration race track during the Battle of the Gauges. It was opened on January 4, 1841, for minerals, and for passenger traffic on March 30. One of the standard gauge champions was a Stephenson long-boiler engine known simply as " Engine A ", or the " Great A ". It had the usual Gothic firebox in rear of the last axle, but was unique, at that time, in having outside cylinders with the 4-2-0 wheel arrangement, nicely calculated to make the notoriously unsteady long-boiler type worse than ever. Those responsible for the demonstration runs, as might have been expected on any line associated with Hudson, tried every conceivable trick to prove the engines capable of the same sort of performance as Gooch's on the Great Western. " Flying starts " were given, so that what ought to have been start-to-stop timings were in fact pass-to-stop; the tenders were filled with nearly boiling water (there were no injectors then), and a wonderful contraption erected for inducing a fierce draught while the engines were standing still.

Under these ideal conditions, " Great A " managed to cover 44¼ miles in 47 minutes. There was a bad derailment in the course of the trials. Stephensons failed to make much of the " Great A " type, though they managed to sell several similar, larger engines to the London and North Western. David Joy of the famous valve gear had an early footplate trip on the " Great A ", which belonged to the York and North Midland company, when he was a young engineering student in Leeds in 1845. " No coat, nothing on, I popped on to the engine, and away we went, so jolly. This was my first fair run on an engine with a train; only to Castleford, still it was fine " (*Joy Diaries*). I like Joy, and those who knew him loved him. His pleasure and anger were alike ebullient; he went for life, people and engines with joyful zest.

The Thames was at last linked to the Tyne by the completion, in 1844, of a line between Darlington and Gateshead, originally divided in ownership between the Newcastle and Darlington Junction Railway, which extended northward for $27\frac{1}{4}$ miles to Washington (Co. Durham), the Pontop and South Shields Railway (1834), $5\frac{1}{4}$ miles to Brockley Whins, and the Brandling Junction Railway (1839) over the final $6\frac{1}{4}$ miles along the south side of the Tyne. The N. and D.J.R., which absorbed the B.J. in 1845 and the P. and S.S. in 1846, coincided in part with the present East Coast main line, and in part with the Leamside line diverging therefrom north of Ferryhill. This carried all the East Coast traffic prior to 1872, though Brockley Whins was cut out by a line diverging at Penshaw. On June 18, 1844, a through train was run from London to Gateshead, and though it started from Euston, it might, without too much licence, be recalled as the first East Coast express. A Travelling Post Office service between Tyne and Thames was started in the following year. It was diverted to the new St. Pancras station in 1868, continuing thus instead of following the normal East Coast Route to King's Cross.

In 1845, too, there was some very remarkable running over the route, arising out of the egregious Hudson having been elected M.P. for Sunderland. James Allport, later general manager of the Midland Railway, decided that this was an opportunity for standard-gauge trains to show what they could do, the Battle of the Gauges being in full blast. He ordered successive special trains to be ready with steam up at the principal interchange stations. The polling returns were in by five o'clock p.m. of the day of the election. Allport started immediately for London with copies of the returns, reached the city about midnight, drove straight to Printing House Square, and within two hours was starting back for the north-east with copies of *The Times* containing the election result and a leader thereon. He reached Sunderland about ten o'clock in the morning. Including the two hours in London, he had covered some six hundred miles in 15 hours.

Next stage in the jigsaw assembly of the East Coast Route was in Scotland, and involved a considerably heavier piece of construction than anything between York and the Tyne. It was generally felt, in the 'forties, that the construction of a railway from Edinburgh to England along the east coast depended on whether or not one was built to the West Coast Route at Carlisle. The traffic, it was believed, could not possibly support two railways. For that the North British Railway *was* built to Berwick in those years, posterity must in all fairness thank George Hudson. One of his lines was the nascent Newcastle and Berwick, so he naturally put all his weight in favour of a line which should link Berwick with Edinburgh, and was elected a director of the North British company. The Hudson Empire was consolidated on May 10, 1844, by the fusion of the Midland Counties, North Midland, and Birmingham and Derby Junction Railways into the Midland Railway, and, on July 1, 1846, the York and Newcastle was formed by the Newcastle and Darlington Junction taking over the Great North of England. With the formation of the Newcastle and Berwick company in 1844, Hudson was in control of every railway that was working or being built between Rugby and the Tweed. His backing of the North British was to the extent of £50,000 in £25 shares, which was transferred to the York and North Midland account. On July 19, the North British Railway Act was passed, and on August 12 construction was begun on the original N.B.R. main line, 57½ miles from a terminus by the old Waverley Market, under North Bridge, Edinburgh, to Berwick, with a short branch from Longniddry to Haddington.

Upon the Border hills and upon the broad lands of the Lothians descended the navvy army, and these were fiercer, grimmer navvies than the jolly, drunken, murderous English navvy. They were Highlanders driven to the Lowlands by improving landlords, men who had seen things more cruel than the brief blood-bath of Glencoe; they were Irishmen from the Glasgow slums or from remote places haggard with famine. They were Presbyterian Gaels and they were Catholic Gaels. What better reason was there for them to be perpetually at war? Down in England, Deptford Jemmy might decide that the time had come for him to make the world a better place by eliminating Gloucester Jack; a ring would be formed and everyone would be happy. But when, in the green hills above Cockburnspath, someone mentioned the Pope, or referred to John Knox; when Jock of Kildonan and Mike from Collooney had the whisky in them and a bottle and a razor between them, it became an international incident, and there would be a real battle.

Between the fighting, the North British Railway was built, a fairly gentle up and down for some 35 miles south, then a sharp rise at 1 in 96 from beyond Innerwick to a summit between the tunnel at Penmanshiel and Grant's House* station. Over ancient battle-

* Now called Grantshouse.

fields it went, by Prestonpans, where in 1745, just such wild High-
landmen as those now building the North British Railway had
routed Sir John Cope's men along the line of the oldest railway in
Scotland,* whence, Prince Charlie artlessly recorded, they *ran like
rabets*.

Down from Grant's House it went in long stretches at 1 in 200,
and thence by the rocky coast around Burnmouth to walled Berwick
above the Tweed. On June 18, 1846, the first North British train
rolled out through the Calton Tunnel to Dunbar and Berwick,
followed later in the morning by another, likewise conveying
distinguished guests. The two trains returned to Dunbar in the
afternoon, and there the guests enjoyed the inevitable beano of
cold meats, sherry and iced champagne. In the station house,
some 700 guests are reported to have sat at meat, though how
they managed to do so must remain a mystery. The " high table "
for the directors was on the platform, and possibly there were other
means of overflowing. *The Scotsman* distinctly recorded, however,
that the main feast was in one " lofty and cool " room, at three
long tables.

Ordinary traffic on the North British began on June 22, and
passengers were booked through to Newcastle by combined railroad tickets available on the stages between Berwick and the Tyne.
Through Northumberland work progressed on Hudson's new baby,
the Newcastle and Berwick, that line which to this day can give
the waking traveller an electrifying glimpse of sunrise over Lindisfarne, or, on dark, clear winter mornings, one of an illuminated
fishing fleet glittering like a phantom city, miles out across the
cold North Sea. The York, Newcastle and Berwick Railway was
formed by amalgamation in 1847. Trains started running from
Newcastle to Tweedmouth on July 1 of that year, and thus, over
two months before the rival Caledonian was open even from
Carlisle to Beattock, it was possible to travel from London to
Edinburgh by rail, with but two waterbreaks, formed by Tyne
and Tweed. Special omnibus services were run for the through
passengers between Tweedmouth and Berwick stations, and likewise
they had to cross between Gateshead and Newcastle.

This last passage was replaced in 1849 by the first of the great
bridges which were later to be a feature of the East Coast Route
from the Mimram Valley to Montrose, namely the High Level
Bridge. It has never had another title. Neither Victoria, nor

---

* The " narrow cart road " described by Sir John before the ensuing court-martial
was in fact the colliery tramroad between Tranent and Cockenzie Harbour, built in
1722. Hence came the reference " gang tae the coals in the morning " in the old Jacobite
rant *Hey, Johnnie Cope !* (Kenneth Brown).

Albert, nor yet King Hudson bestowed their names on it. T. E. Harrison and Robert Stephenson were the joint designers, and it was the first example of a large bridge carrying both a main-line railway and a road. For a century now it has stood, unchanged under all the changing traffic, 1,372 ft. long, with its six 125 ft. main spans composed each of four iron arches supporting the three railway tracks on top and the roadway in the middle, with foot-paths between the inner and outer arches. The height above high water is 112 ft. It was formally opened on September 28, 1849.

There remained the Tweed gap. Here was a different pro-position and a different construction; a wide valley with a shallow salmon river, though indeed the northern bank was precipitous. Robert Stephenson designed a great viaduct of 28 arches, each of $61\frac{1}{2}$ ft. span, and with a height of 126 ft. above high-water level, carrying a double track. This most beautiful bridge was formally opened by Queen Victoria on August 1, 1850, and with it was closed the last break in railway communication between London and Edinburgh via York and the Tyne. The royal engine, N.B.R. Crampton No. 55, was painted in Royal Stewart tartan, and ran thus for a long time thereafter.

Ere this, the North British had suffered a major misfortune, the first of several inflicted by unkind Nature. Less than four months after its opening from Edinburgh to Berwick, in the autumn of 1846, a tremendous storm washed out three bridges in the Dunbar-Linton area, together with long stretches of embankment on the big climb through Cockburnspath, and severely damaged six of the seven bridges by which the line crossed and recrossed the Eye Water on the stretch down from Grant's House. For some time stage coaches had to ferry passengers between Linton and Grant's House. This calamity was repeated, with all sorts of uncanny resemblances, 103 years later, in the first year of State ownership, when trains were stranded and through traffic had to be drastically re-routed, chiefly via the end-on branch connections which, years before, the North Eastern and North British companies had built between Tweedmouth, Kelso and St. Boswells. Then one saw the great East Coast expresses, proudly headed by streamlined Pacifics, plodding over the single track beyond Kelso, and such-like prodigies.

Before considering how the East Coast line came to extend beyond Edinburgh and into north-eastern Scotland, let us turn to the southern end. The Great Northern Railway now enters our picture, that line which began at King's Cross with one of the most outstanding post-Georgian buildings in London, and ended, accord-ing to its first chairman, Edmund Denison, " in a ploughed field four miles north of Doncaster ". He was referring, not to the later junction point with the North Eastern at Shaftholme Junction, but to Askern, where the original East Coast expresses from King's Cross passed on to the Lancashire and Yorkshire Railway, over which they had to run for 14 miles to reach our old friend the York and North Midland.

In the early eighteen-forties, there was quite a fight for the enterprise of building a railway from London to York, or thereabouts. Three concerns were got going, the London and York, the Great Northern, and the Direct Northern. The London and York absorbed the Great Northern, whose title was actually dropped in May, 1844. Joseph Locke was appointed engineer, and advised in favour of the route subsequently adopted. One Friday night late in September, 1844, Mr. Denison received a letter from Locke in France, containing his resignation. The outlook was disastrous, for the rival Direct Northern was still on the warpath. Eligible engineers had their hands full in 1844, but Denison believed that William Cubitt might be available. Calling for the carriage, he went bowling off through the midnight streets of London to Clapham Common, where Cubitt lived. The house was in darkness, so Mr. Denison banged and rang until a window flew up on the first floor and a very angry Mr. Cubitt, in a long tasseled nightcap, thrust out his head.

" Who the devil are you, sir ? Go away ! "

" Ah, that you, Cubitt ? Will you be the engineer of the London and York ? "

" Eh ? What ? What's happened to Locke ? "

" Resigned. Will you take his place ? "

" Yes, I will come and see you in the morning."

So they parted politely; the appointment was confirmed next day, and announced on Monday.

In May, 1846, the rival Direct Northern was comfortably absorbed, the discarded title of Great Northern Railway was revived, and the company got its Act on June 26. Flat as was the country on the map, construction was not easy; some of it south of Peterborough was unreclaimed fen. Near Whittlesea Mere there was " a quaking bog you could stand upon and shake an acre of it together ". Tom Brassey, who had the contract for the London-Peterborough section, used the old Chat Moss technique of hurdling.

The Great Northern Railway, straightforward though it seemed on the map, was opened piece by piece. The first section, on March 1, 1848, was a bleak and fenny oddment in the Louth neighbourhood, not at any time part of the East Coast Route.

Next came the celebrated 4½ miles from Doncaster to the Askern ploughed field, then the long cross-country line from Louth down to Peterborough. In August, 1850, there was completed the southern part of the present main line, between Peterborough and a temporary London terminus at Maiden Lane. Very soon after, through Great Northern carriages were being run from London to Edinburgh via Peterborough, Boston, Lincoln, Retford, Doncaster, Knottingley, Church Fenton, York and thence by the present route except for the Leamside line.

Two important things happened in 1852; in August, the direct line from Peterborough to Retford via Grantham and Newark was opened for through traffic, and on October 14, the new and magnificent King's Cross Station was opened. Cubitt's nephew, Lewis, was the architect, and as is well known, he based the design of his two great roof spans on the roof of the Imperial Riding School in Moscow. The arched members were not girders, but were built up of planks bolted together. Consequently they produced the effect of a cantilever spring bent like a bow, and tended to push the eastern arched wall out into the street. On the western side there was more solid support from the main office block. During 1869 and 1870, the wooden roof was replaced by iron on the eastern side, and in 1886-7 the same was done on the western or departure side. As originally built, the station had two platform roads only, for departures and arrivals, with the wide intervening space filled with fourteen carriage sidings connected by short turntables. Later years brought additional island platforms, and suburban platforms outside, but the main structure has suffered little change from then to now. German air bombing took a slice out of the departure side at 3.21 a.m. on May 11, 1941, but one would scarcely guess it today. The great clock on the summit, which the G.N.R. bought out of the Great Exhibition of 1851, still rises proudly above the pigsty of jerry-building which came to obscure the station's fine façade. For over eighty years it kept exemplary time, but a tradition has now arisen that it had some sort of a nervous breakdown in 1936, when it looked across London and saw the Crystal Palace burning on Sydenham Hill.

There was some murmuring, when it was new, about the extravagance of having so magnificent a station, though in fact it turned out to have been remarkably inexpensive. It stood on the site of an old smallpox hospital. The " King's Cross " which furnished it with a name was in fact a cross-roads with a highly cravatted statue of George IV for decoration.

So the First Gentleman came down, and was banished to

whatever sort of an Elysium Victorian London thought fit for him, and the great station came in his place. The first train to leave it was the 7 a.m. Parliamentary for York on October 14, 1852, and the daily service then consisted of thirteen trains each way, three of them expresses and the rest slow. The new Great Northern Railway had no ferocious gradients, though it was not quite such a playground as the Great Western, starting as it did with a sharp rise at 1 in 110 to Holloway, and having a long climb at 1 in 200 from Wood Green to Potter's Bar. Over the Mimram Valley by Welwyn stretched the largest viaduct near London, with its forty brick arches carrying the track 89 ft. above the bed of the stream. The line brought also a sufficiency of tunnels, with seven between King's Cross and Potter's Bar, and two more north of Welwyn. Who can think of the East Coast Route without tasting its particular brand of sulphur? A more particular figure of the late Middle Ages is that of the man who, on up expresses, used to come through the older corridor trains in the Hitchin-Stevenage neighbourhood, carrying a perilous looking taper with which he lit the enormous gasoliers one after another.

So the East Coast Route was completed, in its original, somewhat circuitous form. A queer thing happened in the late 'fifties. As we have seen, the original course had been over the Midland Counties and North Midland lines, but in 1858 the Midland Railway itself started running over the Great Northern into King's Cross, gaining entry to London via Bedford and Hitchin. It continued to do so for ten years, until it had completed its own London extension, and the terrific Gothic of St. Pancras, with a rival giant clock, had soared into the patient London sky next door to King's Cross. During that intervening decade, with one double line and the simple signalling arrangements of the 'sixties, the congestion on the southern portion of the Great Northern Railway was menacing in its magnitude. On the night of June 9-10, 1866, there was an unholy smash in the northern Welwyn tunnel. A down Great Northern goods collapsed a tube; a following Midland goods ran into its back, and a trainload of Scotch beef and mutton, southward bound, careered into the wreckage. A fierce fire broke out, eruptions of flame and smoke poured out of a ventilating shaft, high upon the hill, and went on doing so all next day. It was a great barbecue, with unfortunate loss of life.

Until the 'seventies, all trains had to use the Knottingley and Leamside lines; the direct line from Doncaster to York via Selby was brought into use in 1871, and through Durham to Newcastle in the following year. The Team Valley line from Newcastle to

C. Hamilton Ellis

The Royal Crampton: North British Railway No. 55, heading an up East Coast express near Dunbar in 1851

Durham was opened in 1868. For many years the old High Level Bridge provided the only access to the latter place for through trains from the south. The present line deviating northwards from a point near Bensham and crossing the Tyne on the King Edward Bridge, was not opened until 1906. York, too, for many years had a terminal station inside the walls, through which a wide arch was cut. In 1877, it was turned over to coaching storage, and old buildings adjoining it contain the famous railway museum established there by the London and North Eastern Railway. York became a through station, outside the walls, and one of the largest of its kind in the country. It was designed by Thomas Prosser, and opened on June 25, 1877. The roofing closely resembles that of Paddington, though the great sweeping curve on which it was built distracts one's perceptions from this. The longest platform is 1,500 ft. between ramps.

Physical changes apart, the most important development on the East Coast Route during Mid-Victorian years was the formation, in 1854, of the North Eastern Railway Company by amalgamation of the York, Newcastle and Berwick, the York and North Midland, and the Leeds Northern (which gave the West Riding access to the main East Coast line at Thirsk). To these were added the ancient Stockton and Darlington Railway in 1863, bringing doubtless a wholesome Quaker leavening to the previous Hudsonian mixture. The S. and D.R. for long retained virtual autonomy.

Turning back to the northern extremity of the East Coast line, the terminus in Edinburgh did not remain one for long. The Edinburgh and Glasgow Railway had been terminating at the Haymarket, Edinburgh, since 1841, but while the North British Railway was under construction, the E. and G.R. likewise was at work on the long tunnel east of Haymarket and the line passing through the ravine that separated the Old Town and the New Town. Six weeks after the opening of the N.B.R., Edinburgh and Glasgow trains began running into the same station between the North Bridge and the Waverley Bridge. It became known as the General Station, and had its entrance and offices on the Waverley Bridge. Through carriages were run from Glasgow to Berwick, and it became obvious that neither Edinburgh nor Glasgow were to be monopolised by one group of railway interests where traffic to and from the south was concerned.

On May 17, 1847, the Edinburgh, Leith and Granton Railway* opened a station called Canal Street, close to the " General " but

---

* Originally incorporated as the Edinburgh, Leith and Newhaven Railway, its first section was opened from Scotland Street (then called Cannonmills) to Trinity in 1842.

at right angles to it, and approached by a tunnel rising towards it at 1 in 27, under the New Town, worked by rope haulage. This gave direct, if very wearisome access to the north by a ferry between Granton and Burntisland. Granton Harbour was built by the then Duke of Buccleuch. On the opposite shore, railway transport had begun with the Edinburgh and Northern Railway, incorporated in 1845 to build a line from Burntisland to Ladybank Junction, with divergent routes thence to join the Scottish Central near Perth on the one hand, and through Cupar to Ferryport-on-Craig on the Firth of Tay, giving access to Dundee via Broughty Ferry. It was opened on May 7, 1848. In the following year, this Edinburgh and Northern absorbed the Edinburgh, Leith and Granton, and restyled itself Edinburgh, Perth and Dundee Railway. The line could hardly be regarded yet as being of national importance, although it was later to become a very considerable part of the through East Coast Route. Travelling by it from Edinburgh to Dundee in Mid-Victorian years was a waesome business. One started at the Canal Street terminus, a dreich place at right angles to the General Station. Thence the carriages, without locomotive, but with special brake-wagons attached, tobogganned slowly down through a steep tunnel to Scotland Street. There the brake wagons were taken off, a locomotive came on, and drew the train forward for a couple of miles to Granton. Having made this bright start, the passengers, with all their luggage, had to transfer to the ferry steamer which took them across the Firth of Forth to Burntisland. With the water choppy and a bitter east wind howling up the firth, it beat Hell. Heavy luggage was conveyed as far as Burntisland by *through trolleys*, which were run on and off fish wagons. Having reached Burntisland more or less alive, the happy travellers once more entrained, and their conveyance doddered on its weary way to Ladybank Junction. Here a couple of carriages would be detached for Perth, and those who were not in too great a hurry to reach Dundee could go round that way, picking up the Dundee, Perth and Aberdeen Junction Railway, though in early days this necessitated taking a cab at Perth to reach the Schoolhill Station across the river. Passengers who had bravely committed themselves to a direct attack by sea invasion stayed in the main part of the train, which crawled on to Tayport and there unloaded them and all their chattels on another bleak and east-windy quay, with another singularly comfortless steamer in readiness. The process seems to have resembled that undergone in modern war by certain people engaged in certain *special duties*. When these have been heartened, praised, and patted on the back after accomplishing some touchy mission, the bladder of their conceit is unkindly punctured. True, they are given a chance of backing out gracefully (as were the Dundee passengers at Ladybank Junction) but thereafter they must be prepared to board the aeroplane which will in due time parachute them back into a pitch-black country under hostile occupation. What a relief was one's entrainment at Burntisland after just living through the Forth crossing ! But how one's heart and stomach must have dropped on that final approach to the ferry at Tayport, with the fury of the skies and the upheavals of one's cherished inside to be faced all over again ! So it was, in the days before the Forth and Tay Bridges had been built. The sad survivors eventually reached Broughty Ferry, and joined their third train, which crawled up the branch, reversed, and staggered into Dundee too late for high tea. True, there was a " fast " service. It left Edinburgh at the unholy hour of 6.25 a.m., and occupied 3 hours 12 minutes. In the up direction it left Dundee at 12.50 p.m. Of course things were not always so frightful; occasionally the journey could be very pleasant, but the climate of eastern Scotland has never been fairly comparable to that of the Aegean.

A few gentler ghosts of the old Edinburgh, Perth and Dundee Railway survived in various forms. The Scotland Street tunnel, cut out by construction of a more circuitous but more practical line by Leith Walk, became, at various times, a wagon storage, a mushroom farm and a composite air-raid shelter, first-aid post and emergency traffic control centre. The railway was taken into the North British system in 1862, and the N.B.R. achieved an absolute monopoly of the ancient Kingdom of Fife. Granton station was closed on November 2, 1925. When the Forth Bridge had come into being, and the direct route thence to Perth via Mawcarse Junction, the line from Ladybank Junction became more of a backwater than ever, and was for long a favourite hunting-ground for the lover of antique locomotives. One of these was the royal Crampton, which ended her days in the present century as No. 1009, but which had originally been No. 55. She had been very severely converted, and only her carrying wheels were recognisable from her brave days in tartan. Some of the intermediate stations in Fife, like many others in Scotland, have long had a reputation for beautiful gardens on the platforms. At Cupar, function overlapped with adornment, with the result that, on its up platform, the station boasted what was probably the most beautifully situated cast-iron convenience in the world.

Between Granton and Burntisland plied the ferries *Leviathan*, *Balbirnie*, *Kinloch* and *Midlothian*. The last-mentioned carried 40 wagons on the train deck. *Leviathan*, though not appearing in *Lloyds Register* until 1874, was built and engined by Robert Napier in 1849, and plied until 1890 when the Forth Bridge was opened and she was sold for breaking up. She was a paddle steamer of 399 tons gross, with a two-cylinder 210 h.p. engine. On this most ancient train ferry service, a movable jetty, running up and down rails on an inclined plane, transferred the wagons between shore tracks and the open deck of the steamer, at all states of the tide. Passenger coaches were not taken.

North of the Tay, what was to become the East Coast line to Aberdeen went through the same piece-by-piece sort of construction, including that of some of the oldest railways in Scotland. The Dundee and Arbroath Railway Company was incorporated in 1836, opened from Arbroath to Craigie in 1838, and completed into Dundee on April 2, 1840. Nobody thought that it would later have more than local significance, and the Dundee and Arbroath saw no reason why it should not, like the Great Western, have a gauge of its own. In a truly liberal spirit of compromise, with the neighbouring Arbroath and Forfar, it chose the 5 ft. 6 in. gauge, and its original track, laid on stone blocks, was arranged for right-hand running instead of left. The gauge was narrowed in 1847.

The railway's subsequent history was extraordinary, for it belonged for many years to the West Coast camp. The old Dundee, Perth and Aberdeen Junction Railway leased it shortly before it was opened, then the Caledonian had it; in 1850 it began twelve glorious years of independence, but in 1862 it was merged into the Scottish North Eastern, and came thereby for a second time into the Caledonian creel. In 1880, it was placed under a joint committee of the Caledonian and the North British companies, and as the Dundee and Arbroath Joint Railway it survived, latterly under the L.M.S. and the L.N.E.R., until the end of company ownership. It is an unexciting line, running flatly along the north shore of Tay. It had one tragic event in its history, during the great snowstorm in the winter of 1906, when an East Coast express turned back at Arbroath and with the engine (N.B.R. No. 324) running tender first, collided at full speed in the blizzard with a stationary Caledonian local.

Contemporary with the Dundee and Arbroath, and built to the same broad gauge, was the Arbroath and Forfar, which eventually and naturally became a branch of the Caledonian Railway. It deserves mention in that it provided the first East Coast connection to Aberdeen. The direct line from Arbroath, through Montrose to Kinnaber Junction on the Caledonian, was not open for all traffic until May 1, 1883,* by which time the first Tay Bridge had come and gone.

Not there, along that harsh coast of the Scottish north-east, do we find the straight lines and civilised gradients of the East Coast Route farther south. When, in 1895, East Coast and West Coast raced one another, night after night, from London to Aberdeen, the toughest job was that of the North British engines north of Edinburgh. The only easy stretch is that of just over 15 miles, straight and dead-level practically throughout, from Camperdown Junction, Dundee, almost to Arbroath. Between Burntisland and Ladybank Junction are two sharp humps, with considerable stretches at 1 in 100-105, and steepest gradients of 1 in 67, for a short stretch, near Thornton Junction, and 1 in 95 between Falkland Road and Ladybank Junction, both rising in the southbound direction. From near Arbroath to Kinnaber Junction, there is a profile like the edge of the executioner's axe in *Annie Protheroe*, and the line which finally combines East and West Coast routes on the last 38 miles into Aberdeen is stiffly undulating, and quite violent enough in places.

* St. Vigeans Junction—Letham Grange, November 1, 1880, thence to Lunan Bay on October 8, and to Kinnaber, though not for through East Coast expresses, on March 1, 1881.

CHAPTER SEVEN

The Great Bridges and the Waverley

AT intervals through history, proposals were made for bridging the Firths of Forth and Tay, and of the railway age, the outstanding early planner was Thomas Bouch, who, as far back as 1854, when he was engineer to the Edinburgh, Perth and Dundee Railway, described in detail to his directors how both tasks could be undertaken. Such projects were beyond the company's means. It was not until 1869, when the North British Railway was the controlling force, that the decision was taken to bridge the Firth of Tay between Wormit in Fife and Dundee Esplanade, with Bouch responsible for design. Restrictions by Government at first required a headway of not less than 100 ft., but this was reduced to 88 ft. after some wrangling. The North British company was most anxious to supersede at least one of the awful ferries bequeathed by the Edinburgh, Perth and Dundee Railway. At best, and as we have seen, the 46-mile journey from Edinburgh to Dundee occupied 3 hours and 12 minutes of solemn humiliation and repentance.

There was much more of these last-mentioned commodities to come, had people known, but they did not know; certainly not the sanguine Bouch. He satisfied himself, after several preliminary borings, that he had to reckon with substrata of hard clay, gravel and rock. Thereon he proposed to erect a viaduct of 89 spans resting on twin cylindrical piers of stone and brickwork. So construction began, and all went happily until the fifteenth pier from the Fife side was reached. Here and hereafter, the fine solid bottom began to grow rapidly less fine and solid, and it became painfully clear that it would by no means support the massive red brick pillars originally intended. The alternative was a much lighter pier, on a wider masonry base, and for the superstructure of these piers Bouch chose slender cast-iron columns. There was no particular reason why these should not bear the weight to be superimposed. The strain exerted by high winds blowing broadside was another matter, which did not come into the amended calculations.

At the same time, the design of the bridge's middle section was modified. Here, to give the required headway, the rails were carried inside the lattice girders instead of on top. The number of high spans was reduced from 14 of 200 ft. to 11 of 245 ft. and two of 227 ft. As the iron columns were erected, they were filled with concrete. The bridge was formally opened on May 31, 1878. It was on a falling gradient, from the high cliffs of the Fife shore to the level banks on the Dundee side, which it approached, as does the present bridge, on a sweeping right-hand curve to a new station at the back of Dundee Esplanade. It had two approaches at the Fife end; one connecting with the old Tayport line of the erstwhile Edinburgh, Perth and Dundee Railway, and the other forming a direct line from Leuchars Junction on the latter, through St. Fort. The total length was 11,653 ft.

So the great bridge stood across the Tay, one of the wonders of the world. Queen Victoria passed over it, and after her safe translation she knighted Bouch. In the public eye, all was very well, and Bouch had already undertaken to bridge the Firth of Forth just east of the Queensferry Passage, with a monstrous steel suspension bridge, carrying, like the Tay Bridge, a single-track railway. Work was begun on this, and a brick pier was built on Inchgarvie.

On the afternoon of Sunday, December 28, 1879, a tremendous gale beat up over Central Scotland. Chimneys came down, slates whirled in the air like cards, barns were unroofed. The wind swept through the girders of the Tay Bridge, making it sing like a vast Æolian harp. But none feared for it, save perhaps some of those who had watched the wet concrete swelling in the iron columns so that these cracked, and had to be bound with wrought-iron bands. There were few Sunday trains on Scottish railways at that time. The mails had to be carried, and Dundee duly sent the up mail to Burntisland, whence it returned, behind the Dundee spare engine, N.B.R. No. 224, late in the afternoon. The train reached Wormit Junction, where the enginemen received the train staff at 7.13 p.m. and continued slowly on to the shuddering bridge. From the Wormit signalbox, Signalman Barclay and Ganger Watt followed its lights until they reached the high girders in the middle. The red tail-lamp winked and vanished in the girders.

Within those girders, the train presented with them a solid sail against the force of the wind, which rose in those moments to a hurricane gust. The iron columns broke. The concrete that had never dried spilt out of them. A few people, looking out by chance, saw a ruddy flash of fire falling, then darkness.

In the station at Dundee, people waited to meet those who were coming in by the train. The signalman who had received

" Train in section " from Wormit likewise waited. Anxiously, he tried to " talk " to Wormit on the old-fashioned telegraph. The line was dead. People peered out over the wind-lashed waters. Brief flashes of moonlight showed what seemed a great cloud of vapour or spray, which in fact came from the Newport water-main, laid beside the rails across the bridge and broken when it broke. Some said that they could see a great void where the high girders had been; others said " Och, get away ! "

Stationmaster Smith of Dundee Tay Bridge, and Mr. Roberts, the district locomotive superintendent, made their way on to the bridge, clinging to the iron parapets as they went. With their hands cut and bruised, their clothes soaked by the great gobs of sleet borne down by the storm, they went far enough to see that at least some of the high girders and their supporting piers had vanished. With news of this they returned to Dundee, and though the wishful clung to information that the mail engine was fitted with steam brakes and might have halted and held her train even as the gap yawned ahead, it became clear that part of the bridge had fallen, taking with it the train and the 73 people aboard. Dawn broke, and showed that all 13 of the high girders had gone. Across the fairway, their piers showed as a string of broken stumps, lashed by the waves.

A little later, the mail bags were washed up at Broughty Ferry. Some of the dead were cast ashore, with bits of panelling and carriage doors. After the storm had blown itself out, divers went down to investigate. They found the train lying inside the sagging girders on the bed of the Firth. It was still roughly in line; the engine was on her side in full forward gear; the carriages lay battered and unroofed, with no sign of their passengers. Some months later, pieces of North British coachwork drifted ashore on the Norway coast, giving rise to a legend still current in Scotland that an entire coach body crossed the North Sea and was thriftily put to a useful after-life by the Norwegian State Railways. In the spring of 1880, first the tender, then the engine, were raised and re-railed at Tayport, taken to Cowlairs, and repaired. North British No. 224 survived the calamity by forty years, being withdrawn at last in 1919.

The inquiry into the accident was long, and the published findings were massive. The gist of them was that the soundings had been quite inadequate, many of the caissons had not been sunk nearly far enough and severe scouring had taken place at the bases of certain of the piers, that lamentable miscalculation had taken place in estimating lateral wind pressure, that the quality of the cast iron used had been questionable, and that the bridge had been badly designed, badly built, and badly maintained. Technically, that divided responsibility between Sir Thomas Bouch, the contractors, and the North British Railway, but in fact Bouch had assumed previous responsibility for all three. At the end of the inquiry, he suffered a nervous collapse. He went into seclusion at a house in Moffat, where he died.

The fall of the first Tay Bridge inevitably brought to an end its designer's plans for a steel suspension bridge across the Firth of Forth and the works were at once abandoned, at heavy loss. The unfinished brick pier still survives on the island of Inchgarvie. But the improvement in east Scottish communications brought by the Tay Bridge, while it had lasted, had shown that its repair or replacement must be undertaken as soon as possible. One proposal was for the duplication of the existing foundations, uniting them with the old brick arches, and superimposing new masonry piers and wrought iron girders. It was a makeshift, avoiding recognition of the fact that the old caissons were inadequate in themselves, and that rubble had to be dumped round their bases at intervals to prevent them from being undermined. The Parliamentary Committee set up to consider the future of the Tay Bridge connection recommended the building of an entirely new bridge on the upstream side of the old one. The Board of Trade required the complete removal of the old bridge before work should start on the new one.

W. H. Barlow and Crawford Barlow, his son, were entrusted with the design of the new bridge, with William Arrol and Company as contractors. After some polite wrangling with the Board of Trade, they were given permission to use what remained of the old bridge for carrying materials to the new construction, after which the original piers might be cut down to about high-water-mark. Practical experiments made on the site included the sinking of a trial caisson to a depth of 20 ft. in soft silt, where the bed of the Firth was at its worst, putting in a concrete bottom, and loading it to twice the maximum expected for the new bridge. Five and a quarter inches of settlement was recorded, then no more, though the weight was kept on for ten weeks. Also, two of the old piers were loaded with old rails, giving a gross pressure on the piers of $3\frac{3}{5}$ tons per sq. ft. One pier, standing in clean sand, settled $\frac{1}{4}$ in., and the other, in micaceous sand, sank a little over 2 in. The river bed, which was found to have sunk round the old piers since their construction, was exhaustively surveyed, and its nature exactly ascertained.

Plans of the Barlows' bridge were ready in the autumn of 1880. It was placed 60 ft. upstream from the remains of the old bridge and was arranged for double track, consisting of wrought-iron piers on concrete cylinders, with steel girder spans above. Some of the old girder spans, which were ascertained to be sound, were transferred to the new bridge and enclosed within the new girders. The test weight imposed on each of the largest piers amounted to 2,438 tons. So came the new Tay Bridge, 10,711 ft. long, or 151 ft. over two miles, 83 ft. high at the southern abutment, 26½ ft. high at the land end of the northern curve of 21 chains radius, with its level middle section of five spans at a height of 79 ft. The longest spans are eleven of 245 ft. Rocker bearings at intervals of about 500 ft. allow for expansion and contraction under changes of temperature. Work on components began in Arrol's yard at Glasgow in June, 1882; the foundations were begun in July, 1883. The first goods train crossed the bridge on June 12, 1887, on June 18 it was tested and passed by the Board of Trade, and passenger traffic began two days later. Since then it has stood fast.

An examination, in the light of later experience, of Sir Thomas Bouch's design for a steel suspension bridge over the Firth of Forth suggests to a generation wise after another event that it would probably have fallen or broken as disastrously as the old Tay Bridge. The impression one gets from published drawings is that of immense drying poles, 600 ft. high, with an exaggerated sag to the lines.

In the early 'eighties designs were invited by the Forth Bridge Railway Company, an undertaking backed by the three East Coast companies and the Midland Railway, and, as is well known, the winning design was that submitted by Sir John Fowler and Benjamin Baker. Tancred, Arrol and Company had the contract, and the caissons were sunk in 1883. The cantilever bridge, like the suspension bridge, is of great antiquity, and may still be seen in its primeval form in parts of China. But Fowler's and Baker's cantilever bridge across the Firth of Forth was on a scale never before attempted; the nearest approach to it at that time was the Lansdowne Bridge over the Indus at Sukkur. Of the three great towers supporting the cantilevers, one stands on Inchgarvie, one on the north shore, and the third in the bed of the Firth, which at the Queensferry Passage is about 4,000 ft. wide at low water. Each tower is 361 ft. high from high-water-mark, and the deepest piers reach to 70 ft. below low-water-mark. The two main spans between the central tower on Inchgarvie and the others are each 1,710 ft. long, the end cantilever spans each 689 ft. 9 in., the girder spans between the cantilevers are each 350 ft. long, and their height above high water is 180 ft. Of the high lattice-girder approach viaducts, two spans are of 179 ft., two of 173 ft. and eleven of 168 ft. The masonry approach viaducts at each end contribute 521 ft., and the overall length of the Forth Bridge is 8,296 ft.

Construction went on through the middle and late 'eighties, by night as well as by day, with the monstrous tubes and girders ablaze with the fitful violet glare of hundreds of arc lamps. Into the piers went 120,000 cu. yd. of Arbroath stone and granite; about 45,000 tons of steel went into the tubular members and girders, and some 8,000,000 rivets. One inch per 100 ft. was allowed, all over the bridge, for expansion and contraction under changes of temperature, and the structure is calculated to withstand a lateral wind pressure of 56 lb. per sq. ft. The bridge proved to be a killer during construction; 56 men were lost, compared with 13 on the Barlows' Tay Bridge. The total cost came to approximately £2,500,000.

On March 4, 1890, a grey, gusty, wet day, the Marchioness of Tweeddale drove North British engine No. 602 on to the bridge, with the first train to cross. On the bridge, the Prince of Wales (afterwards Edward VII), top-coated, silk-hatted and majestic, ceremonially drove the last of those millions of rivets in a howling squall, the company entrained again, No. 602 and her train moved forward to the other shore, and the East Coast main line was complete from King's Cross to Kinnaber.

From that day forward, the Forth Bridge has stood unchanging in a mutable world. It is among the few prodigies of civil engineering that cannot be exaggerated by graphic brush or pen. It truly fills the sky above the village of North Queensferry. From the air it is still vast. Remotely enormous, it crops up in the Lothian landscape. From the Calton Hill in Edinburgh it shows up like three distant, gigantic termitaries. When seen broadside, up or down the Firth, it is a thing of delicate beauty. At night, with a train passing over and the ruddy glare from an open firedoor catching the topmost girders, its splendour is awful. In an era which has brought other enormous bridges in many parts of the world, there remains therein nothing quite like the Forth Bridge.

Bridging the last gap in the East Coast Route brought greatly increased through traffic to the Waverley Station at Edinburgh. At that time it was still, in most respects, the old, inadequate General Station dating from the physical union of the Edinburgh and Glasgow Railway with the North British. The old Canal Street station at right-angles to it was closed when the Abbeyhill and Leith Walk line to Leith and Granton was opened in 1868. Thereafter, the main station was somewhat extended and improved though it was still no stately monument. William Morris, obliged to linger there on his way to Iceland in July, 1871, after the doubtful comforts of a journey overnight from King's Cross in the third class of the period, recorded: " the station is a trifle more miserable looking than the worst of such places in England ". A more racy disapproval was that expressed by Professor Foxwell in his survey of express trains in the Royal Statistical Society's papers (1888).* " On the platforms of the Waverley Station at Edinburgh may be witnessed every evening in summer a scene of confusion so chaotic that a sober description of it is incredible to those who have not themselves survived it. Trains of caravan length come in portentously late from Perth, so that each is mistaken for its successor; these have to be broken up and remade on insufficient sidings, while bewildered crowds of tourists sway up and down amongst equally bewildered porters on the narrow village platform reserved for these most important expresses; the higher officials stand lost in subtle thought, returning now and then to repeated inquiries some masterpiece of reply couched in the cautious conditional, while the hands of the clock with a humorous air survey the abandoned sight, till at length, without any obvious reason and with sudden stealth, the shame-stricken driver hurries his passengers off into the dark."

At the time of which Foxwell wrote, the Forth Bridge was still being built. When it was opened, the congestion of the Waverley Station became chronic, when before it had been more or less seasonal. In 1892, its metamorphosis began. Quadruple tracking was carried out on both approaches, through the Mound and the Calton Hill tunnels. The old station between the North Bridge and the Waverley Bridge was replaced by a very large island station, with its offices in the middle, two separate terminal portions for north and south traffic, and through lines and platforms on either side. The North Bridge was rebuilt at the same time, and its line fell across the middle of the new station. The style of the place was somewhat cramped by *servitudes* (corresponding to *ancient lights* in England) so that its 11½-acre glass roof was restricted to a height of 42 ft. above rail level. It became the largest railway station in Great Britain, excepting Clapham Junction, which was then really two stations, much of whose acreage was taken up by carriage sidings, and this distinction it retained until London's new Waterloo Station was opened in 1922. Of the Waverley's four signal-boxes,

* Quoted by E. L. Ahrons in *The Railway Magazine* of August, 1920.

with a total of 565 levers, the East Box, with 260 levers, had what was the longest single locking frame in the world at the time of its construction. The old signalling was replaced by modern colour-light equipment, extending from Haymarket East to Abbeyhill Junction, during the nineteen-thirties.

Thereapart, and saving the building of the magnificently ugly North British Hotel with its superb clock (completed in October, 1902), the place has changed little with the years. The roaring cable trams (delicious mystery to a boy !) have gone for ever from the streets outside, but those streets are still reached by the same windy flights of stairs, where the north-easters do the same things with your best grey trilby or your lady's Post-New-Look as they did with Uncle Willie's flat-top-bowler and Aunt Janet's petticoats. Down below there is the same gauntly magnificent booking hall, with its mosaic pavement having the North British Railway's coat of arms in each corner. One of them is cracked across; how one could have cracked that massive device by any means short of dropping a battleship on it passes comprehension, but there it is, characteristic after all these years of the shabby splendour which used to distinguish the more imposing flights of the North British. Trains going north steam out through the tunnels in the Mound, once the city's garbage heap and now supporting the National Gallery, the buses and the tub-thumpers. They sweep proudly through Princes Street Gardens and under the Castle Rock on their way to Aberdeen, or Perth, or Inverness. Trains going south pass out below the battlemented remnants of the Calton Gaol, which tourists always fondly imagined to be the castle itself. For all its gloomy magnitude, the Waverley remains one of the most impressive metropolitan stations in Europe. Milan tried to be sublime, but succeeded only in being colossally ridiculous.

The Waverley is also the best placed city station in the country. Not here do you find the like of London Bridge, sprawling between Tooley Street and Guys, or Paddington sitting on the trailing skirts of Bayswater, or London's northern termini lurking furtively beyond Bloomsbury. The Waverley is *in* Edinburgh. It is a fascinating place. Last time your author was there, he leant over the garden parapet above the Mound Tunnel for so long, looking down at the trains and the signal lights, that a stately policeman ranged up with a fatherly look in his eye, apparently ready to point out that things were not quite as bad as that.

CHAPTER EIGHT

Of Mr. Sturrock's Dream, and its Fulfilment

PERVERSELY, for such changes as there be are for the better, I like to think of King's Cross and its trains as they were over thirty years ago. The scene is easy to recapture, for only the trains have changed very much. It was never the cleanest station in London, and Scandinavians arriving from Newcastle, having gradually recovered from their impressions of the Tyneside, were properly horrified at the first glimpse of London vouchsafed to them by King's Cross. But the tropical green of the Great Northern engines, an incredibly luscious green it was, quite different from the darker shades of the Great Central, the Great Western and the South Eastern and Chatham, or the faintly yellowish green of the South Western, caught the youthful eye and held it. The acridity of South Yorkshire coal, at which one's elders railed, was heavenly in a boy's nostrils, and when he saw his first Great Northern Atlantic-type engine, previously known only in post-cards and picture books, he felt, had he known it, like the tourist who sees for the first time the Jungfrau, and discovers that she really does blush at sundown. Then round the back, patiently shunting empty coaches, there was a domeless Stirling 0-4-4 tank engine with a bright brass safety-valve casing, and *that* produced the same sort of excitement as one's first view of San Gimignano.

Of course, there were the carriages; stately sleeping cars with their teak sides polished like a baronial dining table, embellished with proud coats of arms and the mystic legend E.C.J.S.; older, more florid twelve-wheelers, with clerestories ornate in figured frosted glass, and glaring gasoliers with ponderous equipment for dimming them at night. Here and there were carriages which did not belong to London at all; North Eastern carriages, which were a credit to any railway, and North British ones, which were not.

In their earliest days, all three of the East Coast railways had an incredible collection of engines. The Great Northern was nearer uniformity than the others, for it began business with a large number of Sharp's and Hawthorn's standard types. It was briefly let in for the embarrassing services of Mr. Bury, but his little tar-boiler engines did not flourish here as they had done on the London and Birmingham. He afterwards claimed to have originated the characteristic Great Northern carriage, with its panels unpainted and highly varnished. This clung to the East Coast Route for nearly a century; almost at the very last, the London and North Eastern was building steel carriages, then carefully painting and graining their outsides to look like varnished teak, even putting on imitation mouldings, a quaint converse to the American practice of the early nineteen-twenties, which was to coat old wooden coaches with tinplate, securing it with massive nails intended to resemble rivets. In spite of the *Daily Express*, the British public never got really anxious about wooden coaches.

The Great Northern Railway was fortunate in getting the services of a very eminent locomotive man at an early stage of its history. Archibald Sturrock, as shrewd a Scot as ever came out of the broad links of Angus, had been second in command to Daniel Gooch of the Great Western during the Battle of the Gauges. From Swindon he brought the excellent precept, somewhat ignored in the 'forties and 'fifties, that the best way to make an engine go was to give it a larger boiler and a high pressure. " The finest gun ", he said, " is no use unless there be plenty of powder." That simile was characteristic of the man, for Sturrock was ever a good gun, and liked to appear even on official occasions dressed as if he were just going off to a shoot. He went to the Great Northern in 1850, and soon after the opening of King's Cross Station he dreamed a dream, then announced publicly that he saw no reason why the new East Coast expresses should not run thence to Edinburgh in eight hours. In proof of his belief, he built a big 4-2-2 bogie engine, No. 215, with 7 ft. 6 in. driving wheels, 17½ by 24 in. cylinders, 1,718 sq. ft. of heating surface, and a working pressure of 150 lb. per sq. in. At that time, on many lines, 80 lb. was considered a respectable pressure. The only British standard-gauge engine bigger than G. N. R. No. 215 up to that time was the Crampton white elephant *Liverpool* on the London and North Western. What the Great Northern directors really thought of their locomotive super-intendent's proposals must remain unrecorded, but it is unlikely that the partners in the East Coast, the York, Newcastle and Berwick and the North British, would have welcomed the idea. Poor old 215 ! She became a sort of current account for spare parts, and her big driving wheels finished up in a Stirling single.

Sturrock's ordinary express engines were smaller, but still out-standing of their period, and the 150 lb. pressure was perpetuated.

91

In 1863 he made a very remarkable innovation in some heavy 5 ft.
0-6-0 goods engines, in which the six tender wheels were also
coupled, and driven by a smaller pair of cylinders supplied through
flexible connections from the main boiler, to give increased tractive
force on starting and getting the heavy London coal trains under
way. The arrangement made rather undue demands on the boiler
of that time, even a Sturrock boiler; the men complained that the
footplates were unpleasantly hot, and that they were being required
to look after " two engines at once ". Even so, the arrangement
was a remarkable anticipation of the booster principle. In con-
ception, it was ancient.

Sturrock was responsible for the Great Northern carriages as
well as the engines, a consideration of £250 a year being added to
his initial stipend of £500 a year when he joined the company,
on this account. After the manner and means of Mid-Victorian
locomotive engineers, he managed to amass a considerable fortune
while in office, and by 1866, when he was exactly fifty years old,
he decided that the time had come for him to retire on this, plus,
one assumes, a liberal pension from a properly grateful company.
So wee Archie Sturrock of Petruchie, became Squire Sturrock, J.P.,
of the big house. Twenty-two years later, the Great Northern's
distinguished pensioner was still hunting. Thirty-five years later,
finding that his hand was not as steady as of yore, he regretfully
laid down his gun. He continued to dispense justice, a strange,
moustachioed old man, dressed as ever, in light hill checks with a
watered-silk stock, scarifying poachers, and upbraiding patient
policemen because he could no longer hear their evidence. He
just outlived the year of 1908, his ninety-third.

The coming of Patrick Stirling to Doncaster Works, Great
Northern Railway, from the remote bush of the Glasgow and South
Western, brought marked changes in the design of the standard
Great Northern engines. The domeless boiler remained, though
it was flush-topped now, instead of having the raised casing over the
firebox after the fashion of Swindon. Outside bearings disappeared
from driving axles; goods engines had inside frames; all engines
had cabs. There had been little shelter on a Sturrock engine, as
on the old broad-gauge engines of the Great Western. Stirling
made a simple and effective cab in two sheets, one forming the
spectacle-plate and the other the roof and both sides. The first
Stirling cabs were rectangular in elevation, with a round window
each side, but soon after, cutaway side-sheets succeeded this, giving
an easier lookout at the expense of a slightly shorter roof. It was
a simple cab; long reversing lever to right, one gauge glass to left,

Between the Welwyn Tunnels : Up East Coast express, Great Northern Railway, in the 'nineties, headed by Patrick Stirling's 7 ft. 7 in. single No. 235

injectors, pressure gauge, and, dominating all, the big two-handled pull-out regulator.

Certain Stirling features seemed retrograde. Neither pressures nor heating surfaces showed any marked tendency to increase, rather the reverse. Yet old Great Northern drivers swore by the Stirling engines with a loyalty seldom known elsewhere, except among those who served the London, Brighton and South Coast in Stroudley's time. The fast trains, save exceptionally, were hauled by engines with single driving wheels thenceforward to the late 'nineties, and a series of big coupled engines by Sturrock was rebuilt as singles. Never, in Stirling's time, which lasted from 1866 to his death in 1896, did one see two engines on a Great Northern train. The thing was anathema, and the heavy midday Scots expresses during the mid-ninety summer holiday seasons, which included a set comprising two eight-wheel diners with a six-wheel kitchen car between, were always headed by one Stirling single-wheeler, either an eight-footer or one of the equally competent 7 ft. 7 in. engines (2-2-2 with inside cylinders).

The celebrated eight-footers scarcely need detailed description; they have been, perhaps, the most-written, oftest-sung engines in British locomotive history, and in another book I have given them a chapter to themselves (*Some Classic Locomotives : Pat Stirling's Masterpiece*). The original No. 1, which has survived, and which refreshed public acquaintanceship by hauling a series of special " period " excursions in 1938, is kept at York Railway Museum. She ran in regular service from 1870 to 1907, when she ended her normal active existence as the station pilot at Doncaster.

While Stirling built many heavy six-coupled mineral engines, much of the Great Northern's fast goods traffic was worked by 0-4-2 mixed-traffic engines, of which there were large numbers and several varieties. The 0-4-4 suburban and branch-line tank engines were closely akin to them. Many of the ordinary passenger trains were worked by 2-4-0 locomotives, certain of which survived, with the old Stirling boilers, into the early years of the London and North Eastern Railway, on the level country lines of Lincolnshire.

The Great Northern Railway was the first British company to run a regular dining-car service, with kitchen equipment on the train, which it did with a Pullman car called *Prince of Wales* on the Leeds business expresses in 1879. Diners were much later in coming to the East Coast expresses in Scotland. In 1881, however, Doncaster produced a design for a side-corridor coach, the forerunner of the ordinary British main-line carriage of today, and it was built in the following year, a four-compartment six-wheel first class, with a ladies-only compartment and lavatory at one end, and a fully equipped " gents " at the other. A five-compartment variation, for second and third class, was brought out seven years later. Such carriages were built in very large numbers to the standard Great Northern design for the East Coast Joint Stock, and apparently the G.N.R. at any rate was so pleased with them that they continued to be the regular thing for King's Cross, Edinburgh and Aberdeen for long after eight- and twelve-wheelers were general on the rival West Coast and Midland Routes. Two of them were united to form the first of Gresley's famous articulated carriages in 1907. At first, the corridors led only to Jericho, but the rebuilt examples had Pullman corridor connections and could be marshalled with the much more spacious and comfortable bogie carriages and dining cars built from the late 'nineties onwards.

Among the occasional misfortunes of the Great Northern Railway, there was a very serious accident at Abbots Ripton on January 1, 1876. The up Flying Scotsman ran into a shunting coal train in a blinding snowstorm. Although destruction of vehicles was severe, there was no worse casualty among the passengers than a broken leg. A few minutes later, the evening down Leeds express, headed by an eight-footer, ran into the wreckage, and in this second collision 13 lives were lost. The accident is historically interesting, in that one of the contributory causes was a doubtful indication given by one of the old signals with the semaphore pivoted in a slotted post, the slot having become choked with hard snow. The Great Northern, and most other railways, abolished the slotted signal during the years following, likewise the white light for a *line clear* indication, adopting instead of the latter the old cautionary green. The Great Northern went one further, using thereafter a signal in which the board was centrally pivoted on an extension at right angles to the post. The North Eastern Railway, on the other hand, retained the slotted signal, or its lattice-post equivalent, and one can still see it in plenty between Humber and Tweed.

While there was a fair uniformity among Great Northern loco-motives, it was not so with the North Eastern. Until the middle 'eighties, the variety of North Eastern engines was staggering. Even those specifically belonging to the same class differed one from another, and needed different spare parts. Something of it had to do with the formation of the company by amalgamation ; more had to do with the character of the locomotive engineer, Edward Fletcher, who had come into the business via the York and North Midland Railway. He was an amiable, fatherly character, who liked to run his extensive locomotive department as a sort of federation of autonomous principalities, each stemming from one or other constituent of the North Eastern Railway. They even painted the engines in different styles.

Gateshead was Mr. Fletcher's Imperial General Staff head-quarters, and Gateshead engines were painted light green, with red-brown frames, the former with bands of dark green and black, with vermilion and white lines, and the latter with vermilion lines. The flat-fronted smokebox doors were of the ancient rectangular shape. The chimney was of wrought iron with a plain top ; there was a big bell-mouthed dome casing of iron, with spring-balance safety-valves, and an additional safety-valve in front of the cab, either of lockup type in a decanter-shaped brass casing, or of Naylor's design on a circular manhole cover. Darlington engines inherited much of the tradition of the Stockton and Darlington Railway, whose locomotive superintendent, William Bouch, had continued to carry on much as he pleased after the amalgamation in 1863, producing the once famous 4-4-0 bogie outside-cylinder engines known as Ginx's Babies. Here, the engines were painted a lighter green, with a darker brown below ; they had plain chimneys, much wider at the top than on Gateshead engines ; the bell-mouthed domes were enormous ; the smokeboxes had dished circular doors. The cab was an unprepossessing tin box, though the memorable S. and D. 4-4-0 engines *Brougham* and *Lowther*, of 1860, had begun their careers with large and really beautiful side-window cabs.

York engines were much neater in appearance, and their colour scheme was almost identical with that of the Great Northern, with the same claret-coloured underframes lined out with vermilion. Leeds engines were a vivid emerald green, lined out in yellow, but otherwise of an even plainer, more Quakerish aspect than those of Gateshead and Darlington. To make up for this, many of the North Eastern engines in Fletcher's time were elaborately decorated by the enginemen, with brass dog-collars, stars, crescents, monarchs of the glen, a picture of Mr. Gladstone, and on one briefly glorious occasion, a lovely lady *in the altogether*.

The East Coast expresses, in Fletcher's time, were worked at first by archaic single-wheelers with outside sandwich frames, and latterly by very admirable 7 ft. 2-4-0's, but never by bogie engines, which were confined to Mr. Bouch's Stockton and Darlington dependency and to the Whitby line. Fifty-five of the celebrated seven-footers were built between 1872 and 1882, the later ones with $17\frac{1}{2}$ by 24 in. cylinders. No. 910, a 17 in. engine built in 1875, took part in the Railway Jubilee celebrations of that year,

and is now in the Railway Museum at York, lovingly restored to
her original form. Of Fletcher's other designs, a most notable one
was that of his fast goods engines, of the o-6-o type with 5 ft. 8 in.
wheels, 17 by 26 in. cylinders and 140 lb. pressure. They normally
worked between York and Newcastle, and were fitted with the
Westinghouse brake for handling heavy passenger trains when
needed. One of the several quaint and archaic features of all
Fletcher locomotives was the fitting of exhaust cocks, which diverted
some of the exhaust steam underneath the engine while running,
resulting in a softer blast in smokebox and chimney, and less
dispersal of the fire over the countryside.

Mr. Fletcher was a diplomat as well as an engineer. Seldom
was a railway so free from friction and labour disputes as the
North Eastern in the 'seventies. Enginemen and directors alike
trusted Old Ned, and abode by what he said. Even the Egyptian
Government accepted him as arbitrator in a row over some engines
exported by a famous British firm. When, therefore, he retired in
1882, full of years and loaded with gifts, and was succeeded by
Alexander McDonnell, a serious Gael from Inchicore on the Great
Southern and Western, with pronounced views on discipline, there
was trouble. The first manifestation seems to have been a general
notice that all unofficial embellishment of the engines be instantly
removed ; next, Gateshead works was to be reorganised ; soon there
were many other signs that Father's old chair now held a man of
wrath. So the men of York, and of Leeds, and the tough Geordies
of Gateshead, who would do anything for one who was nice to them,
began a cold war with the severe idealist set in office over them.

As might have been expected, the new chief produced engines
quite unlike anything before seen on the North Eastern Railway.
Bogies were in. Exhaust cocks were out. Yea, though the new
engines had much in common with those in Ireland, which were
doing very well there, somehow they would not " go " when
handled by the men of York and of Gateshead. The trouble lasted
for eighteen months ; it ended with the triumph of the Geordies,
and the resignation of the disgusted martinet.

An interregnum followed, during which time the N.E.R.
drawing office produced a very creditable express engine which
was in most respects a modernised Fletcher seven-footer. The men
liked the new class well. The engines were known as the Tennants,
after the then general manager, Henry Tennant. One of these, also,
survives at York Museum. Thomas W. Worsdell took command
in 1885, coming from the Great Eastern, and though he, too, had
ideas on locomotives quite different from what had gone before,

with his arrangement of the Von Borries system of compounding, this time all was well. North Eastern enginemen were accustomed to Quakers, and Mr. Worsdell, an imposing, upright sort of a man with a patriarchal beard, seems to have been a reasonably tolerant one ; also, he had not to contend with the first shock of old Father Fletcher's departure. The latter had been on the North Eastern or on one of its constituents for forty-seven years, and few, at the end, could remember having led working lives without him. Though the compound locomotive has seldom flourished in these islands, the Worsdell two-cylinder compounds on the N.E.R. were a more reasonable proposition than Webb's on the London and North Western. They included the first single-wheelers built for the North Eastern for many years, a bogie design of 1888, some handsome 6 ft. 8 in. 4-4-0's built in the previous year, and several types of mixed-traffic, goods and tank engine. The bogie singles were of two varieties. The first, class I, had 7 ft. drivers and cylinders 18 in. and 26 in. (h. and l.p. respectively) by 24 in. The second batch, of larger engines, had 7 ft. 7¼ in. drivers and the cylinder diameters increased to 20 in. and 28 in., and was known as class J. They were in marked contrast to the erratic and sometimes sluggish Webb compounds on the West Coast Route ; No. 1518 was timed at a top speed of 86 m.p.h. with eighteen carriages on level track, at the time a record.

The younger Worsdell, that was Wilson Worsdell, a gentleman with a mighty moustache and a mountain retreat in Norway, had been on the North Eastern in McDonnell's time, and he succeeded T. W. Worsdell as chief mechanical engineer in 1890. Of his engines built during the following decade, the best remembered are the very successful 7 ft. 1¼ in. 4-4-0's of Class M, beginning with No. 1620 in 1892 and consisting of twenty engines. The larger Q class appeared in 1896, the first two, Nos. 1869 and 1870, being unique in having four coupled wheels 7 ft. 7¼ in. All these had the handsome and roomy Worsdell side-window cab, with a clerestory roof in the Q class.

During the 'eighties and early 'nineties, the North Eastern Railway had some of the most comfortable ordinary carriages in the country. Only those of the Midland Railway could compare with them. Certain saloons and sleeping cars were built with semi-elliptical roofs, though during the 'nineties, under David Bain, these were dropped in favour of a beautifully designed clerestory. The company's contributions to the East Coast Joint Stock closely followed Great Northern conventions, and were often much less prepossessing than the article for home consumption, but they included, in 1894, the prototype of the modern first-class sleeping car, with single- and double-berth compartments, and a side corridor. For about two decades previously, East Coast sleepers had been chiefly of the Pullman type, plus some oddments produced by the Great Northern. But, as previously noticed, the very first sleeping car on the East Coast Route and, indeed, in Great Britain, was built by the North British Railway in 1873, a six-wheeler having two first-class compartments joined by a passage between lavatories, and each containing three folding bed-chairs, of the French *lits-salon* type. Pulling the seat-backs out and down disclosed the beds on the other sides, while the chair parts folded up underneath. There was a luggage compartment at one end, and a servants' second class at the other. Both these historic sleeping cars are illustrated in *Nineteenth Century Railway Carriages*, on pages 145 and 65-66 respectively.

In the days before the opening of the Forth Bridge, locomotives of the North British Railway had little to do with the East Coast expresses, for by virtue of an old arrangement, North Eastern engines ran through to the Waverley, their working being balanced by North British engines off the Border Counties line working over the N.E.R. from Hexham to Newcastle. Indeed, the only fast trains the North British Railway possessed in the late 'seventies and early 'eighties, were those over the Waverley Route to Carlisle, not presently germane, and some between Edinburgh and Glasgow, which conveyed through carriages and sleeping cars from King's Cross. For these, Dugald Drummond built his very first engines, in 1876, two very fine 7 ft. singles called *Glasgow* and *Berwick*. The much better-known Drummond 4-4-0 express engines were normally on the Waverley Route trains, though two of them worked north of Dundee during the brief existence of the old Tay Bridge. Built between 1876 and 1878, they were rebuilt during 1902-3, and lasted usefully until the nineteen-twenties. Between Burntisland and Tayport or Dundee, much of the work was done by Drummond 0-4-2 (later 0-4-4) tank engines, but the trains they hauled could not be called East Coast expresses by any stretch of the imagination.

During the 'eighties, Matthew Holmes, who succeeded Drummond at Cowlairs Works, N.B.R., began the building of numerous handsome 4-4-0 passenger engines and capable six-coupled goods, the latter in particular following Drummond practice very closely. Among the passenger engines were some most imposing seven-footers, starting with No. 592 in 1886, and including that No. 602 which was first across the Forth Bridge, but the most numerous were those with 6 ft. 6 in. coupled wheels, starting with some small ones

(574 class) in 1884, and built with increased cylinder and other dimensions, and greater boiler power, from 1891 onwards. The 633 class of that year had 18 by 26 in. cylinders and 140 lb. pressure (raised to 150 lb. in further, similar engines built in 1894-5). They equalled the Worsdell engines in the beauty of their lineaments, but the North British colour scheme of pea-soup (officially " dark gamboge ") was less happy.

The pre-Drummond engines were noteworthy more for their wild variety than for their size and puissance. Among the most successful were legacies of the Edinburgh and Glasgow Railway— 2-4-0's of S. W. Johnson's design, dating from the early 'sixties, others with which William Stroudley is believed to have had something to do, and some excellent little 6 ft. 6 in. singles, generally ascribed to Paton, but of characteristic Beyer design. Thomas Wheatley had built a number of very useful 5 ft. goods, some 6 ft. 2-4-0's, and two classes of 4-4-0, all with inside cylinders. The first Wheatley 4-4-0, built in 1871, was that No. 224 which fell with the old Tay Bridge, and was also the first of this afterwards characteristic British type, with inside cylinders and inside frames, apart from tank engines, to run on a standard-gauge railway in these islands.

Turning now to train services, and to some samples of loco- motive performance on the East Coast expresses of last century, we have seen that right back in the early 'fifties, Archibald Sturrock had envisaged eight-hour expresses between King's Cross and Edinburgh, even though the old York and North Midland and Leamside lines formed parts of the route. But for years, there was nothing so heroic as this. Moreover, at that time, both the North Eastern and the North British companies had curious reputations in the matter of punctuality.

The Flying Scotsman, the famous ten o'clock day train between King's Cross and Edinburgh, began running in June, 1862, and it made the journey in 10½ hours. It conveyed some through carriages for Manchester as far as Retford, and made a half-hour luncheon stop at York. The corresponding up train in the same year, for no obviously good reason, took an hour longer. It may be remarked that although Flying Scotsman has for many years been the official name of the morning East Coast express, the title was quite loosely bestowed during the last century on all sorts of Anglo-Scottish expresses. It was certainly applied in the Nottingham neighbour- hood to the Midland Scotch expresses, though north of the Border these were always called the " Pullmans ". The London and North Western Railway at least semi-officially applied it to the rival ten o'clock out of Euston, as late as the early nineteen hundreds—

about the time that the same company was trying to impose the rather unfortunate title of " Wild Irishman " on another train.

The East Coast Scotsman was originally a first- and second-class train. Third-class passengers were briefly admitted in the summer of 1872, but this concession was dropped and not revived until November, 1887. The best time made in 1872, in the autumn accelerations, was 9 hours 20 minutes from King's Cross to Waverley, including the dining interval at York. By 1876, there were more of Patrick Stirling's celebrated eight-footers at work, and Edward Fletcher's admirable seven-foot coupled engines were likewise in sufficient numbers, 39 having been built in four years. The Scotsman was accelerated to make the journey to Edinburgh in 9 hours. At this time it loaded 10 six-wheel carriages, but this might be increased to 15 in summer. There were no lavatories on the train, and the law of displacement had to be observed in the rush of the dinner interval. No man drank beer before a long journey unless he was a fool, and ladies had to be careful about tea. Though such things were never mentioned in contemporary literature and conversation, many curious artifices were tacitly recognised.

The late Mr. Ahrons described the Fletcher seven-footers as really excellent engines, in both performance and fuel economics, and quoted two runs made with 180-ton trains in the middle 'eighties. With the up Scotsman, one of the older engines covered the 80¼ miles from Newcastle to York in 92 minutes, making up 10 minutes on booked time, and on the old racing ground between Darlington and York, another averaged 55⅓ m.p.h. start-to-stop. One day in 1907, following failure of the regular modern engine, No. 844 of the class averaged 55·9 m.p.h. on a 200-ton train over the same section, with wet rails and a side wind.

The first race to the north began with the East Coast companies announcing that, as from July 1, 1888, the Flying Scotsman would make the run to Edinburgh in 8½ hours. The quickest run made in that merry year was 7 hours 26¾ minutes ; a 7¾ hours schedule was maintained for a while, and was observed for longer with certain night trains for destinations beyond Edinburgh, but 8½ hours became the standard fastest time, and was reduced to 8¼ hours in the early nineteen hundreds.

When racing broke out again in 1895, these times were very considerably cut. The opening of the Forth Bridge in 1890 had put the East Coast in a position to compete for the favours of Aberdeen, and the opening of the Glenfarg line likewise gave it a new advantage with the Perth and Inverness traffic. The day service gave an arrival at Dundee in 10 hours 25 minutes, and at

Aberdeen in 12 hours 20 minutes. At the end of the wild scramble into which acceleration of the night trains had developed, the East Coast reached Aberdeen in 8 hours 40 minutes, with a train consisting of six ordinary E.C.J.S. six-wheelers and an eight-wheel sleeper. The West Coast train, which on the following night, bettered this by 8 minutes, was of absolute minimum weight, and made what was described as an *exhibition run*.

In the East Coast run of August 21, 1895, Great Northern eight-footer No. 668 ran to Grantham and No. 775 thence to York, which was reached in 181 minutes for the 188·25 miles, with a four-minute stop at Grantham for changing engines. The finest performance on the North Eastern was with 4-4-0 No. 1620 (class M) which averaged 66 m.p.h. start-to-stop over the 124¼ miles from Newcastle to Edinburgh. On the difficult road north of Edinburgh, with its continual undulations, its severe slacks over the Forth Bridge and through Inverkeithing, and its single-track section beyond Arbroath, Matthew Holmes's 211 class (the 150 lb. variety of the 633 class) worked all the racing trains. With 147½ tons, engine No. 211 ran at average speeds of 50·25 m.p.h., Edinburgh to Dundee; 52·3 m.p.h., Dundee to Arbroath; and 50·4, Arbroath to Aberdeen. On the last night, with the Arbroath stop cut out and the load down to about 100 tons, one of the same class, the number of which is unfortunately elusive, averaged 60·25 m.p.h. to Dundee and 56·25 m.p.h. thence to Aberdeen. Both the runs quoted were most praiseworthy for such a road, and fully up to the quality shown farther south.

Some very fine work by North British engines took place in the late 'nineties, what time the North British company had a stramash with the North Eastern, and stopped the running of the latter's engines north of Berwick. The North British bound itself to keep time on the existing schedules, in spite of the stop for changing engines at Berwick. The merrymaking began on January 14, 1897, and lasted for a little over a year, while the lawyers enjoyed themselves. On several occasions, the 57½ miles were covered at 60 m.p.h. start-to-stop. The up afternoon dining-car train was allowed 72 minutes, and on one occasion, with one engine and 230 tons behind the tender, made the run in 62 minutes 37 seconds. The faster trains invariably had two engines. Holmes's 633 class was generally used; more occasionally the seven-footers or the old Drummond bogies.

The next phase in the history of East Coast locomotives and trains, though it opened in the last years of the Victorian Era, belongs more properly to that which succeeded.

CHAPTER NINE

From the Atlantic to the Pacific

THE turn of the century saw a more abrupt change in the locomotive practice of the Great Northern Railway than was apparent on any other main-line railway at that time. In the mid-'nineties, as remarked, every East Coast express in or out of King's Cross was headed by *one* engine, with single driving wheels of 7 ft. 7 in. or 8 ft. diameter. By the end of the decade, the same engines were working in pairs (Mr. Stirling having died, and been succeeded by H. A. Ivatt from Ireland), and the large Atlantic-type engine had arrived, initially in the form of No. 990 (afterwards called *Henry Oakley*). Late in 1902 came No. 251, with a much larger boiler and a wide Wootten firebox, containing 2,500 sq. ft. of heating surface (firebox 141 sq. ft.) and a grate area of 31 sq. ft. In all, 93 large-boilered Atlantics were built thenceforward by the G.N.R., later improvements including the use of superheaters. The big wheel was out, superseded by four 6 ft. 7 in. wheels front-coupled. Variations were played on the Atlantic theme, including a trial of compound expansion and four-cylinder simple expansion.

At the bottom of this revolution was a simple first cause. During the late 'nineties, much heavier coaching stock was built for the Scotch and Leeds expresses, including many twelve-wheelers of that sumptuous clerestory style mentioned at the beginning of the previous chapter. The Flying Scotsman became a very heavy dining train in 1900, and the midday train had included such facilities since 1893, acquiring the new heavy clerestory stock in 1896. An eight-coach train, Pullman vestibuled and with automatic couplers, tared 276 tons, which, though not heavy by present standards, was a tough proposition for the old single-wheelers, designed for light six-wheel stock plus, perhaps, a solitary Pullman car. Mr. Ivatt did indeed build twelve singles, a larger-boilered, bogie version of Stirling's 7 ft. 7 in. type, but their life was short, they lasting less than twenty years. The Atlantic was to be the regular East Coast express engine (for the North Eastern and North British companies both took it up) for longer than this.

In 1901 there was an enlargement of the Great Northern heavy goods engine, in the first of the Long Toms, Ivatt's 0-8-0 coal engines, with 4 ft. 8 in. coupled wheels and 19¾ by 26 in. cylinders. Judged by dimensions, they were the goods equivalent of the earlier 990 class Atlantics. Ivatt's last goods engines, which were for some time perpetuated by his successor, H. N. (later Sir Nigel) Gresley, were an enlargement of the ordinary 0-6-0 type. They were more generally useful engines than the powerful but plodding Long Toms. Fast goods trains were frequently worked by Ivatt's 4-4-0 engines, which, like the bogie singles, were in some respects Stirling derivatives. But all Ivatt's engines had large domes on the boilers, as inevitably as Stirling's, save long ago on the Glasgow and South Western, were domeless. Some of the old Stirling engines received domes in the course of rebuilding, others not. Ivatt's cab followed Stirling's, in having the side-sheets and roof in one piece (Holmes's cabs on the North British, up to 1903, were identical) but the Ivatt version had the top extended backwards to give a more adequate roof.

Herbert Nigel Gresley took command of the Great Northern carriage department before he succeeded Ivatt in charge of the locomotives, and at an early stage he made two important contributions to coaching design. In 1906 he adopted the high elliptical roof with domed ends. In the following year he rebuilt six old carriages as twin units. Between each body, the headstocks were strengthened, and a steel bracket mounted on each in place of the usual drawgear and buffers. One bracket overlapped the other, and through them passed a king-bolt forming the pin of a single bogie common to both carriages. The coaches chosen for experimental rebuilding were a pair of standard East Coast corridor six-wheelers, a couple of Great Northern lavatory composites, and two 45-ft. non-bogie eight-wheelers of a type first built in 1885. The arrangement was soon after adopted extensively on the Great Northern; new suburban trains were built with it, and in 1921 a very magnificent quintuplet dining car set was built for the Leeds service. It was perpetuated for many years by the London and North Eastern Railway, and taken up to a lesser extent by the L.M.S.R. and the Great Western.

After the ornateness of the 'nineties, with its flights of green plush and gilt ironwork, its twining ivy imposed on ground glass, and what-not, a solid severity distinguished main-line coach interiors under Gresley. The ordinary Great Northern carriages had always been so, but new coaches built for the Flying Scotsman in 1914 were of Cromwellian plainness. There was to be a sharp reaction, but not yet. Lighting was much improved, and no more gaslit carriages were built after 1907, the year following a very serious accident, with an outbreak of fire, to a night Scotch express at Grantham.

This disaster was one of three inexplicable derailments—the others were those at Salisbury on the South Western and Shrewsbury on the North Western—initiated by the overturning of an express engine at full speed on a curve. At Grantham, the train did not make its booked stop and the engine, standard Atlantic No. 276, was overturned on the crossover. The death of the enginemen in this, as in the other accidents mentioned, prevented any satisfactory explanation afterwards, but there was evidence to suggest, at Grantham, that the driver had been suddenly taken ill on the footplate.

On the North Eastern and North British Railways during the early nineteen hundreds, there were several parallels with the Great Northern in locomotive practice, both companies making much use of the Atlantic-type engine on the best expresses. Unlike the Great Northern, however, the other partners built many large-boilered 4-4-0 engines. On the North Eastern, Wilson Worsdell produced his 6 ft. 10 in. class R, which was developed in 1908 into the very imposing class R 1. Of the original R class, 60 were built between 1899 and 1907. At the same time as the first of these, Worsdell built the first 4-6-0 express engines to belong to any railway in the United Kingdom, though David Jones's big goods, of this type, had been running on the Highland Railway since 1894. The Worsdell 4-6-0's, however, were later transferred to fast goods traffic, and painted black for this purpose, the Atlantic, as remarked, becoming the normal heavy express engine, used on the East Coast expresses between York and Edinburgh.

Several very interesting experiments were carried out in the younger Worsdell's time, including the first application of Smith's system of compounding. W. M. Smith had been with Wilson Worsdell on the North Eastern in Fletcher's day, and was allowed a fairly free hand. One three-cylinder compound had been built, or rather rebuilt from a large two-cylinder compound, in 1898. It was the forerunner of the numerous Smith and Smith-Deeley compounds on the neighbouring Midland Railway, and in 1906 Smith designed for Worsdell two very handsome four-cylinder compound Atlantics.

The ordinary North Eastern Atlantics began with Wilson Worsdell's class V, in 1903, with the usual 6 ft. 10 in. coupled wheels, 20 by 28 in. cylinders (two) with piston valves, and very large boilers for that time. Two of them, Nos. 784 and 742, between them worked the royal train from Shaftholme Junction to Edinburgh when they were new, in September 1904. Reversal and engine changing was then still necessary at Newcastle. Following the opening of the King Edward Bridge, one of the Smith compound Atlantics, No. 730, took the royal train from Edinburgh to York, with one service stop at Newcastle, on October 17, 1906. The bridge had been opened on October 1.

Some of the most spectacular locomotive work on the East Coast Route at that time was on the relatively local Newcastle to Sheffield expresses, over the old flat straight from Darlington to York. The 12.20 p.m. up was for some years timed to cover the 44·125 miles in 43 minutes. Its timekeeping was described as "almost monotonous in its excellence". On February 4, 1911, the run was made in 41 minutes, or at 64·57 m.p.h. The engines used were R or R 1 class 4-4-0's. In 1903, for the first time, the York stop was cut out of the schedule of the first part of the summer Flying Scotsman, which then ran from Doncaster to Newcastle non-stop, with, of course, a North Eastern engine.

In 1901, Wilson Worsdell adopted the 0-8-0 heavy mineral engine, like Ivatt on the Great Northern, and several series followed, culminating in Sir Vincent Raven's large three-cylinder class T 3 of 1919. Raven's most famous express engines were the Z class Atlantics, the first of which came out in 1911, with three 16½ by 26 in. cylinders. The first ten were saturated engines, but these were afterwards superheated and became identical with later engines of this class, of which fifty were built, the last in 1918. A similar policy of superheating had been adopted with the Great Northern Atlantics. The North Eastern variety, unlike the Great Northern, always had narrow fireboxes. The last engine of class V, No. 2212, had Uniflow cylinders, an improved form of an arrangement of Stumpf Uniflow cylinders which Raven had fitted to a No. 825 heavy 4-6-0 of class S 2. These last, which came out in 1911 and 1912, were the only six-coupled passenger engines built by the North Eastern Railway between the Worsdell 4-6-0's of classes S and S 1 (the latter with 6 ft. 8 in. coupled wheels) and the Raven Pacifics built right at the end. Even the heavy passenger tank engines were 4-4-4, though the L.N.E.R. rebuilt them as 4-6-2.

The Raven Pacifics, the last express engines to be built for the North Eastern Railway, numbered five, but the class was not completed until after the formation of the London and North Eastern Railway. In some respects, the design was a much elongated Atlantic, but for the first and only time, Sir Vincent Raven adopted in these the wide firebox which the Great Northern Railway had used for so long. The L.N.E.R. did not perpetuate the class, which was not so successful as the Atlantics had been. The men called them " Skittle Alleys ", for reasons explained elsewhere.*

Later North Eastern carriages, as on other railways, except the Midland, showed a sharp reaction from the clerestory type during the nineteen hundreds. Some flat-sided corridor composites turned out for the East Coast Joint Stock during 1905-6 would have been better had they never left the drawing board, but for provincial express services, a little later, the company built some very fine corridor carriages with domed and bowed ends, as on the Great Northern, and with entrance through end vestibules only. The dining cars that went with these were most imposing vehicles, with the steel frames each side in the form of an inverted bow. Coaches for the joint stock were finished in varnished teak instead of the usual North Eastern crimson, and this applied on the North British also, which built some joint carriages to Great Northern designs.

Matthew Holmes on the North British had cautiously enlarged his standard 4-4-0 engine; the final version, the 317 class of 1903, rather resembling the later Dunalastairs on the Caledonian, had the unusually high boiler pressure of 200 lb. per sq. in. On these he substituted a large side-window cab for the Stirling type which he had used for nineteen years previously. These engines worked the East Coast expresses north of Edinburgh until the coming of the first North British Atlantics in 1906.

These, designed by W. P. Reid, were most splendiferous engines. The restrictions of the North British loading gauge, causing their chimneys and domes to squat on their backs, made them seem bigger than they were. To a youthful eye, they were indeed engines worthy of the Forth Bridge. What names they had—*Aberdonian, Bon Accord, Auld Reekie, Bonnie Dundee!* How beautiful were they in the hands of enginemen who put polished stars and thistles on their sturdy chests for the love of it !

W. P. Reid, who had succeeded Holmes, and later rebuilt some of the latter's old engines, had fourteen Atlantics built in Glasgow by the North British Locomotive Company in 1906, and six more by Stephensons in 1911, having superheaters, with which the older ones were fitted subsequently. The last two were built in 1921, after Reid's retirement. They had 21 by 28 in. cylinders and 6 ft.

* *Some Classic Locomotives*, page 132.

9 in. coupled wheels, 3 in. larger than the usual North British standard. The fireboxes were of the Belpaire type, the only example of its use on the North British. The Belpaire, indeed, was rare on the East Coast Route; it was unknown on the Great Northern; on the North Eastern it distinguished the two Smith compound Atlantics.

Apart from the Atlantics, North British locomotive practice followed the Drummond type to the end, whether in express, goods or tank engines. The Scott and Glen classes were Drummond engines with much bigger boilers and piston valves, in short, muchly what Drummond himself built for the London and South Western in 1912. The final big goods engines were the same. The later passenger tanks, whether 4-4-2 or 0-4-4, were elongated developments of Drummond's 4-4-0 and 0-4-2 tanks of the 'seventies and early 'eighties, and they served the North British Railway very well. It is not so easy to write a eulogy of the North British carriages. Those used on local, and on many ordinary main-line trains, including the sample in which your author made his first crossing of the Forth Bridge, are best forgotten. There were some fairly good non-gangwayed corridor coaches, and the Aberdeen expresses, apart from the through trains from the south, had some handsome twelve-wheel stock with hot water in the lavatories, built in opposition to the celebrated " Grampians " on the Caledonian. Some of the dining cars were cast-offs from the East Coast Joint Stock, but to these were added some ponderously armour-plated fireproof twelve-wheelers, late in the 1914-18 war. They were about the heaviest carriages ever used in ordinary steam services on a British railway. I saw one of them being broken up at Cowlairs a few years ago. It was rather like cutting up an old dreadnought, only, maybe, a tougher job. In the meantime, the L.N.E.R. had faithfully painted its battleship sides to look like varnished teak.

The locomotive practice of Sir Nigel Gresley, as he became after making 100 m.p.h. a relative commonplace on the rail, is recent and well-documented, Mr. O. S. Nock having devoted a learned book to it. Gresley succeeded Ivatt and after building some 0-6-0's, went on with some useful 2-6-0 mixed-traffic engines in 1912. The type had been represented previously only by a batch of American-built Moguls bought by the Great Northern during an acute locomotive shortage at the turn of the century. New features were the raised platforms, above outside Walschaerts gear and piston valves, and this distinguished all new Great Northern main-line engines, and most standard L.N.E.R. types, thereafter. These were followed in the next year by a heavy 2-8-0 goods, with two cylinders, though the next engine of this class, built in 1918, had three, with further examples built in 1921. They were designed for the haulage of 1,300 ton coal trains between New England and London.

So far, the Atlantics continued to handle all the heavy express trains. A very large 2-6-0 with three cylinders was the nearest approach to a new express engine before the appearance, in 1922, of the famed No. 1470, *Great Northern*, the first Pacific on the East Coast, just preceding the Raven " Skittle Alleys ", and the first in the country to be a class prototype. With a total heating surface of 3,455 sq. ft., $41\frac{1}{4}$ sq. ft. of grate, three 20 by 26 in. cylinders, and an all-up weight of 148 tons 15 cwt. it was easily the largest engine in the country.

Gresley served the London and North Eastern Railway as its chief mechanical engineer through most of its history, and will be remembered by many for having designed some of the most beautiful locomotives of modern times. His Pacifics were perfectly balanced to the eye. A characteristic feature was his modification of the Walschaerts valve gear so that on three-cylinder engines the inside valves were operated through tailrod extensions and rockers from the outside piston valves on one side. That reminds me of a breakdown, going to Edinburgh one winter night in 1927, when something happened to the inside parts of *Merry Hampton*. The trouble, which sounded like a broken valve, shook us out of our innocent slumber on the climb from Reston Junction, fortunately very near the top, with the train crawling spasmodically along and the engine's lively 6/8 rhythm turned to an awful one-two-BURR-one-two-BURR. Thus we staggered into Grantshouse station, where there was a hurried council of war down in the cess, where lay about a foot of snow. Sounds of ironmongery being manhandled ensued during about a quarter of an hour; the driver believed he could make Dunbar if something were sent out from St. Margaret's to meet us there. Then the train started with a jerk that sent eight passengers, standing curiously in the corridor of my coach, over like a set of skittles. Unfortunately I was standing next to an extra-large guardsman, with a petite Scots lass on the other side. While the guardsman was peeling himself off the wreckage, the engine limped over the summit with her twelve-coach train, and we tobogganed very cautiously down Cockburnspath bank. For our relief, St. Margaret's shed had provided one of the old 211 class Holmes 4-4-0's, which was faithfully awaiting us at Dunbar. Having recovered my wind by then, ascertained that most of my ribs were intact, my right ear not beyond repair, and

Edinburgh Waverley
Station

(Photo :
Topical Press Agency)

INSET TWO

25. Eastern end of
the old Waverley
Station, Edinburgh
in the 'nineties,
with a prospect of the
Calton Gaol

(*Locomotive and General
Railway Photographs*)

Northern end
the old Joint
Station at
Aberdeen ;
eat North of
land carriages
foreground

*ocomotive and
neral Railway
Photographs*)

27. The
   Brid
an early
   photog

(Valenti
   Son

28. Barlow's Tay Brid

(Photograph by the
   Author)

29.
" The Bri
North Br
engine No
with the
train, on
old Tay Br
Decembe
1879

(Wash dr
by the Au

. Flying
tsman at
g's Cross
t Northern
ailway
e 'nineties.
Stirling
ht-footer
o. 221 ;
on left
East Coast
ing car of
1894

ocomotive
ishing Co.
Ltd.)

Great Northern
excursion train
headed by
mall-boilered
ntic-type engine
No. 257

omotive Publishing
Co., Ltd.)

32. Press run of the Silver Jubilee train, L.N.E.R., in 1935 ; engine SILVER LINK

33. Up East Coast express on Dundee and Arbroath Joint Railway in the 'nineties, double-headed by N.B.R. Holmes 6 ft. 6 in. 4-4-0 engines Nos. 262 and 213

(*Locomotive and General Railway Photographs*)

34. Up Sunday East Coast express leaving Aberdeen in 1932; ex-North British engines THANE OF FIFE and CALEB BALDERSTONE

(*Photograph by the Author*)

35. The last lap. East Coast express near Stonehaven, L.M.S.R., in the nineteen-thirties; three-cylinder 2-8-2 engine THANE OF FIFE which replaced the N.B.R. Atlantic shown above

(*Photograph by F. R. Hebron*)

36. Royal Albert Bridge from Saltash, Great Western Railway

(*Locomotive and General Railway Photographs*)

37. College Wood timber viaduct Falmouth branch

(*British Railways Photograph*)

38. Viaduct replacement on the Cornwall Railway; the piers of the old timber-top structure still stand alongside the newer stone arches

(*Locomotive and General Railway Photographs*)

39. Exeter St. Thomas's ; a beautiful example of the old timber-roofed stations on th
former broad-gauge railways, and still extant.   Photographed about 1912

40. Moretonhampstead, Great Western Railway, showing the timber roof and an early
G.W.R. motor bus for Chagford

41. Starcross atmospheric pumping station of the old South Devon Railway, now a chape
(*All from Locomotive and General Railway Photographs*)

42. The great cliff fall between Dawlish and Teignmouth, 1862; passengers transferring between two South Devon trains

(From an old coloured lithograph)

43. The branch engine at Clevedon, Bristol and Exeter Railway, in the 'sixties

(Locomotive and General Railway Photographs)

44. Pearson's nine-foot single tank engine No. 42, Bristol and Exeter Railway, after the Weston Junction accident, April 18, 1865

(Locomotive and General Railway Photographs)

45. One of the last broad-gauge expresses into London, in Sonning Cutting; eight-foot single engine with four narrow-body convertible carriages and a wide-body composite at rear

(*British Railways Photograph*)

46. G⟨reat⟩ Western ⟨train⟩ from Sal⟨isbury⟩ approac⟨hing⟩ Batham⟨pton⟩ headed ⟨by a⟩ converted ⟨—⟩ class er⟨—⟩ (origi⟨nally⟩ o-4-4 t⟨ank⟩

(*Locomotive⟨ and⟩ General R⟨ailway⟩ Photogr⟨aphs⟩*)

47. North-to-west express on the sea-wall at Dawlish, Great Western Railway, headed by a Duke class 4-4-0 engine, second vehicle is an early dining car

(*Locomotive and General Railway Photographs*)

the young person likely to recover, I quite enjoyed the valiant antics of the little engine with the big train.

That year of 1927 had seen the first radical improvement on the original Great Northern type of Pacific, with the rebuilding of No. 4480, *Enterprise*, the eleventh of the class, with 220 lb. pressure instead of the original 180 lb., and the number of superheating elements increased from 32 to 43. Leading dimensions, apart from the boiler, remained unchanged, with the coupled wheels at 6 ft. 8 in. and the three cylinders 20 by 26 in. The experiment was successful, and this, with the cylinders reduced one inch in diameter, remained the standard form of the L.N.E.R. Pacific until the coming of the streamlined engines in 1935.

Before the Pacifics supplanted the North British Atlantics north of Edinburgh, as eventually happened, the L.N.E.R. supplemented the latter with a number of inside cylinder 4-4-0 engines practically identical with J. G. Robinson's Director class on the Great Central Railway, and for some years these did good work both on the fast Edinburgh and Glasgow trains and to Perth. The last London and North Eastern four-coupled express engines, the three-cylinder Shire and Hunt classes, have likewise done good work, though not normally on the heaviest trains. Lentz poppet valves were fitted to some of these, with rotary-cam gear, beginning with two Shires in 1929, and extending to the Hunts.

The most remarkable experimental engine of this period was a four-cylinder compound, of the 4-6-4 type, with a 450 lb. pressure Yarrow watertube boiler. It was numbered 10000, and appeared at the back end of 1929. Fuel economy through the use of unconventional high-pressure boilers was in the wind just then; the L.M.S. produced *Fury*, a compound Royal Scot with a Schmidt high-pressure boiler, which had a most unfortunate accident therewith while running its trials. No. 10000 was rebuilt with a large ordinary boiler and a streamlined casing in 1937.

In May, 1928, certain of the higher-pressure Pacifics on the L.N.E.R. were equipped with corridor tenders in order to provide a stunt service with the Flying Scotsman, namely, running it from King's Cross to Edinburgh, 392·7 miles, without a stop, with a relief driver and fireman taking over half-way. The thing had several ridiculous highlights. The L.M.S. let off a rocket by running non-stop to Edinburgh, just for a lark, with a little Midland compound, a few days before. Then the gentlemen's agreement between East and West Coast meant that stop or non-stop, the train must not take less than 8¼ hours on the journey, so nothing was to be gained except a long loaf, sans intermission, at an average speed of 47·6 m.p.h., in the course of which you longed for the engine to break down, or for someone to fall out, or for an aeroplane to crash on the track—anything, however drastic, to break that interminable rumble. On a night train, the arrangement would have had its points, but as things were, a barbers' shop, a cocktail bar and a super " ladies " were put on the train to beguile the most tedious railway journey in Great Britain. The second part of the train made the usual stops, was much heavier, and took the same time.

From 1932 onwards, long desirable accelerations took place. In the summer of 1937, the time was down to 7 hours each way. The time at the outbreak of war was 7 hours 20 minutes, with the old stops properly observed.

In Scotland, the nineteen-thirties saw the passing of the North British Atlantics from East Coast express service. As they went, they were scrapped, for unlike the Scott and Glen 4-4-0's, they were not suitable engines for secondary services. The first new design for expresses north of Edinburgh, since the appearance of the Atlantics twenty-eight years before, appeared in the summer of 1934 with the *Cock o' the North*, a 6 ft. 2 in. 2-8-2 with 6 ft. 2 in. coupled wheels, three 21 by 26 in. cylinders, 220 lb. pressure, double blastpipe and chimney, and a streamline casing to the boiler. She was the first eight-coupled engine in the country to be designed for fast passenger traffic, although, as previously remarked, the Great Western 2-8-0 mixed traffic engines were sometimes thus employed. The original engine of this most imposing class had poppet valves with rotary-cam gear. On the picturesque side, all of the class were favoured with high-sounding Scottish names; even the *Wolf of Badenoch* descended on the East Coast Route from his island fortress on Loch-an-Dorb.

So this was the great Gresley's contribution to Scottish locomotive history; save when they were new and being run in, the engines were never seen south of Edinburgh. There were variations; the front end of the streamlined casing underwent some metamorphosis, and the poppet valves with R.C. gear were not perpetuated. The only other 2-8-2 tender engines to run on a British railway were also Gresley's work, a pair of heavy goods, originally booster-fitted, and somewhat on the lines of his earliest Pacifics. Both are scrapped now.

Main-line goods traffic was handled by the usual 2-6-0's and 2-8-0's on the Great Northern section, and by 0-8-0's and 4-6-0's on the North Eastern, but from 1936 on, the line saw remarkable use being made of the large-wheeled 2-6-2 type of Gresley's design

(Green Arrows), which had many features in common with the later Pacifics, and seemed equally at home with the vacuum-fitted express goods or with some of the fastest passenger trains. Suggestions of unsteadiness were made about them in official reports on several accidents due to permanent way defects, and some modification has been made recently to the leading truck arrangements. On foreign railways today, where engines having a single leading carrying axle followed by a coupled axle, are employed for express trains, it is usual—in some countries compulsory—to mount these on a Krauss-Helmholtz bogie.

The grand spectacle of East Coast passenger services during the inter-war years was provided by the special streamlined trains from 1935 onwards. For these, Gresley produced a modified Pacific, with a whaleback casing to the boiler and smokebox, and the platforms in an aerofoil shape (later with the side valances cut out to give better access to the valve-gear).

Practical experience in the running of very fast trains had been gained in some trial runs with the existing Pacific *Papyrus*, which showed a four-hour timing between King's Cross and Newcastle to be entirely feasible, and touched a top speed of 108 m.p.h. In the new engines, the pressure was bumped up to 250 lb. and the cylinder diameter reduced from 19 to $18\frac{1}{2}$ in. What the general populace most readily noticed was the silver colour of engine and train (it was really fishbelly rather than silver) and the sonorous chime whistle. This had previously appeared on the 2-8-2's, but they were far away in Scotland.

The story of what happened on the trial run is such common property, with its pass-to-pass average of 100 m.p.h. for 43 miles and its two maxima of $112\frac{1}{2}$ m.p.h., that to give it all again in detail would be, of its kind, a bore. But there was nothing boring about it at the time, and in common with others who went on that merry run to Grantham and Barkston Junction, your author has his treasured memories. Among the scrawled notes in one of those grubby little books that one keeps, and never quite likes to throw away, is: " What were we doing at Hitchin " ? We were doing 107 as it happened, with the speed steadily rising to its first top-notch at Arlesey, but plenty of people were manipulating formidable-looking chronometers; I was content to sit back and take their word for it. The second time we exceeded 112 m.p.h. was at Sandy, where we overtook an L.M.S. goods train at that speed. It was the oddest sight, appearing to be going backwards against its own wheels.

All sorts of flashes there were, like that. Faces—everywhere faces ! They gazed out of other trains, over hedges, out of windows; they stared and vanished. At Barkston, where the engine ran round on the triangular junction before making the return trip, an entire school, or it may have been two schools, had camped out for the afternoon, and boys and girls together pursued the *Silver Link* as she moved round between the three connections. It was a triumphant homecoming at King's Cross. I have but once, and since, known anything like it; and that was the return of the " period " Flying Scotsman from Cambridge, behind Stirling eight-footer No. 1, in 1938.

So came the Silver Jubilee, bringing with it the first *real* acceleration the East Coast line had seen since the 'nineties. It also brought back to England the practice of charging supplementary fares for fast trains, and nobody grudged this. With it, the ornately decorated railway carriage, too, was firmly back in favour, indeed, this pleasant reaction had been going on for the previous five or six years, beginning with the startling appearance of a French Baroque first-class diner on the Flying Scotsman. The quality of its floridity greatly improved on that of the old Victorian style (old G.N. diners, it will be remembered, were excellently ugly) and delighted the eye of the traveller jaundiced by years of that stodgy austerity which, at the time, was hailed as *tasteful simplicity*. Bad cess to the fanatic of function ! Truly, the most functional appointments of a railway carriage are the toilets; or at least, they should be, though in fact they are often very badly designed.

Outwardly, the Silver Jubilee train was much less beautiful than inside. Its aluminium finish was scarcely suited to the warren of tunnels leading into and out of London. Not until the Coronation began running between London and Edinburgh, painted in two shades of blue, could we fully perceive the beauty of Sir Nigel Gresley's streamlines. Even this train had its absurdity, for its beaver-tail observation car, as far as observation was concerned, was the most unfunctional example of consciously functional design yet achieved. Incidentally, it bore not the remotest resemblance to a beaver's tail.

Up to 1937, the fastest time ever made between King's Cross and Edinburgh had been 6 hours 19 minutes, with one of the racing trains of 1895, taring only 105 tons behind the tender. The Coronation, put on in July, 1937, weighed 312 tons, and it was timed to reach Edinburgh in 6 hours, with departure from King's Cross at 4 p.m. The up train left the Waverley at 4.30 p.m. At first there was one intermediate stop only, at York, but soon after, a Newcastle stop was inserted. On the up journey, the train ran non-stop from Newcastle to King's Cross. Its timings were thus: King's Cross to York, 188·2 miles in 157 minutes (the fastest booked run in the Empire); York to Newcastle, 80·1 miles in 77 minutes; Newcastle to Edinburgh, 124·4 miles in 120 minutes. The up train ran from Newcastle to King's Cross, 268·3 miles, in 3 hours 57 minutes.

Internally, in my opinion, its decorations in aluminium and different colours on a flat surface, were less agreeable than the engaging baroquerie that had gone before, but Oh blessed virtue, it was fully air-conditioned! The streamlined engines used for this and other services were beautiful things, in their garter blue with claret-coloured wheels. They added, too, something to the sights of London, the newest of which was the vision of the Coronation express and the four o'clock down Leeds express leaving King's Cross side by side.

Sir Nigel Gresley died quite suddenly on April 5, 1941. He had been in charge of the locomotives of the Great Northern and of the London and North Eastern Railway Companies for 29½ years, and, as we have seen, he had previously made a lasting mark on East Coast coaching practice. Without disrespect to the great coachbuilding profession, it may be remarked that seldom does a promoted " carriage man " subsequently exert, over a long period, a deep influence on locomotive design. James Holden and Harry Wainwright on the Great Eastern, and South Eastern and Chatham respectively, were wont to depute work when it came to engines; Joseph Beattie of the London and South Western was fairly comparable, becoming an advanced exponent of boiler economics.

Gresley's last engine, which came out shortly before his death, was the light 2-6-2 *Bantam Cock*, a miniature edition of the Green Arrow class, and carrying in her modest-looking boiler a pressure of 250 lb. Almost at the same time came that large electric locomotive which has so far spent most of its working life on loan to Holland, but this, destined for the Manchester-Sheffield line, has no place in East Coast history. It may be recalled, however, that the former North Eastern Railway considered main-line electrification very seriously, and contemplated electrifying the East Coast main line from York to Newcastle. Sir Vincent Raven got to the length of building an experimental 4-6-4 (more correctly 2-Co-2) electric locomotive, but the necessary motive force was not forthcoming under the L.N.E.R.

Reverting to Gresley, he was not above learning by comparison. In 1925 he was party with C. B. Collett to a locomotive exchange with the Great Western, the active agents being the former's No. 4474 (later *Victor Wild*) and the latter's *Pendennis Castle*. It was an undoubted Great Western victory, which impartial spectators, already feeling slightly sick with overdoses of the usual Great Western flashy publicity, felt to be rather a pity, but its practical results included the fitting of the high-pressure boiler to the L.N.E.R. *Enterprise*, of longer laps to its *Gay Crusader*, and increased valve travel on *Centenary*, all of which things had lasting influence.

Edward Thompson succeeded as chief mechanical engineer of the L.N.E.R. at a time when the job was scarcely enviable. The country was in a state of siege; trains of enormous length and fantastic states of crowding, growing steadily more shabby, rumbled up and down that long East Coast main line where once brilliant blue engines had cut their 100 m.p.h. dashes. From the passengers' point of view, travel by the East Coast expresses during the war years was more acutely unpleasant, of a more deliberate-seeming discomfort, than on any other British railway. For no apparently good reason, third-class compartments were labelled off as firsts, while for third-class passengers the L.N.E.R. produced more of those abominable bucket-seated saloon coaches than we ever believed it to possess. The things had appeared, originally as excursion stock, in the early nineteen-thirties. Ten years later, they were the mainstay of the day and night Scotch expresses in and out of King's Cross. From the locomotive man's point of view, one engine had to do something like the work of two; lifetimes will pass before those twenty-two-coach trains, stretching out of King's Cross into the tunnel, are forgotten.

Much of the heaviest passenger locomotive work at this time was done by the large Gresley 2-6-2's, and from the same years one recalls the proud Pacifics with their racehorse names, smothered in dirt, plodding along with the heavy goods in company with British and American 2-8-0's and such unlikely immigrants as King Arthurs off the Southern. Mr. Thompson made his mark on London and North Eastern locomotive practice by rebuilding the magnificent Cock o' the North class 2-8-2's as mixed-traffic Pacifics with the cylinders in rear of the bogie. The metamorphosis was regarded by many as regrettable.

In July, 1946, A. H. Peppercorn succeeded, as the last C.M.E. of the London and North Eastern Railway. He was no stranger to the East Coast Route, having served under Ivatt, Gresley and Thompson, and for it he brought out the first of his 6 ft. 8 in. Pacifics in 1948. Like the later Gresley Pacifics, there were three cylinders 19 by 26 in., centred on the bogie, but the derived motion for the inside valves was not perpetuated after the close of the Gresley period. The pressure was 250 lb. per sq. in., and double blastpipes and chimneys were fitted, as on Gresley's streamlined Pacific *Mallard*, which, on a special run in July, 1938, attained a fastest-ever speed for a steam locomotive, of 126 m.p.h. If Peppercorn's engines lacked the grace of Gresley's, they were at the same time the most imposing express locomotives the East Coast had ever seen. With them one must finish this sketch—for it is no more —of a great chapter in locomotive history.

For a closing picture, let us take a summer evening at Tweedmouth in 1948. The great washout had taken place on the Berwick-Dunbar section, and I had spent the afternoon getting down from St. Boswells; in a goods brake as far as Kelso, with a Great Northern 4-4-0 and a North British 0-6-0, both tender-first, heading the train, and thence in a two-coach local drawn by a North Eastern R class 4-4-0. It had been a strange journey, and strange, too, was the shuttle service over the Royal Border Bridge, worked by a North Eastern 0-4-4 tank with two carriages, one a Great Central clerestory relic.

There was a melancholy about the place; the Hudsonian-Gothic of Tweedmouth station stood up spikily against the sunset; one was conscious of those wrecked bridges and marooned trains in the hills to northward, and passengers for the South, who had crossed the Tweed in the little shuttle train, shivered in the evening chill. Then round the curve of the Kelso branch, that quiet byway which had suddenly become the main line to Edinburgh and Aberdeen, came the train that was to bear us away; a glittering, pre-war train of choicest carriages, headed by *Kingfisher* in gleaming garter blue. Most majestic was she, like something out of a Brahms symphony transmuted into steel and steam, and I found myself trolling an august air as the noble engine swept past me.

How graciously gleamed the carriage lights on fine fabric and handsome woodwork ! How gratefully one sank back upon softly superior upholstery ! How magically the up platform of Tweedmouth vanished like a cobwebby dream ! How comfortably a bottle of Bass clinked against its glass ! How supremely civilised were all these things ! The Lindisfarne light flashed out to sea as the train raced southwards in the gathering darkness. The East Coast Route, for all its wounds, stood where it did.

PART THREE

PART THREE

CHAPTER TEN

Broad-Gauge Glory

ALONE among the main-line constituents of British Railways on December 31, 1947, the Great Western had kept its original identity for over eleven decades, since the beginning of railways as we know them. One felt that there would always be a Great Western Railway, just as there would always be an England. And the name will surely die hard. Though the next following chapters are concerned mainly with the route to the West of England, their opening remarks go for the whole system. Probably, years hence, when the rising generation is quite hazy on whether the Grand Junction was a constituent of the North Western or the L.M.S., inquiring youth will still ask: " Father, what was the *Great Western* really *like* " ?

Father's reply will probably depend on various things; on whether he lived on the Great Western main line, or on a branch, or merely used the railway once a year to reach Torquay, or Salcombe, or the Tregenna Castle Hotel. It may depend slightly on long-ago first impressions. My father said: " The first time I ever saw a broad-gauge train ? Oh, the engine looked bandy-legged, and the carriages were all squat, like a cake that hadn't risen ". And this: " There were four of us in the compartment for the night, but we could all lie down without kicking each other too badly ". O magnificent broad gauge ! Those who had grown up with it swore by it, and the Cornishman of 1892, with its peculiarly archaic, sandwich-framed, eight-foot-single engine, was yet one of the most impressive trains in the world. Throughout its history, out of all its virtues and faults, there emerged a singular quality of the Great Western. It was a majestic railway.

Now for some less reverent observations, beginning with your author's first impression of a journey on the Great Western, gained as a very small boy being taken to a boating party at Wargrave. My brother had prepared me for the fastest and most magnificent railway in the world. There was indeed a shadowy splendour about our third-class carriage, with its big, box-like clerestory roof containing a prodigious gas pendant. When, just outside Paddington, we passed *Princess Maud* and *Princess Louise* coupled together, this was something like the railways in the picture-books, and I gazed on those copper-crowned giantesses in awe and worship. But something had gone wrong with the " fastest " part, especially after stopping at Ealing Broadway. I think that was where someone informed me, for the first time, that " our engine's having a drink ".

Thence we dawdled on, over Hanwell Viaduct, and through the flat nursery gardens. I was shown a dim something on the skyline and was told that it was Windsor Castle. My brother pointed out another engine bearing what seemed to me the engaging name of *Winnie Peg*. I was told: " That's Maidenhead ! " and, immediately after: " Our engine's having a drink ".

We got to Twyford somehow and after crossing over and joining the Henley branch train, whose engine counterfeited the least mentionable noises, I looked back at what had brought us thus far. I think it was taking water. Between the carriages and the engine, a County 4-4-0, was a long line of extraordinary things on wheels. I know what they were, now. They were gas wagons, going down on that fine Sunday morning to replenish the lighting outfits of most of the Great Western carriages belonging to Reading and points west. Then the strange vision was blotted out by something vast and unending, which tore through towards London at 90 miles an hour—or so I guessed.

Nor did the years belie that first impression. A distinguished colleague of mine who went to live on the Great Western a few years back was much shocked at his homeward train service. So he took the trouble to dig up the timetable of 1855, and found that in that year he could have got home in several minutes less time. Boldly he mentioned this, at a business binge, to a very high officer of the company, who replied: " Eh ? Ha ? Well, you know, old boy, the trains are much heavier nowadays ! " Dear old Great Western ! Line of great expresses and paralysed locals ! Pompous, gaslit, lovable old humbug !

Before they hurl my book at the picture of Great Aunt Emily, let me hastily agree with irate readers that the greatness of the Great Western was very great indeed. Throughout its history, in both its grand aspects, and in funny little things, something of the spirit of Brunel brooded over the railway. There was a superb personality who conceived all his finest projects on a vast scale. The layout of the Great Western and its allied lines, their massive stations, great viaducts, and the most stately Royal Albert Bridge over the Tamar—all these things were magnificent. Yet Brunel, like other artists of many parts, more than once struck a buffoon note. His essays in the locomotive line were disastrous, and one trembles to think what might have happened had not Daniel Gooch come to the rescue. Of Brunel's original—very original—permanent way, nobody could say a good word. It was simply a very clever permanent way to invent. His broad gauge, like his huge steamer *Great Eastern*, was dogged by bad luck, though both were grandly heroic conceptions.

What a surprising number of important things were begun in Great Britain by the Great Western Railway! For it, in 1839, Daniel Gooch carried out the first locomotive tests by dynamometer car. It was the first railway in the world to regard 50 m.p.h. as a normal, practical average speed for passenger trains. In 1852, it built the first main-line eight-wheel carriages. In 1863 it worked the first city underground train service in the world, using thereon the first workable condensing locomotives. For its constituent, the Cornwall Railway, Brunel built one of the world's first long-span bridges, some thirty years before Fowler and Baker built the Forth Bridge. In 1891 it built the country's first completely gangwayed side-corridor train. It built at Swindon the country's first stationary testing plant for locomotives, and until recently the only one. It was the first British railway to instal automatic train control throughout its main lines, and the first to use diesel traction for regular, including fast, passenger services.

This last was quite a shock to the public when it came. We had always regarded the Great Western as a solidly steam line. We had another shock a little later when the company clinched a disagreement about the price of South Wales coal by announcing its intention to electrify all lines west of Taunton, presumably including the Culm Valley, Kingsbridge and Helston branches. Just a threat, maybe, but what a threat! It was like the Head in *Stalky & Co.* undertaking to thrash the entire Upper School on the day the College broke up, for it was *epic—immense!*

Yet, on the other side, and for all their faults, the Great Western branch lines have always held a great charm for all those who seek charm in railways. I came to know the Great Western by sight through one of them, the Salisbury branch, of which I have two particularly intimate recollections from the days when it was full of outside cranks, brass domes and clerestories. One is of a dear, prim old lady—one of the vanished generation whose hands in repose were always clasped, and who spoke so precisely the English of a Trollope character—reading aloud the report of an accident at Warminster. For her to use the word *telescope* as a verb was unthinkable. She paused, gently coughed, and told us that he carriages had been driven into one another telescopically.

The other memory is of watching a train coming into Wilton one bright afternoon in 1918, headed by an old brass-dome engine. My viewpoint was a down slow, leaving the South Western station. I noted with interest the big single driving wheel, which I had never before seen on a Great Western engine, save in pictures. Years after, I painted a nostalgic picture of just such a train, and *The Railway Magazine* made a nice reproduction of it. Then, and only then, I heard that the last Great Western six-wheel single had been scrapped some years before 1918. In a most courteous comment on this oddity, the C.M.E. of the Western Region suggests that what I saw was probably a Barnum 2-4-0; the last Great Western single, a 4-2-2, departed in 1915, and the last 2-2-2 before that. But I love to believe I saw one. After all, if Miss Jourdain and Miss Moberly could see Trianon in its prime, if John Buchan could look down at his feet on the shores of a silent loch and see eighteenth-century buckled shoes, if Edith Olivier could see Avebury Fair (abolished in 1850) and drive a car from Beckhampton along the avenue of megaliths (vanished before 1800), why should I not see so agreeable a phantom as an Armstrong or early Dean single? Mr. E. W. Twining tells me that the last 7 ft. single (157-166 series) was on Swindon dump as late as 1920.

Literary cadenzas must end, and business-like recording begin, but it is difficult to approach the more prosaic side of the Great Western because of the very reason that its history has been written and published so often. Like several other early railways, it was originally a two-party enterprise, sponsored by business interests in London and in Bristol City, then still the great port for the Americas.

As far back as 1800, four years before Trevithick first made a locomotive run on rails, a trunk railway with horse traction was planned between Bristol and London by Dr. James Anderson. Two years later, the scheme was revived with the important improvement of cable haulage by steam. For the next thirty years, such projects cropped up at intervals, and that which was in truth the genesis of the Great Western main line originated with a deputation formed in Bristol, which issued a circular as follows:—

> The Gentlemen deputed by the Corporation, the Society of Merchant Venturers, the Dock Company, the Chamber of Commerce, and the Bristol and Gloucestershire Rail Road Company, to take into consideration the expediency of promoting the formation of a RAIL ROAD from BRISTOL to LONDON, request you to favor them, in writing, with such information as you may be able to

afford, respecting the expediency of the proposed Rail Road, addressed to the Chairman, in time to be laid before an adjourned Meeting of the said Deputies, to be held at the COUNCIL-HOUSE on Thursday, the 31st Instant, at Twelve o'Clock.

I am, &c.

JOHN CAVE,
Chairman.

Bristol, 21st January, 1833.

A copy of this, the birth certificate of the Great Western Railway, survives at Paddington. The old Bristol and Gloucestershire company mentioned in the circular built a horse tramway of 4 ft. 8 in. gauge from the Floating Harbour to Coal Pit Heath and neighbouring collieries, about 10 miles long in all; it was authorised in 1828 and opened in 1835. It became part of the Bristol and Gloucester Railway, opened in the broad gauge in 1844, but eventually, through the Birmingham and Gloucester Railway, taken into the Midland Railway.

It is quaint that this sponsor of the original Great Western should have passed subsequently into the ownership of another very large and important English railway, but so it was, and for this reason the original western terminus of the Great Western became, and remained to the end of company ownership, a joint station.

There was at this time a young engineer, Isambard Kingdom Brunel, son of Sir Marc Brunel of Thames Tunnel fame, who had attracted Bristolian attention with his plans for bridging the Avon gorge, which had been chosen in preference to those of the august Thomas Telford. That was in 1831, when he was only 25. Two years later, on March 7, 1833, the Bristol Railway Committee chose him to survey and plan its proposed main line. Within a month, and in face of the usual savage reception always promised and frequently given to railway surveyors at that time, he had completed his preliminary survey and mapped out a route via Swindon and Didcot, following the lines of the Avon valley, the Wilts and Berks Canal and the Thames, and piercing the oolite ridge by Box. This was substantially the course along which the line was subsequently built.

The name " Great Western Railway " was first officially used (instead of " Bristol and London Railroad ") at a meeting of the Bristol and London committees in the magnificent counting house of Antony Gibbs and Sons at 47 Lime Street, in the City of London, when a prospectus was issued. There were twelve directors each

123

from Bristol and London respectively, including the very energetic
George Henry Gibbs; Charles Saunders was London Secretary;
and W. Tothill, Bristol Secretary.* The first prospectus showed
Brunel's main line from Bristol to the neighbourhood of Taplow,
whence there were two routes into the Metropolis, one to cross
the Thames at Kingston and to run thence to a terminus near
Waterloo Bridge, a portent, as it happened, of the later London
and South Western Thames Valley lines; the other projected
Great Western line was to run directly to the West End. " Probable
branches " were from Didcot to Oxford, Swindon to Gloucester,
and Chippenham to Bradford-on-Avon. The Waterloo Bridge
project was dropped early, and when the first Great Western
Railway Bill came before Parliament, the proposed terminus was
at Vauxhall Bridge, whence the line would run to West Drayton
via Pimlico, Brompton, Hammersmith and South Acton, starting
on a four-mile viaduct. There was to be a tunnel through Sonning
Hill, where the great cutting afterwards came, and four crossings
of the Avon between Bath and Bristol, instead of the two actually
made. While making his detailed survey, Brunel had practically
lived in a huge travelling carriage specially arranged for the conveyance of himself, his assistant Hammond, and all their equipment, and including as a fixture a great leather-covered cigar case.
He described himself as being rarely much under 20 hours a day
on the job, and smoked most of the time.

The Pimlico extension was abandoned owing to lively opposition
from Belgravian landowners, and the site of the terminus shifted
to some open ground behind the old Brompton pub, the *Hoop and
Toy*. There was plenty of opposition from widely differing bodies,
but with the landowners in full force. There was opposition from
Windsor because the line did not come near enough, and from
the Provost of Eton College because it came much too near. The
London and Southampton Railway promoters likewise led a violent
attack, they having their own eyes on Bristol and the West Country.
In that Parliamentary session of 1834, with neither railway incorporated, let alone built, was born a feud between them which was
to last in greater or lesser strength for a century.

To give instances, as one should always do: In the nineteen-
twenties, the otherwise admirable maps of the Great Western
" Through the Window " booklets either omitted Southern lines
altogether (a common sort of inter-railway courtesy) or else, when
running powers gave an excuse, claimed them for the Great Western.
The Southern was equally polite in its way. Nobody in the latter's

* This office lapsed later.

The Stately Days of Dean : Down Bristol express between Corsham and Box, Great Western Railway, in 1897 ; engine No. 14, *Charles Saunders*

station at Salisbury could ever tell where and when a Great Western train for Westbury and Bath was going to start. By then, of course, the motor transport industry was beginning to play Old Harry with the receipts of both railways.

Jumping back to the last century: a proposed branch to Windsor, pacifying the citizens of that royal borough, aroused such disproportionate wrath on the part of the Provost and Headmaster of Eton that it was dropped. The Headmaster, Dr. Keate, said that it would be impossible to " keep the boys from the railroad in their hours of liberty ". The Headmaster added craftily: " I may also say that the passengers themselves will be placed in a situation of great danger in consequence of the thoughtless tricks which the boys will play ". Mark that *will!* The Great Western Bill, earnestly supported by Daniel O'Connell on account of the great benefits which such a railway would confer on Irish commerce, passed the second reading in the Commons, but was thrown out by the Lords.

Another prospectus was pluckily issued in the autumn of 1834, describing a line more nearly approximating to that eventually built. It differed in that its London approach was to be made over the route of the London and Birmingham Railway to the latter's terminus by Euston Square, from a connection near Kensal Green.

After a very stiff Parliamentary fight, the Great Western Railway Act received the Royal Assent on August 31, 1835. The broad gauge was born in the same year, though but for the failure of the previous Bill, it might never have been heard of. In consequence of the ancient coal cart gauge of 4 ft. 8 in., or 4 ft. 8½ in., having become general in the North through George Stephenson having favoured it for the Stockton and Darlington, and the much more important Liverpool and Manchester Railway, already a clause was inserted in each new Railway Act designed to secure national uniformity as railways extended and linked up. This clause was omitted from the final Great Western Bill. Brunel had successfully persuaded Lord Shaftesbury, Chairman of Committees, to drop the clause, citing the London and Southampton Railway Act, which lacked it apparently by an oversight. As soon as the Act was passed, Brunel astutely trotted out his hobby horse, which was the adoption of a considerably greater width between the rails.

Thus, he considered, could be allowed an engine less cramped and therefore potentially more efficient, a more solid and steady road, and carriages with their bodies entirely between the wheels, producing less friction because of the diameter of these being

9

practically unlimited, and a low centre of gravity through the bodies being quite near the ground with, perhaps, the axles passing through them. This last was never put fully into practice, indeed, all the ordinary carriages of the Great Western were mounted above the wheels, with the bodies extending over them laterally, as on other railways. But Brunel won his point, which he had been nursing ever since he made the preliminary surveys, and a Great Western minute of October 29, 1835, ran: *Resolved that the embankments, bridges and other works to be constructed of such dimensions as to admit of rails being laid to the extreme width proposed by Mr. Brunel, viz., 7 ft.* The actual gauge, as is well known, was 7 ft. 0¼ in.

It will be remembered that the arrangement of Brunel's original permanent way was as much out of the ordinary as its width. The iron bridge rails, in lengths of 14 to 17 ft., weighing 43 lb. per yd., were bolted to longitudinal baulks of pine in 30 ft. lengths, 12 to 14 in. wide and 6 to 7 in. deep. A tapered plank between rail and baulk gave the former a cant of 1 in 20. Gauge was maintained by pine cross transoms bolted to the baulks, either singly or in pairs, at 15 ft. intervals, and common to both up and down roads. The double transoms fell automatically where the 30 ft. baulks came together. They were bolted in turn, and housed into, 9 to 10 in. diameter piles of beech, varying in length, according to whether they were in cutting or on embankment, from 8 to 18 ft. The object of the piles was to hold the track firmly down into the ballast, which was packed fine under the longitudinals. On paper it was indeed a permanent way, designed to last for ever.

The broad gauge was liable to cause trouble with the proposed connection with the London and Birmingham by Kensal Green, but other differences arose between the companies ere this. Immediate plans were made for an extension to Paddington, and work was begun on this, wherever landowners consented, before Parliamentary sanction was obtained (July 3, 1837). The first Paddington terminus lay to the west of the present Bishops Road Bridge, where the goods depot now lies. A goods shed, on the other hand, was placed north of Eastbourne Terrace (then called Spring Street) and east of Bishops Road.

Brunel undertook all engineering activities in the early days of the company, including the locomotive side. As we have seen, he had pronounced theories of his own, especially in regard to reducing friction and providing low centres of gravity, and though he did not design the first Great Western locomotives, he made certain stipulations which the makers had to follow as best they could. The resulting collection of monstrosities is too well known to need particularisation here, but it may be recalled that the only normal reliable engines the Great Western had in its earliest days were the two famous Stephenson singles *North Star* and *Morning Star*, and their advent was accidental, for they had been intended for the 5 ft. 6 in. gauge New Orleans Railway and left on the builders' hands owing to financial panic.

The first engine to be in steam on the Great Western was *Vulcan*, a freak with 8 ft. driving wheels and 14 by 16 in. cylinders, having the driving axle-boxes and horns above the main frames. Built by Tayleur of Newton-le-Willows, she was shipped to London River, and thence to West Drayton by barge, together with *Premier*, by Mather Dixon, arriving early in November, 1837.* By this time, having ordered the engines, Brunel had taken on the young Daniel Gooch to deal with them on arrival, and make them work as best they could. Gooch's first task was to hoist *Vulcan* and *Premier* off their barges and get them about a mile overland to the railway at Drayton. On December 28, 1837, *Vulcan* was given a trial trip near Iver, over a mile and a half of completed track.

The superior *North Star*, however, was the first Great Western engine to haul a passenger train. She had 7 ft. driving wheels (substituted for the original 6 ft. 6 in. wheels when the engine was converted to 7 ft. gauge) and 16 by 16 in. cylinders. It was of the *North Star* that Brunel wrote to T. E. Harrison, patentee of two super-freaks built by Hawthorn's, emphasising the importance of beauty in locomotive lineaments:—

> " . . . we have a splendid engine of Stephenson's, it
> would be a beautiful ornament in the most elegant drawing
> room and we have another of Quaker-like simplicity
> [possibly Mather Dixon's *Premier*] carried even to shabbi-
> ness but very possibly as good an engine, but the difference
> in the care bestowed by the engine man, the favour in which
> it is held by others and even oneself, not to mention the
> public, is striking. A plain young lady however amiable is
> apt to be neglected. Now your engine is capable of being
> made very handsome, and it ought to be so."

Tom Harrison's engines, *Thunderer* and *Hurricane*, were those which had the boilers and the " works " on separate carriages, thus destroying whatever powers of adhesion they might otherwise have possessed. The former had four-coupled wheels geared up to give

* The event is recalled by " The Engine " public house at West Drayton, which has for its sign a handsome picture of Gooch's *Acheron*.

the equivalent of more than 16 ft. diameter. The latter had 10 ft. single drivers. G. H. Gibbs had an enjoyable trip on *Thunderer* before the opening and recorded in his diary:—

> "Along the greater part of the four miles the engine ran beautifully smooth and for some way we cleared sixty miles an hour."

Both engines, like most of the other monsters, were hopeless failures and quite useless for regular traffic. As the reason for most of the failures was to be found in Brunel's eccentric theories —light weight entailing insufficient boiler power, gearing, low piston speed and so forth—and following Gibbs's apparently satisfactory experience with the worst of the engines, it is not surprising that the unfortunate Gooch was early in quite undeserved trouble over them. It must be added that Brunel, who might easily have made him a scapegoat, loyally stood by him when Gibbs was on the warpath. The truth was that without Gooch's patience, experience (though he was not yet of age) and slogging hard work by day and night, the Great Western might easily have suffered a complete stoppage of traffic at the very beginning. Enough has been described to indicate what sort of equipment it had when it hopefully began operations in the summer of 1838.*

On the initial section, from Paddington (old station) to a point on the Thames opposite Maidenhead, 22 miles, 43 chains, the principal work was the handsome viaduct across the valley by Hanwell, with eight 70 ft. arches supported on parallel square brick pillars having a slight batter and set in pairs. It was named after Lord Wharncliffe, Chairman of the Lords Committee on the Act of Incorporation, and his arms were carved and mounted in the middle of the south side. It was completed in 1837, some time before the rest of the London-Maidenhead section. Construction of the complex permanent way, with its attendant pile driving, was very slow. Long extracts from Gibbs's diary, and much other interesting material, provide a well of information in MacDermot's *History of the Great Western Railway* (1927).

On May 22, the Directors had a joy-ride from Bull's Bridge, Hayes, to Maidenhead, and on May 31 there was the formal opening, when a large and select party went down from Paddington to Maidenhead behind the *North Star*. There was high junketing

---

* Charles Saunders said before the Parliamentary Committee on Railways in April, 1841: "At the opening in 1838 we found the engines were so inefficient that time-table working was hopeless; one or two engines might keep time, the other eight or ten were always out of time. So we suspended time-tables till the locomotive power became sufficient."

in a large marquee, under the influence of which (*The Times* sweetly recorded) one of the Bristol directors, T. R. Guppy, got on top of the train and walked all along the carriage roofs while it was going at full speed. The outward journey averaged 28 m.p.h., and the return trip was made at 33½ m.p.h., without any unfortunate incidents *in re* Guppy. On June 4, the public opening took place, the first train being taken by the Tayleur engine *Aeolus*.

The long and bitter progress of the Battle of the Gauges belongs more properly to histories of the Great Western company than to one of its West of England main line *per se*. It was fought in Parliament and it was fought on the lines themselves, and in general it was the "Narrow Gauge" party that distinguished itself by sharp practice and jiggery pokery, with at least one example of active sabotage. The trouble arose, of course, as soon as Brunel's broad gauge came into contact with Stephenson's standard, as at Gloucester, where the old Bristol and Gloucester made connection with the Birmingham and Gloucester. The transfer of passengers was bad enough, that of goods was worse, and the Birmingham company was out to make them worse still in order to stir up trouble. Its goods manager, J. D. Payne, hearing that a Parliamentary Committee was coming down to investigate, " arranged for the unloading of two trains already dealt with, as an addition to the usual work, and when the Members came to the scene, they were appalled by the clamour arising from the well-arranged confusion of shouting out addresses of consignments, the chucking of packages across from truck to truck, the enquiries for missing articles, the loading, unloading and reloading, which his clever device had brought into operation ".*

But before ever the troubles of break-of-gauge were heard of, there was sorrow enough over Brunel's ingenious pile-driven road. Instead of holding the track securely down in the road-bed, it stayed firmly put while the road-bed itself settled down comfortably on the bosom of Mother Earth, leaving what amounted to a continuous trestle. Progress became more and more like the Witching Waves at a fair as the baulks and rails sagged under pressure between the unyielding piles. So the piles had to go, and as the cross transoms were housed into them, this was no mere Saturday afternoon sawing job.

In Brunel's greater works, there was no such absurd fiasco, though many people awaited, with relish, the collapse of Maidenhead Bridge under its first train. It is—for its original arches still stand—a most beautiful structure. Brunel designed for it two of

* G. P. Neele, *Railway Reminiscences* (1904).

the largest and flattest brick arches ever built, having a span of 128 ft., each with a rise of only 24½ ft. The bridge was completed in 1839, on July 1 of which year the line was opened to Twyford for Reading and Henley.* East of Reading came the great cutting through the hill by Sonning, originally intended to be tunnelled. The rest of the line between London and Bristol was opened by stages. Reading was reached on March 30, 1840, Steventon on June 1, and Faringdon Road (now Challow) on July 20. At the western end, where the country was much more difficult, the line was opened from Bristol to Bath on August 31, 1840, and on December 17 the eastern section was extended from Farringdon Road to Hay Lane, 80¼ miles from Paddington.

In the uncompleted gap was the fearsome Box Tunnel, another of those works which pessimists agreed would never be completed. Yet this bore through marl and oolite proved less disastrous for those concerned than Kilsby on the London and Birmingham. Though it was still unfinished when the first train rolled eastwards out of Bristol, it was completed and opened, with the Chippenham-Bath section, on June 30, 1841, the Hay Lane to Chippenham section having been opened previously on May 31. So there was the Great Western Railway, complete in its intended form, one of the most ambitious, most majestic works of its time, 118¼ miles long. Nearly everything was on the grand scale. To the glory of Maidenhead Bridge was added those of the bridges and tunnels in the Bristol-Bath district; even the embankments and the viaducts at Basildon and Cholsey were clearly built to last ten centuries. Box Tunnel was 1 mile, 70 chains in length, dead straight, on a gradient of 1 in 100 falling towards Bath and Bristol, and very soon there had been established the superb tradition that once a year the sun shone straight through it soon after rising—on Brunel's birthday, April 9. Incomparable Isambard ! You were quite capable of surveying the tunnel with that in mind !

The grading of the Great Western line was on the same grand scale as everything else. In just over 77 miles from London to Swindon, there was no steeper gradient than 1 in 660, and most of it was far easier than that, with long level stretches and rises ranging from 1 in 1,204 to 1,760. It was a locomotive man's dream.

The summit came just beyond Swindon, between there and Rushey Platt, whereafter the line generally fell to Bristol City, with two downward inclines of 1 in 100 (beyond Wootton Bassett and again through Box Tunnel), and one upward, through Chippenham to the level preceding Box Tunnel. Ostentatious attention was

* The Henley branch was not opened, however, until 1857.

paid to tunnel portals in the Bath and Bristol neighbourhood, and at the stations at these places, also, magnificence was in the ascendant. Bristol Temple Meads, in particular, was given a superb hammer-beam roof, and both this and Bath initiated a Great Western tradition for massive timber station roofs, covering trains and passengers alike. All over the West Country were they to rise, proudly in their buff-coloured paint. A great one was to span the tracks at Newton Abbot and to survive there until the early nineteen-twenties. A little one was to do the same at the branch terminus of Moretonhampstead—and likewise throughout all of what became the immense Great Western system. Here and there we find them today, and though they may afford beggarly shelter on a wet day, we may regard them with strange affection, and feel sorry when they come down in favour of modern and much more efficient platform roofing. Could not one have become the hall of a newer station, as at Stockholm ?

The first Paddington, however, had none of the splendours of Temple Meads, nor could it hold a candle to Bath. It was not until 1854 that it was replaced by the stately Brunelian terminus (seeming somehow to have the Brighton Pavilion and the Crystal Palace for its parents) which was immortalised by Frith, and which, with additions, has survived to this day. Venerable Paddington ! You have known Gooch and Brunel; Cuthbert Bede, and, long after, Compton Mackenzie, passed through you before they came to write *Verdant Green* and *Sinister Street*; you have seen the broad gauge in its prime, and you have seen its end; of trains you have seen so many—eight-footers and cigar-boxes, brass domes and clerestories, Zulus and Cornishmen; your bronze soldier from one war has stood firm while the next war took a slice out of the General Offices and laid most of Eastbourne Terrace low. Beloved old diehard !

Let us rest our glowing vocatives, however, the more soberly to consider the building up of this great English main line. Bristol formed the end of the original Great Western Railway, but by no means the end of broad-gauge advances to the West, and where they were, there was the hand of Brunel. The year after the formation of the Great Western company, there was incorporated the Bristol and Exeter Railway, and sixteen days before the final G.W. section was opened, the first of the B. and E. began operations between Bristol and Bridgewater.* The B. and E. terminus at

* Some time in the mid-nineteenth century, Bridgewater apparently gave its middle E to Folkstone, a town then suffering from an unfortunate anagram discovered by Queen Elizabeth, for today they are undoubtedly Bridgwater and Folkestone.

Bristol, with imposing general offices in choice Early-Victorian-Tudor style, was at right-angles to the Great Western Temple Meads station, with which it was connected by cross tracks and turnplates. Opposite it, on the north side, was the Great Western goods depot, alongside a dock connecting with Floating Harbour, and 12 ft. below main-line level, four wagon-hoists being in use. A spur connected the Great Western main line with that of the B. and E.R. for through running, and its curved course is followed by the main platforms of the present Temple Meads through station. This layout dates from the beginning of 1878, the original one from 1845. In 1933, the station was very much enlarged and modernised, but ancient relics are still there.

Having reached Bridgewater via Weston-super-Mare on June 14, 1841, the Bristol and Exeter pushed on to Taunton (July 1, 1842), Beambridge (May 1, 1843), and to Exeter, 193¾ miles from Paddington, with a barn-like wooden station on the site of the present St. Davids, exactly a year later. The general aspect was Great Western, emphasised by the broad gauge, though there were visible differences. One of the Bristol and Exeter's trademarks, the use of earthenware finials for the telegraph poles, survived the original company by many years. At first, the Great Western was the working company, but in 1849 the B. and E.R. provided its own engines and vehicles, continuing to do so until it became merged with its powerful ally in 1876. Two early branches of the Bristol and Exeter were those to Clevedon and Tiverton, opened in 1847 and 1848. The second-named is noteworthy as having been worked by Bridges Adams's celebrated steam car *Fairfield*, the first practical example of a self-contained rail car, such as the Great Western was to use in large numbers for local traffic during the present century.

Beyond Exeter, Brunel was active again with the South Devon Railway to Plymouth, which was initiated with considerable joint support from the Great Western, the Bristol and Exeter, and the Bristol and Gloucester. It was opened to Teignmouth, with its celebrated passage below the red cliffs, on May 30, 1846, to Newton Abbot on December 30, and to Totnes on July 20, 1847. On May 5, 1848, the very hilly line thence to Laira Green, Plymouth, was opened. The Torquay branch followed on December 18, and the main line was completed into Plymouth and to the Millbay terminus, 246¾ miles from Paddington via Bristol, on April 2, 1849.

Neither the Bristol and Exeter nor the South Devon could show anything like the near-billiard-table gradients of most of the original Great Western main line. The first stretch of some ten miles out of Bristol contained the up-and-down through Flax Bourton, with steepest gradients of 1 in 180 down and 1 in 146 up. Thereafter came an almost continuous level to the site of Creech Junction, followed by the almost continuous rise to Whiteball, culminating in some 3 miles at 1 in 80 to 90 and a little over half a mile at 1 in 127 through Whiteball Tunnel. On the eastward rise from the Exeter direction, the stiffest part was the final two-mile rise at 1 in 115. Beyond Exeter, the line was made largely level to Aller Junction, though curvature was severe in places. Also the red cliffs of Devon have always been inclined to spill themselves on to the permanent way. There was a very bad cliff fall in the winter of 1862, illustrated now by a contemporary lithograph. The nearer engine there shown is one of Gooch's bogie saddle tanks (q.v. *post*), attached to an early third-class carriage of average dastardly design.

The use of such relatively heavy and powerful engines on the South Devon Railway a century ago (the first two appeared in 1849) was dictated by the very heavy gradients beyond Aller Junction, where there was first the short but violent rise to Dainton Tunnel with a corresponding fall beyond, including short stretches at 1 in 36 to 38. West of Totnes came the great 19-mile hump with its summit at Wrangaton, with a ruling gradient of 1 in 46 in the down direction. In the up direction, a stiff climb between Plympton and Hemerdon was mostly at 1 in 42 (about a mile and a half), with half a mile at 1 in 41.

The prospect of these severe gradients let the South Devon Railway in for another of Brunel's brain-waves. While the South Devon Railway was under construction, Clegg and Samuda's patent atmospheric system of traction was calling attention; in an evil hour, Brunel became interested in it both as an engineer and as a business man, though business had never been a strong point of the Brunel family.* The principle, though disused for more than a century now, is well known. Briefly, it involved the laying of a continuous cast-iron pipe between the rails, from which the air was exhausted by steam pumping stations at regular intervals. Along the top of the pipe was a continuous slot covered by a greased leather flap forming a valve. Through this slot, the traction carriages were connected to internal pistons, and the connection, by lifting the flap, admitted air in rear of the piston, causing it to

---

* In 1821 Mr., afterwards Sir Marc Brunel, I. K. Brunel's father, was committed to the King's Bench Prison for debt. In later years, according to Lady Celia Brunel Noble, this episode was "referred to mysteriously as 'The Misfortune', being otherwise unmentionable". Cf. Lady Noble's *The Brunels, Father and Son*.

shoot forward along the tube wherein the pumping engines maintained a constant vacuum. A roller on the train closed the flap-valve in rear, and after the carriages had passed out of each section the air was quickly exhausted again in readiness for the next train.

Difficulties which should have been immediately obvious were those entailed by junctions and points. These, on another railway which got bitten by the atmospheric bug, the London and Croydon, resulted in the building of the world's first flyover junction. Marshalling of vehicles, and the operation of goods traffic in particular, was likely to be a laborious business, even with the ever-ready help of poor Dobbin. But atmospheric traction had taken the volatile Brunel's fancy, and, particularly as the South Devon gradients promised heavy work for locomotives, the South Devon Railway had to have the thing.

It was not ready when the first sections of the line were opened, and the passage of ordinary steam trains held up the work. Trials with light atmospheric trains were held in February, 1847, and a maximum speed of 70 m.p.h. was claimed. Quite probably it was so, and certainly it encouraged the atmospheric enthusiasts. On September 13, 1847, regular atmospheric trains began running from Exeter to Teignmouth, and to Newton Abbot on January 10, 1848, thus working over 20 miles of route. The apparatus was a new wonder of the age. Here at last was the perfect railway, swift, smokeless, and silent save for the comfortable rumble of the wheels.

Then things began to happen. The neighbouring rat population suddenly discovered, in the continuous greased-leather flap, an apparently inexhaustible supply of delicious food. What the rats spared, the salt sea air spoiled, and breakdowns became as regular, and as troublesome, as those of locomotives on the original London-Maidenhead line ten years before. The despised and rejected locomotive had to come to the rescue, and on September 10, 1848, after just under a year of working, the South Devon Railway was obliged to scrap its atmospheric traction, at a capital loss of £400,000.

Before we go on into the Duchy, we should notice some subsequent history of the Bristol and Exeter and the South Devon companies. The former made spasmodic efforts to occupy North Devon, but was too suspicious of its great and benevolent ally, the Great Western, to present with it a fully united front to standard-gauge penetration, at the back of which was the London and South Western Railway. It gained control of and absorbed the Chard and Taunton Railway before its opening in 1866, but the South Western had already reached Exeter before the C. and T. was incorporated. Thereafter followed a purely defensive campaign; the Chard line was kept broad-gauge for long after other branches east of Exeter had been converted to block possible South Western expansionist tactics such as the obtaining of running powers to Taunton via Chard. Though the B. and E.R. ran trains over the Exeter and Crediton Railway, it failed entirely to gain control of the important North Devon Railway thence to Barnstaple, which fell to the London and South Western, broad gauge and all, as will be described in the story of the South Western main line.

The South Devon Railway, by controlling and taking over locally promoted lines, all on the broad gauge, got entry to Tavistock in 1859, and Launceston in 1865, but failed to produce this line to Wenford, on a mineral branch of the ancient Bodmin and Wadebridge Railway, which would have given North Cornwall to the broad gauge party. Macaulay's map of the British railways, published in the 'sixties, optimistically showed the Launceston-Wenford connection as being " in progress ", and as an appendage of the Cornwall Railway, to whose ownership, also, the Bodmin and Wadebridge was quite improperly credited, for it was indeed a sort of " cell " which the South Western maintained deep in the heart of the broad-gauge empire.

This Cornwall Railway, solidly broad-gauge, belonged to a company incorporated in 1846, and was jointly leased, from its opening on May 4, 1859, to the Great Western, the Bristol and Exeter, and the South Devon companies. In its length of 53½ miles from Plymouth to Truro, it came to exhibit some of Brunel's most memorable work as a civil engineer, indeed, what was perhaps his greatest single work, the Royal Albert Bridge across the estuary of the Tamar from the environs of Plymouth to Saltash in Cornwall.

The bridge, of single track at a high level, was proposed by Brunel in preference to a floating bridge across the Hamoaze. This had first been suggested for a railway planned back in the 'thirties, which was to run westward from Basingstoke, and which would have given the London and South Western the road to southern and western Cornwall which it never got. The Cornwall Railway Company itself had revived the floating bridge idea before Brunel became its engineer. Work on the great high-level bridge was formally inaugurated in 1857 by Prince Albert, for whom it was named. The river at this point is 1,100 ft. wide and 70 ft. deep in the middle at high water. Needless to say, Admiralty requirements were exacting, allowing a minimum span of 300 ft. and height of 180 ft. above high water. Brunel complied with them by placing a single pier in the middle deep, connected to the shore piers by two 455 ft. spans. Sinking of the first trial caisson had taken place as far back as 1849, but construction had been suspended in the post-mania depression. The archetype was the bridge which Brunel had built over the Wye at Chepstow for the South Wales Railway in 1851-2. Royal Albert Bridge, as is well known, is a combination of tubular and suspension construction, the suspension chains being anchored to the ends of two great, slightly arched tubes, from which the side girders and decking are additionally suspended by vertical members and cross-trusses. With its approach viaducts, comprising 17 spans varying from 70 to 90 ft., it has a total length of 2,190 ft. Like the famous flat-arch bridge at Maidenhead, it stands today, carrying loads never contemplated when it was new, and without alteration beyond the strengthening of the floor members in 1905. Though still at the early age of 53, Brunel was sickening to his death when it approached completion, and only saw it in its finished state from a chair in a wagon on which he was propelled slowly across. He died on September 15, 1859, of shock at the accident on his huge ship *Great Eastern*, of which some miserable person told him as he lay desperately ill after a stroke. Thus passed this brilliant, fallible, admirable engineer, the creator of the Great Western Railway, little more than four months after completion of his last great work, and England knew the little man with the great forehead, the great hat and the great cigar no more. Of his successes and his failures, the *Morning Chronicle* wrote: " The history of invention records no instance of grand novelties so boldly imagined and so successfully carried out by the same individual. He was less successful when he was less bold. Many of his lesser contrivances turned out not only unsuccessful, but blunders. Brunel could make an engineering epic, but not an engineering sonnet."

With the completion of the Cornwall Railway's branch to Falmouth on August 24, 1863, the building of the original broad-gauge line to the West was concluded. Apart from Royal Albert Bridge, its most prominent feature was a magnificent series of timber viaducts, some entirely of wood and others with a wooden superstructure on masonry piers, and all built on lines laid down by Brunel, though some came after him. Five were on the South Devon Railway main line, but the Cornwall Railway mustered forty-two, and there were ten more on the West Cornwall Railway, to be described shortly.

Some of these timber viaducts were of tremendous size, where they crossed the deep Cornish valleys running down to the sea; others, around Plymouth, had piling going to a great depth in the mud of the tidal creeks. The longest on the Cornwall Railway was the last but one before reaching Truro, 1,290 ft. between abutments, and the highest was St. Pinnock, near Doublebois, with the rails 151 ft. above the deepest part of the valley. The timber components, of yellow pine, were so arranged that all could be replaced as required under normal occupation by the Engineer's Department. These were no flimsy " trestles ", such as the wild Pawnee used joyously to burn down in the path of the Bad-Medicine-Wagon; they were built to last, and so they did until the price, and difficulty of obtaining suitable timber, made replacement necessary many years after. Including those on the Launceston branch of the S.D.R., and ten on the West Cornwall Railway, next described, there were sixty-seven of them altogether. The last to remain on the main line was the Stonehouse Pool Viaduct, between Plymouth North Road and Devonport, replaced in 1908. Collegewood Viaduct, on the Falmouth branch, survived until 1934, the last train to pass over it being the 10.50 p.m. up, on August 24. A detailed article on these famous viaducts was included in the special issue of *The Railway Gazette*, dated August 30, 1935, and commemorating the centenary of incorporation of the Great Western Railway.

The West Cornwall Railway remains to be described. Its history began with the Hayle Railway, of standard gauge, opened in 1838 for mineral traffic with steam locomotive traction, and officially for passengers on May 22, 1843, though passengers had been carried for at least two years previously. Extending from Redruth to Hayle, it failed in an attempt to extend in both directions to Truro and Penzance. The new West Cornwall Railway was incorporated on August 3, 1846, the same day as the Cornwall Railway, with powers to absorb the Hayle Railway, make deviations to cut out its steep gradients, and duly to link Truro with Penzance. The W.C.R. was built to standard gauge, but made capable of conversion to broad. To this end, Barlow's sleeperless track was at first employed. It was opened from Redruth to Penzance on March 11, 1852, and to Truro on August 25. On August 1, 1859, the West Cornwall trains began to run into Truro Cornwall Railway station, though there was a break of gauge between the two railways. The C.R. was entitled to running powers over the West Cornwall, and early in 1864 it required the latter to mix the gauges from Truro to Penzance, an expensive operation beyond the means of the West Cornwall, which sold out to the broad-gauge confederacy in the following year. Broad-gauge goods trains began running over the West Cornwall on November 6, 1866, and on March 1,

1867, the first through express train from Paddington to Penzance, 325½ miles via Bristol, made its inaugural run.

Now was the broad gauge at its flood tide, and all too soon the ebb was to begin. It had indeed begun in other parts when, on June 1, 1877, the short branch was opened from St. Erth to St. Ives, the last line ever to be built on Brunel's stately, most uniquely English gauge of 7 ft. o¼ in.

CHAPTER ELEVEN

The Gooch Heritage

IT has already been suggested that seldom had a locomotive engineer a less enviable task than young Daniel Gooch when he went to the Great Western. He had to take charge of the truly *doctrinaire* locomotives which Brunel had specified and ordered, make them go, and bow before august disapproval when they broke down. This was the sort of thing that Brunel had stipulated: " A velocity of 30 miles an hour to be considered as the standard velocity, and this to be attained without requiring the piston to travel at a greater rate than 280 ft. per minute ". We have seen what happened when locomotives of that sort were let loose on the infant Great Western. Gooch was just twenty-one. On the rare occasions when he was free of the wretched engines, this shy, serious puritan from the North was favoured with embarrassing acts of kindness by the flamboyant, Gallic Brunel, who got him invited to vast dinners and gay routs that shocked him nearly out of his wits. Not by a long way yet was he near to becoming Sir Daniel Gooch, Baronet, of Clewer. A very lucid account of his progress from the one state to the other survived in the form of a book of his reminiscences put together by his second wife, and rather inaccurately known as the *Gooch Diaries*.

As already remarked, the two Stephenson engines *North Star* and *Morning Star* just about saved the situation, which was further eased when some more " Stars " were hurriedly ordered and delivered. Gooch wisely took for his model this Stephenson six-wheel sandwich-framed engine, with improvements, most importantly the use of an adequate boiler with a good pressure, and the result was the *Fire Fly* and sixty-one similar engines, built between 1840 and 1842 by various firms, with 7 ft. driving wheels and 15 by 18 in. cylinders (later enlarged to 16 by 20 in.). Exactly contemporary with these came twenty-one similar though smaller engines with 6 ft. drivers (the Sun class), while 1841 and 1842 also saw the advent of twenty-two 5 ft. goods engines, eighteen of them 2-4-0 and four 0-6-0. The former were officially known as the Leo class, although the first was *Elephant*, and the four 0-6-0's were called the Hercules class. All had the large Gothic-shaped steam space over the firebox, characteristic of early Gooch practice, and outwardly somewhat resembling the Bury haycock arrangement, though it was not so.

These engines, and twelve " Stars ", did nearly all the work until 1846, and saved the Great Western from chaos and perdition. They formed the basic types for many more engines built during and even after Gooch's time. They also initiated the Great Western's occasional habit of spelling the names wrong. Apparently the practice was to get a dictionary of classical mythology, an astrological almanac, and *Buffon's Natural History*, and extract hterefrom suitable names of demigods, zodiacal signs, birds, beasts and creeping things, throw in a few weapons, volcanoes and biblical personages for variety, and forward these to the makers. As the fitters who fixed the brass letters on were still largely illiterate, there were sometimes funny results. Of the weapons, *Assegai* had become *Assagais* by the time it appeared on one of the Sun class; *Samson* became *Sampson* and *Goliath* was spelt *Goliah*.* This sort of thing went on in later years, when *Estafette*† became *Estaffete*, and *Laocoön* appeared as *Lagoon*, but as the late E. L. Ahrons observed, one name was as good as another, and so they remained. None of the named broad-gauge engines had numbers.

Gooch was mainly responsible for the foundation and growth of the company's locomotive works at Swindon, and the accompanying expansion of a small market town into a great industrial centre. Swindon's first locomotive was the celebrated *Great Western*, an enlargement of the standard single express engine, with 8-ft. driving wheels. The Battle of the Gauges was in full blast, and early in 1846 the Great Western company produced its new, prodigious engine in thirteen weeks, with no proper drawings. Her only weak point was the weight on the leading axle, which caused its breakage while running near Shrivenham. The frames were then lengthened and an extra carrying axle put in, making the engine 4-2-2. On the altered design was based that of the *Iron Duke* (April 1847), the prototype of a very famous class, numbering thirty engines, including the original modified *Great Western*. They were built over several years up to July, 1855. One of them, the *Lord of the Isles*, was shown at the Great Exhibition of 1851, and is portrayed in the famous frieze of the Albert Hall. With 18 by 24 in. cylinders, 1,919·47 sq. ft. heating surface, and a

---

* Possibly in protest, this engine exploded at Plympton in 1849, but survived, with a new boiler, until 1871.

† There was already a *Courier*, and the same class, the eight-foot singles, included both *Swallow* and *Hirondelle*.

working pressure of 100 lb. per sq. in. (later 110 lb.), they were easily the largest and most powerful express engines on regular duties in the world. American engines, at that time, were fairly small and light owing to track restrictions, and Crampton's great *Liverpool* on the London and North Western must be regarded rather as a Battle of the Gauges demonstration than as an engine for ordinary service.

Of the Gooch eight-footers, the *Lord of the Isles* ran until June, 1881, covering 789,309 miles. During the 'seventies and 'eighties, many of these grand engines were replaced by new ones of practically the same design, but slightly larger dimensions, and bearing the same names in most cases. The original *Prometheus* was not scrapped until October, 1887, having been built in 1850. The Gothic firebox casing was not perpetuated in the Iron Duke class. *Lord of the Isles* survived in retirement in the paint shop at Swindon, together with the most venerable *North Star*, until 1906, when, with a vandalism fully worthy of railway officialdom at its worst, both were broken up.* One side of the *Lord of the Isles'* motion was kept for educational purposes, and the driving wheels and one buffer of *North Star* also escaped, to be built, later, into a replica of this engine.

Though the findings of the Gauge Commission were pretty poor from the Great Western point of view, the magnificent engines designed by Gooch made history in the company's efforts to prove the broad-gauge case. One of the seven-foot singles, *Ixion* (October, 1841 to July, 1879) averaged 50 m.p.h. from Paddington to Didcot and 53·9 m.p.h. on return with a 60-ton train. Gooch equipped an improved dynamometer car, which recorded drawbar pull each sixteenth of a mile travelled, timing to fifths of a second, and, by an anemometer having its revolving cups 5 ft. above the roof, speed of the wind relative to that of the train.† In 1848 the new eight-foot single *Great Britain* took a train from Paddington to Didcot in 47½ minutes for the 53 miles, or at nearly 67 m.p.h. start-to-stop. This old record of records was discredited for many years, largely owing to the unfortunate fact that at the time only a short abstract was published of Gooch's monumental paper presented to the Institution of Civil Engineers on " Observations of the Resistances to Railway Trains at Different Velocities ".

---

* For many years the Great Western seemed to hold that history was best forgotten, possibly owing to ancient fiascos. All that survived of the broad-gauge locomotives, and that by accident, was the little coffee-pot inspection engine *Tiny*, of the South Devon Railway, which was at last enshrined on one of the platforms at Newton Abbot.

† Robinson's anemometer dates from 1846. It was therefore lacking on the original dynamometer car of 1839.

In the late 'forties the Great Western was running by far the fastest trains in the world; on the standard gauge, only the London and South Western could approach them in 1848. The Gooch expansive link motion, in use on both railways, doubtless had much to do with the free-running qualities of their locomotives. John Viret Gooch was responsible for the London and South Western engines. In later years both lines were to show a sad deterioration, but in that glorious year, while Continental Europe was busy with revolutions, Paddington to Didcot was covered by the crack West of England expresses at an average booked speed of a fraction over 57 m.p.h. As far back as 1846, Bristol could be reached in 2½ hours, with a ten-minute stop in the interests of Swindon's awful refreshment room, and Exeter in 4 hours 25 minutes. The refreshment room stop at Swindon lasted until 1895. Brunel once wrote to the licensee, denying that he had complained of, or even seen, any coffee at Swindon, and explaining that he was " surprised you should buy such bad roasted corn ".

In 1849, Flying Dutchman won both the Derby and the St. Leger, and the Great Western gave his name to the morning mail train to the West. Although speeds deteriorated during the 'fifties, some local facilities were improved by the use of slip coaches, a practice which the Great Western held in great esteem thereafter. In 1855, too, the first special Travelling Post Office train was inaugurated between Paddington and Bristol, making the journey in 3 hours 44 minutes, with stops at Slough, Maidenhead, Reading, Steventon, Swindon, Chippenham and Bath. Installation of mail pickup apparatus at Slough and Maidenhead in 1866 cut out the stops at these places.

The earliest Great Western trains carried four classes, provided by posting carriage (a sort of saloon with a clerestory roof and the body waisted between the four-foot wheels like an old bus), first class, second-class closed, and second-class open; the last-mentioned being open-sided with a flat roof over. Most of the ordinary carriages were six-wheeled, and for its period the first class was excellent, each compartment containing eight comfortable seats, sometimes with a partition and sliding door in the middle. This last arrangement survived on the Great Western for many years. It made a surprise reappearance in 1925 on the Sligo, Leitrim and Northern Counties Railway. Goods traffic did not begin until August, 1839, and some time after poor persons were allowed on the night goods trains, sitting in open wagons with planks laid across. This was " third class " in its earliest form on the Great Western. Eight of its shivering patrons were killed on Christmas Eve, 1841, when their wretched conveyance, headed by the 2-4-0 engine *Hecla*, ran into a bad earth slip in Sonning Cutting.

Most interesting of the early Great Western carriages were the " Long Charleys ", of 1852, though since they were built primarily for the Birmingham line, they are not strictly within our compass. They were seven-compartment, eight-wheel composites, with the axles equalised in pairs. One is illustrated in my book on *Nineteenth Century Railway Carriages*. The Ocean Mail trains between Paddington and Plymouth had some spacious T.P.O. carriages, with adequate headroom in which the ordinary coaches were sadly lacking. The latter were much wider than they were high, and resembled huge, lumbering oblong boxes, painted in an unrelieved chocolate colour.

Having been worked at first by the Great Western, the Bristol and Exeter Railway provided its own locomotives and vehicles from May 1, 1849. In many cases, the B. and E. engines closely followed Great Western practice, and a slightly smaller version of the standard Gooch 4-2-2 engine worked main-line trains. In 1853 Rothwell and Company built to James Pearson's designs the first of the celebrated Bristol and Exeter 4-2-4 express tank engines. The use of tank engines for fast trains had been initiated just before by John Gooch on the Eastern Counties, and by Joseph Beattie, who succeeded him on the South Western, but Pearson's design was a prodigy, " the boldest departure made up to that time from the accepted canons on locomotive design, other than perhaps Trevithick's *Cornwall* and Crampton's *Liverpool* " (Ahrons).

The single driving wheels were 9 ft. in diameter, and the cylinders, widely spaced under the smokebox, so that the cranks would clear the boiler barrel, were $16\frac{1}{2}$ by 24 in. Details of the boiler are elusive, though Ahrons remarked that it was small for a broad-gauge engine. The bogies were of Gooch's ball-and-socket pivot type, and the driving wheels flangeless, with an interesting arrangement of suspension. Though the main frames were inside, a supplementary frame with a triangular truss extended round the outside of each driving wheel, supporting additional outside bearings. Above the wheel was a pivot and lever connecting two brass-cased rubber springs, one inside and one outside the wheel. Apart from its rather effete-looking boiler, with a very short smokebox, Pearson's baby was a very imposing specimen among ancient locomotives.

Eight of the class were built during 1853-4, and gained a reputation for running at 80 m.p.h. down Wellington bank with the up mails. The specimen illustrated, No. 42, had just been in the

143 Inset Nº 44 pages 108/9

wars. On the evening of April 18, 1865, she had a breakdown while hauling a down express west of Bristol, and, standing at Weston Junction, this train was struck in the rear by the 8.15 local from Bristol to Weston-super-Mare. The leading coach of the express overrode the bunker of No. 42, with the results shown.* They lasted about sixteen years, a short life compared with the Gooch singles on the Great Western, and were replaced in 1868 by four larger 4-2-4 tanks, with the drivers reduced to 8 ft. 10 in. These, though quite unbalanced, had 18½ tons on the driving wheels, and on July 27, 1876, one of them was derailed with the up Dutchman near Bourton. The Great Western, into whose hands they had just come through amalgamation, converted them into ordinary 4-2-2 eight-foot singles. Two survived until the abolition of the broad gauge in 1892. Two smaller 4-2-4 tank engines, with 7 ft. 6 in. drivers, had appeared on the B. and E.R. in 1862, and one of these survived, as such, until 1887.

The practice of Gooch, however, had tremendous staying power; the last Gooch type eight-foot single, the second *Tornado*, was built as late as 1888, and the class lasted as long as did the broad gauge. For the steeply graded South Devon and Cornwall lines, there were numbers of those ungainly 4-4-0 saddle tanks, such as that shown in the cliff fall near Dawlish. The name there given, *Rocket*, would seem to be apocryphal, for *Rocket* was one of the Sun class singles, and worked from 1841 to 1870, while the engine so entitled in the picture appears to be one of the 5 ft. 9 in. *Sappho* class, all of which were named after figures in the ancient literary world. Possibly the artist, with still raw memories of having to write five hundred lines of *Virgil* by teatime, was allergic to such nomenclature. The 4-4-0 tanks in question exhibited several curiosities of old-fashioned design. The short bogie had a ball-and-socket pivot, without sideplay, and sanding the rails was accomplished by the daring and agile fireman getting astride of the saddle tank, lifting the lid off the sand-dome there, and scooping the sand into a small funnel which served both pipes.

Gooch retired from office as locomotive superintendent in October, 1864. He became a director of the company, and was elected chairman in 1865, steering the Great Western safely through very troublous times which it then encountered, and continuing in command until his death on October 15, 1889. He did not flatter himself in his assumption of the title " Father of Express Trains ", for he was so.

Joseph Armstrong succeeded Gooch as locomotive superin-

* More details of this accident were published in *The Locomotive* of July 15, 1937.

tendent, but main-line traction remained very much as before, Armstrong's most noteworthy original designs being standard-gauge engines for the Birmingham and northern lines of the company, and for the South Wales line, which last was converted as early as 1872. In broad-gauge days, some of the fast trains on these were worked by a non-bogie 4-4-0 type of Gooch's design, the Waverley class of 1855. These ran for seventeen to twenty-one years. The Gooch goods engine, from the old Hercules class onwards, was a solid, stolid 0-6-0 with inside frames, and all Gooch engines, after the discarding of the Gothic firebox casing in the 'forties, had domeless boilers. Except for the ugly saddle-tank engines, their appearance, with tall copper-crowned chimneys, and low-sided tenders which made them look much bigger than they were, was most imposing, and quite unlike anything else in the world. The oldest examples, with the Gothic firebox casing, had this covered with bright brass, not copper as some suppose. They had no cabs in Gooch's time at Swindon.

In the late 'sixties, the broad gauge was at flood tide. The next quarter-century years saw its ebb. Thereafter the tide flowed once more, without the broad gauge, and the Great Western was transformed from a somewhat lethargic, old-fashioned railway into something quite different, even in the shape of its main line to the West of England.

London and South Western expansion in the West, carrying thither the Battle of the Gauges in its later phases, was chiefly responsible for cementing the sometimes palsied alliance of the broad-gauge railways, culminating during the middle 'seventies in amalgamation. On January 1, 1876, the Bristol and Exeter was merged into the Great Western. A month later it was followed, for all practical purposes, by the South Devon, Cornwall, and West Cornwall companies, though amalgamation was not confirmed by Parliament until 1878, or, in the case of the Cornwall Railway, 1889. Two Great Western salients into South Western territory were made by the Basingstoke branch (1848) and that to Salisbury (1856). Windsor, incidentally, got its branch in 1849 (the Queen had used the railway at Slough since 1842).

Most interesting was the way in which various branch and other country lines, long unconnected, were gradually built up into a very important whole. For example, Newbury and Hungerford were reached from Reading on December 21, 1847. Few could have guessed that some day the fastest Cornish expresses would pass over it, instead of by Swindon and Bristol. On September 5 of the following year, the Wilts, Somerset and Weymouth Railway

was opened from Thingley Junction to Westbury, continuing to
Frome (October 7, 1850), Yeovil (September 1, 1856), Dorchester
Junction and Weymouth (January 20, 1857). There was at this
time a sort of armistice between the Great Western and the London
and South Western. Although the former had secured a lease of
" Castleman's Snake " (the Southampton and Dorchester Railway)
and proposed to complete it with broad gauge, it relinquished this,
likewise other ambitions south of Basingstoke, in return for the
South Western giving up its territorial demands in respect of West
Cornwall. The opening to Weymouth was made a joint function,
for the South Western trains started running the same day on the
Great Western line with mixed gauge south of Dorchester Junction.
Charles Saunders of the Great Western and Henry Lacy of the
South Western took wine together most amicably. Weymouth
admired its fine Brunelian station with a great timber roof, and
rejoiced at having two railways to London at one glorious swoop.
The South Western had the advantage of distance, $147\frac{1}{4}$ miles via
Castleman's Snake, compared with the Great Western's $168\frac{1}{2}$ on
the broad gauge via Swindon and Thingley Junction. The first
train was the Great Western's 6.15 a.m. up. In return for running
powers into Weymouth, the South Western had to grant the Great
Western running powers over a corresponding distance along its
own line east of Dorchester, with the mixed gauge finally losing
itself somewhere in the neighbourhood of Wool. Of what possible
use it could be to the Great Western or anyone else was never
explained.

Previously, in 1853, the Bristol and Exeter had opened a branch
from Durston to Yeovil. In 1857, Devizes had a branch from the
Wilts, Somerset and Weymouth line, and the Hungerford line was
extended to meet this in 1862. Things remained thus until the
end of the century when, in 1900 a cut-off was opened between
Patney, on the Hungerford-Devizes line, and Westbury. The
South Western had already shortened its own line to Weymouth
some years before. Now the Great Western Weymouth expresses
ran via Hungerford, $154\frac{3}{4}$ miles, compared with the South Western's
$142\frac{3}{4}$ miles via Sway and Bournemouth. In 1905, the Great Western
opened a branch from Castle Cary on the Weymouth line to
Charlton Mackrell, and in the following year it was extended to
Langport, on the Durston-Yeovil line (Bristol and Exeter, 1853).
At the same time, a deviation was put in to bypass Durston, and
on July 1, 1906, the principal expresses between Paddington and
the West of England were re-routed via the new main line thus
built up over so many years.

By the new route, the distance from Paddington to Plymouth was reduced to 225¾ miles, and the London and South Western lost its old advantage. The Great Western had still the easier road, though its profile was much more undulating than on the old line, with a steady, almost continuous rise of 30 miles to Savernake, followed by a fall for nearly 18 miles to a point beyond Lavington. There was no really severe bank, though the final rise to Savernake was at 1 in 106 for about a third of a mile. Beyond Westbury came a stiffish undulation with its summit between Witham and Bruton and a ruling gradient, over a very short stretch in the up direction, of 1 in 78.

In 1868 most of the Great Western lines between Reading and Penzance were purely broad gauge. There was mixed gauge on the West Cornwall Railway, on the North Devon to Barnstaple and Bideford, though this had fallen to the South Western already, and on the Bristol and Exeter from Highbridge to Durston and thence to Yeovil. Mixed gauge extended from Paddington to Reading to accommodate the standard-gauge trains to the North, which then ran through Oxford, and branches to Brentford, Windsor and Basingstoke were also mixed, the second- and third-named to allow for the through royal train journeys between Gosport or Windsor and the Deeside via Banbury. Three other branches, those to Uxbridge, Oxford via Risborough, and Henley, were broad gauge only.

Thereafter, a continual though slowly perceptible process of mixing and narrowing went on, for though the comfort and steadiness of the broad-gauge trains earned many faithful friends among passengers, the break of gauge had become a confounded nuisance where goods traffic and through workings were concerned. The South Wales line was converted in 1872, but the first to come without our present scope was the Weymouth line and its branches, in 1874. The operation lasted three days and was completed on June 25. During that time, the South Western carried Great Western traffic from the Basingstoke branch, over its own line to Southampton, and thence by Castleman's Snake through Ringwood to Dorchester Junction. Except at points and crossovers, the job was chiefly a matter of sweat, involving the cutting of the cross-transoms, shifting the offside baulks and rails inwards to the new gauge, and repacking the ballast.

By 1892, the only unmixed broad gauge left on the Great Western Railway extended from Exeter to the West Cornwall line at Truro. Most of it was on the old baulk road, though there was some cross-sleepered track with bullhead rail in chairs south of

147

Exeter. Mixed gauge existed in the Plymouth district, owing to the running powers of the London and South Western Railway. By that time, about 1,000 miles of broad-gauge route had been converted. On May 20, the down Cornishman—the 10.15 from Paddington to Penzance, made its last journey out of London on the broad gauge, headed by the *Great Western*.* Two photographs purporting to show this train have had wide currency, both appearing, as such, in the handsome G.W.R. centenary issue of *The Railway Gazette*, August 30, 1935. That taken at Paddington is authentic, the train having been stopped half-way out of the station for the purpose. The view of a broad-gauge train at speed in Sonning cutting, now once more reproduced, shows an up train. The shadows are impossible for a down train in the middle of a May morning, and the carriages are different.

During that day, all broad-gauge engines and rolling stock were being evacuated from South Devon and Cornwall, destined for a great expanse of sidings specially laid down at Swindon for their reception, preparatory to conversion or demolition. The Cornishman, in its return through the night from Penzance, acted as a clearing train, and when it completed its journey in the small hours of the twenty-first, broad-gauge travel was finished in the West Country. The last broad-gauge public train was the up night mail, May 20-1, headed by the eight-footer *Bulkeley* of 1880.

The departure of the down Cornishman on May 20 had been the occasion for a remarkable demonstration of regretful affection. People laid pennies, and half-crowns, on the rails in front of it, and the train very fitly received such emotional valedictions as an illustrious old ship on her last voyage. Even the proprietors of *Punch* paid their tribute, with a cartoon by Linley Sambourne showing some navvies burying an engine, watched by the troubled wraith of Brunel. With it were some verses by E. J. Milliken after the form of Wolfe's *Burial of Sir John Moore at Corunna*.

The gauge conversion between Exeter and Truro was accomplished successfully in two days by five thousand men. The third day saw the finishing touches to levelling and packing. During that time, the mails and as much other traffic as possible for Plymouth was carried west of Exeter over the South Western line. One of the first standard-gauge trains to pass over the Great Western into South Devon came from the North, and the appearance of its white London and North Western carriages in such unused country emphasised that whatever had been lost, the virtue of through traffic to other parts had been gained. The last broad-

* An 8 ft. single, replacing the original famous engine of this name.

148

gauge locomotives to be in steam were two 4-4-0 saddle tanks, *Stag* and *Leopard*, used for shunting condemned stock in the sidings at Swindon until 1894.

The St. Martin's summer of the broad gauge was marred by a very violent collision at Norton Fitzwarren, which killed ten people. Through acceptance of the up Cape Mail train when the up road was already occupied by a shunted down goods, the former, running at full speed down the long incline from Whiteball behind the old ex-Bristol and Exeter 4-4-0 saddle-tank engine No. 2051, struck the goods engine, a standard gauge 0-6-0, head-on. That was on November 11, 1890. Fifty years after, short of a week, early on November 4, 1940, the 9.50 p.m. down night express from Paddington via the old route through Bristol (engine *King George VI*) ran through signals and catchpoints where the present quadruple track narrows to double at this same place, and was wrecked, with the loss of twenty-seven lives. There had not been a major accident to a Great Western passenger train for many years previously.

Mention of these two unfortunate smashes brings us to the history of and progress of public safety on the Great Western Railway. Up to 1840, the line relied on hand signals given by the policemen who controlled the early points and junctions. In the autumn of 1840, Brunel introduced what was for many years the standard Great Western fixed signal, revolving on a pivot at the top of an immensely high mast. For " line clear " it presented a round red disc, and for " stop " a horizontal crossbar, white and red lights giving the corresponding indications at night. Two years later, an arrowtail board, known as a fantail, was brought in as a distant signal to give a cautionary indication. There were lesser variations for up and down roads respectively, and for junctions. The Windsor junction at Slough had a remarkable signal known as the Windsor Drum, where a broad ring with a disc inside it, like a great red tambourine, mounted on a horizontal pivot, gave indications equivalent to those of the usual disc and crossbar, and at the same time proof against anything equivocal arising out of its position on the very sharp curve of the junction. The railway's first locking frame was installed at Paddington in 1860.

Gradually, after 1865, three-position semaphores in slotted posts replaced the old discs ; " danger " was indicated by the horizontal, " caution " by a downward inclination, and " line clear " by the stick disappearing in the slot. The " caution " indication was subsequently abolished, and after the 'eighties a very steep downward indication was used on the G.W.R. for " line clear ". The slotted posts gradually disappeared, but the company never used upper quadrant indications. The first all-electric signalbox was opened at Didcot North Junction (Oxford line) in the summer of 1903.

A very great improvement in the main line was completed in March, 1933, namely the provision of avoiding lines which cut out the stations and severe curves at Westbury and Frome. As a result, the West of England expresses pass through no stations of major importance between Newbury and Taunton, a distance of 90 miles. Before opening of the new deviations, practical tests included the running of two of the heaviest express engines (Nos. 6001, *King Edward VII*, and 6029, then called *King Stephen*), side by side at full speed, one of them on the wrong road, a glorious spectacle.

In 1906, first the Henley branch line and then the Fairford branch from Oxford were experimentally equipped with electrical cab signalling, or as it came to be known, automatic train control. After long trial, all the Great Western main lines were so equipped by the autumn of 1931, the company being the first, indeed the only main-line railway in the country to make a complete A.T.C. installation. The system incorporates 40 ft. steel ramps between the rails at the distant signals and connected with them by electric contact. An iron shoe on the engine engages with the ramp. With the signal at " caution ", the ramp is dead, and the lifting action on the shoe automatically applies the vacuum brake throughout the train, sounding also a syren in the cab. With the signal at clear, the ramp is " live "; the current, passing through the shoe, prevents brake application, but sounds a bell in the cab. It will be seen at once that, in the event of electrical failure, it errs on the safe side.

We are thankful for it, and Brunel would have loved the thing.

CHAPTER TWELVE

Of Cornishmen and Kings

LIKE Joseph Armstrong, whom he succeeded as locomotive superintendent of the Great Western Railway in 1877, William Dean found, at first, that his style was somewhat cramped by the lingering death of the broad gauge. For a long time he perpetuated the sturdy sandwich-framed engine, stemming from old Stephenson practice, building 2-2-2 and 2-4-0 passenger types as well as various types of tank engine. More recent sandwich frames contained teak planking instead of the more acid oak, which caused trouble with the bolts passing through it. Some later Dean engines had inside bearings to the coupled wheels, notably the final design of standard goods, which served not only its parent railway, but the British Army in two successive great wars (one was discovered at Schweinfürt five years after being captured by the Germans in 1940 and four ended their days in Italy, having reached it via North Africa). Double frames with outside bearings distinguished all Dean's last and finest passenger engines.

In addition to such as these, Dean built several experimental locomotives, including two tandem compound 2-4-0's, and a much elongated 4-2-4 tank for the standard gauge. The existence of this last was for long flatly denied at Swindon. Earnest inquirers were told that they must be mistaken, and thinking of the old Bristol and Exeter tanks. The truth was that the engine ran off the road ere ever it left Swindon, owing to a certain awkward inability to traverse curved track. Thereafter it was hurried out of sight, and in 1884, its driving wheels and outside link motion turned up on 2-2-2 express engine No. 9. As a 4-2-4 tank it was illustrated by E. W. Twining in *The Locomotive* of January, 1940.

But the most beautiful, the stateliest, and the most famous single-driver engines to be built for the Great Western or even for any railway at this time were Dean's famous 7 ft. 8½ in. expresses. The first thirty, the 3001 class, of the 2-2-2 type with 20 by 24 in. cylinders, came out during 1891-2. They had double frames, and to give ample steam space, the boilers had the casing raised over the firebox and a very large brass-covered dome on the after ring.

Eight of the series appeared as convertible broad-gauge engines, with the wheels outside both sets of double frames, having all the spokes visible, and these worked the same traffic as the antiquated eight-foot singles based on Gooch's design. The others were standard-gauge engines from the first, with outside axle-boxes to all wheels.

One of the class, *Wigmore Castle*, was in an alarming derailment through breaking her leading axle in Box Tunnel, on September 16, 1892, in consequence of which all were converted to 4-2-2 engines, with outside-framed bogies, designed thus to clear the large inside cylinders with the steam-chests underneath. The alteration improved the aspect also; in the handsome livery of that time—green lined out in orange and black, with the frames and splashers a deep red brown and all the external copper and brass finished bright—the engines looked superb.

Very similar was the 4-2-2 3031 class, built during 1894-9, with 19 by 24 in. cylinders. The pressure was 160 lb. These noble bogie singles worked many of the best Great Western expresses during the 'nineties, and some of the lighter ones during the earlier years of the present century. Many of them carried on the honoured names of the old Gooch eight-footers—*Rover* and *Lord of the Isles* lived again where once had been the broad gauge—and with one of them heading a set of the new corridor carriages, boldly cleres-toried from end to end, and finished in the Great Western's in-imitable tea-brown and cream, one could not imagine a train more majestic.

The brown-and-cream style in the painting of the Great Western carriages dated from the end of the 'sixties, when it replaced the old unadorned chocolate. The clerestory had made sporadic appearances in early days, first on the ancient " posting carriages " (saloons) and later on some of the T.P.O. carriages. It became a standard form on the Great Western during the 'seventies, with some handsome 10½-foot-wide eight-wheelers for the broad gauge, and continued so until 1904. The wide eight-wheelers just men-tioned were convertible, being narrowed when the time came by having the partitions and headstocks cropped, sides and solebars moved inwards, and standard-gauge bogies (of Dean's famous pendulum-link type) substituted for the older bogies or fixed axles. James Holden is believed to have been responsible for the arrange-ment. Later, on the Great Eastern Railway, he reversed the process in widening the bodies of that company's suburban coaches to take six persons abreast instead of five.

In 1874, the Bristol and Exeter Railway built some six-wheel main-line coaches with narrow bodies and wide frames and foot-boards, and from 1881 onwards, Swindon did likewise, beginning with a sleeping car built in that year. The sleeper in question was the first in the country to have side corridors serving the sleeping compartments, with no upper berths. The first Great Western sleepers, with wide bodies, and dormitory-like sleeping compart-ments, had been built in 1877, for the night express to Penzance. The design is illustrated in *Nineteenth Century Railway Carriages*, together with other interesting vehicles of the Dean period. The last convertibles, built shortly before the final passing of the broad gauge, were standard-gauge designs in all respects save for the bogies and the wide box-like footboards. The most remarkable carriages of Dean's time were those forming the first corridor train, built in 1891. This had no dining car, the virtue of the corridor lying in easy lavatory access throughout the train and in avail-ability of the guard, but it was the forerunner of the standard British express of later years on all other main-line railways in Great Britain. To give greater elbow room, the sides were " bay-windowed " between the doors. This arrangement was not per-petuated, though in some later corridor stock, of the balloon or clipper shape with tumblehome sides, the doors were flat and recessed, giving a somewhat similar appearance. Under Dean, some excellent composite lavatory carriages were built for through services to branch lines or destinations on other railways, one particularly handsome variety having a spacious first class at one end, with large observation windows, and armchairs in addition to the ordinary seats against the inside partition. It is shown in the picture of *Charles Saunders*.

Dean was a pioneer of the large goods engine, building two 4-6-0's in 1896 and 1899 respectively. They were experimental, and the second one had a high-pitched domeless boiler with a Belpaire firebox. A saddle-shaped sandbox on top of the first boiler ring added to its ominous appearance, and the South African War blowing up in the autumn of 1899, the men called this new and uncouth locomotive " Kruger ". It was the forerunner of Dean's standard 2-6-0 heavy goods engines, the earliest of which were likewise known as Krugers and the final form as Aberdares. They had the then usual double frames, domeless boilers and Belpaire fireboxes, and double bearings to the coupled axles. The type was not built for any other British railway. The Aberdares, later rebuilt with coned boilers and superheaters, did useful work on the South Wales coal trains, and other traffic, for many years.

In his passenger engines for the steeply graded western sections

153

* Page 125

of the main line, Dean was at first less successful than with his more imposing designs. His front-coupled tank engines, with double sandwich frames, first appeared in 1887 as 0-4-2's, with a curious arrangement of the trailing axle (illustrated in Ahrons' *British Steam Railway Locomotive from 1825 to 1925*, Figures 346 and 347). This induced a swaying motion at speed, and was replaced by an outside framed bogie of very short wheelbase, with pendulum-link suspension at the corners, as on the carriages, no weight being borne at the pivot. Some of these 5 ft. 0-4-4 tanks, as they had thus become, were broad-gauge convertibles, and after the abolition of the broad gauge in 1892 the class handled the fastest expresses west of Newton Abbot. They were turned after each trip, like true express engines.

This led to trouble, for on April 16, 1895 the 5 p.m. down train from Plymouth, running at about 50 m.p.h., left the road on a 30-chains radius right-hand curve between Doublebois and Bodmin Road. It was headed by two of these 0-4-4 tank engines, the leading one of which, the original No. 3521, turned over against a cutting slope of the down side while the second, No. 3548, was thrown across both tracks and severely damaged, as were the following coaches. Major A. W. Anderson, who conducted the ensuing inquiry, found that the cross-sleepered track of the down road had been seriously distorted by the previous train (the down Cornishman, headed by two similar engines) and censured the design as being most unsuitable for fast passenger traffic, which indeed it was. He added an unfortunate generalisation condemning 0-4-4 tank engines which " one other company " used for fast trains, though this was unfair to several excellent designs, such as that of the Midland Railway, which ran most steadily with fast trains, notably on the Somerest and Dorset Joint Railway. As a result of the Inspecting Officer's findings, the 0-4-4 tank engines were taken off the expresses, and later underwent an extraordinary metamorphosis. The small bogie, of 4 ft. 6 in. wheelbase, with its leading axle 9 ft. 10 in. to 10 ft. 4 in. in rear of driving axle, was first increased to 5 ft., then was replaced by a much longer one, the cylinders were put at the bogie end and the boiler turned round, and the engines emerged as 4-4-0's with separate tenders. The last one ran in this form until 1934.

More specifically for the main line from Newton Abbot to Penzance, Dean brought out in 1895 his well-known Duke class* 4-4-0 with 5 ft. 8 in. coupled wheels and 18 by 26 in. cylinders.

---

* Originally known as " Devons "; later named for the first of the class (*Duke of Cornwall*).

It was a most handy class, and in its latter days found useful employment on the main line of the former Cambrian Railways, so much so that in 1936 replacement began on much the same lines as that of the old Gooch eight-foot singles. There was much unseemly merriment, at the time, over the Great Western Railway building new engines of such Bronze Age aspect.

Of Great Western expresses, the fabled Dutchman was the grand original, although, as remarked, there was a deterioration in speeds during Mid-Victorian years. The ancient, magnificent timing of 4½ hours between Paddington and Exeter returned, temporarily, early in 1862, to better the London and South Western, which had put on a train making the journey in 4¾ hours. In 1868, the heroic Dutchman vanished, though not for good. Further accelerations in 1871 of the South Western's cherished afternoon express, the Beeswing, produced Great Western retaliation in the shape of a 4¼ hour timing from Paddington to Exeter, making the Dutchman again the fastest train in the world. The Great Western had, however, a very rigid regard for the class system. Up to 1882 it charged extra fares for its best trains, and even thereafter it admitted no third-class passengers to the Dutchman, or its equally speedy junior, the afternoon Zulu. The South Western, by the 'eighties, was carrying third class on all its trains, a most Jacobinical and un-English practice in Great Western eyes. Exeter was brought within 4 hours 5 minutes of Paddington, Plymouth, 5 hours 35 minutes, and Penzance within 8 hours 42 minutes by a new train introduced in June, 1890, and later called the Cornishman. Its up journey was slightly faster, bringing Paddington within 8 hours 35 minutes of Penzance. On July 28, 1896, with the provision of water-troughs, long used on the London and North Western, the first part of the summer Cornishman was scheduled to run non-stop from Paddington to Exeter, via an avoiding line at Bristol which cut out Temple Meads, then the longest run in the world made without halting. In 1899 the non-stop run was continued all the year round, and two years later the Cornishman was accelerated to reach Exeter in 3 hours 38 minutes, Plymouth in 5 hours, and Penzance in 7 hours 52 minutes.

About the turn of the century, coupled bogie express engines came more and more into favour. Dean had built, or rather produced by metamorphosis, four very beautiful 7 ft. 4-4-0 locomotives in the early 'nineties (*Armstrong, Gooch, Brunel* and *Charles Saunders*), but they became general with the Badmintons of 1897, with 180 lb. pressure, 18 by 26 in. cylinders like the Dukes, and 6 ft. 8½ in. coupled wheels. *Waterford* of this class, and subsequent engines, had the domeless boiler with Belpaire firebox which also distinguished the redoubtable "Kruger" goods engine, and which became general for large Great Western locomotives thereafter.

The Badmintons were followed in 1900 by the very similar Atbaras, and these, in 1903, by the celebrated City class, which, though brought out by G. J. Churchward and exemplifying several of the features for which he became famous, were still basically of the Dean type with double frames, outside cranks, and outside-framed bogies. In the City class, the pressure was 195 lb. per sq. in. In 1898 a larger version of the 5 ft. 8 in. 4-4-0 engine appeared in the Bulldog class, which to a certain extent displaced the Dukes on the best trains in the West.

With the retirement of Mr. Dean, and the succession of George Jackson Churchward, the Great Western trains underwent several radical changes in their appearance. Tapered domeless boilers with Belpaire firebox became general on all larger engines. Inside frames and outside cylinders took the place of double frames, outside cranks and inside cylinders. Likewise with the carriages; the familiar clerestory contour was replaced in new stock by large bodies, some of them up to 70 ft. long, with tumblehome sides and roofs deeply semi-elliptical in section. Churchward stated that with clerestory carriages, the condensation on the decklights overhead caused moisture to drip on, and spoil, " expensive ladies' dresses ".

Whichever way one took this last definition, it came to the same thing, and by degrees the old carriages had the clerestory glass painted over, and in some cases removed. The new rounded roofs were cavernous-looking, and unattractive to unused eyes especially, but did not produce the unfortunate effects just mentioned, also, they were more spacious, cheaper to make, and easier to keep clean. With many of the new carriages, the Great Western retained for some years its touching affection for oil-gas lighting.

Changes were made in external finish during the early nineteen hundreds. On the engines, black replaced the handsome dark Indian red colour of frames, outside cylinder casings, steps and so forth, while green supplanted it on the splashers. The three-panel style of painting tender sides, with a very florid " G.W.R." monogram, gave way to a single panel with the company's insignia (composed of the arms of London and Bristol) set between the words " Great " and " Western ". For a few years, new engines came out with plain iron chimneys, though Churchward soon restored the characteristic type with a deep copper cap. On the carriages, the cream upper panels were dropped about the end of 1907, and later on a dark purplish-red replaced the brown.

Below Bodmin Moor: Penzance–Paddington express approaching Menheniot, Great Western Railway, in the nineteen thirties; engine *Tregenna Castle*

From about 1916, as a wartime economy, engines were painted khaki, a disgusting exhibition. At the beginning of the nineteen-twenties, with green restored on the engines, chocolate and cream carriages came back also. The combination weathered much better than the dark colours, as well as looking more attractive.

For some time before he succeeded Dean, in 1902, Churchward had been allowed his head by the former in locomotive design, and his final practice after taking office was a radical departure from what had been regarded as Great Western traditions. The tapered domeless boiler with Belpaire firebox and direct-loaded safety-valves came to stay for all bigger engines. To it was added, early on, the Swindon superheater, giving a moderate amount of superheat. It belonged to the Schmidt family, and was distinguished by having six elements arranged horseshoe fashion in each large flue, facilitating cleaning. Top feed was added to the standard Swindon boiler, with the clacks each side of the safety-valve mounting. Piston valves came into general use, and instead of greatly increasing cylinder diameters, as being complementary to the growing power and capacity of boilers, Churchward went in for a very long stroke—30 in. on two-cylinder engines—long valve travel and long laps. In short, the modern Great Western engine of the nineteen hundreds and after, like the modern Southern Railway engine of the nineteen-forties, resembled nothing else on earth. Indeed, the outward aspect of the first 4-6-0 express engine on the Great Western seemed as grotesquely outrageous to the amateur engine-fancier of its day as did that of Mr. Bulleid's Pacifics on the Southern forty years after.

Churchward was truly a Great Western man. Born in South Devon, he rose through the G.W.R. locomotive department to the top, on which he had more influence than any other save possibly Gooch. Nor did he leave it after his retirement in 1922, for he went on living in Swindon, going across to the works whenever he could, to see how his successor was getting on. This, indeed, brought his life to an end for he was knocked down by one of his own engines while crossing the track on December 19, 1933. He was a first-rate experimental as well as practical engineer, installing the famous stationary test plant at Swindon in 1905, and building or ordering during that decade, a number of locomotives for the purpose of making comparative tests. In this he was much more fortunate than Dean. He carried out dimensional standardisation as far as possible.

Churchward's original design for a 4-6-0 express engine was carried out pending Dean's retirement, and appeared in 1902. In 1903 a 4-4-2 de Glehn compound engine, following the well-known Nord design (No. 102, *La France*), was obtained from France, and two more (*President* and *Alliance*), of the larger Paris-Orleans type, followed in 1905. Churchward carried out extensive comparative trials between these French engines, and 4-4-2 and 4-6-0 express engines of his own design. The French compounds were later rebuilt with standard coned boilers and Swindon superheaters. Finally, for fast passenger traffic, Churchward standardised on the 6 ft. 8½ in. 4-6-0 simple engine, in two varieties, namely, the Star class with four 14¼ by 26 in. cylinders, and the Saint class, with two cylinders 18 by 30 in. The pressure was fixed at 225 lb. per sq. in., only exceeded at the time by the French compounds with 227 lb. Between them, these two standard classes, during ensuing years, did some of the best work in the world.

Goods, mixed traffic, and tank engines were all two-cylinder, and, apart from the Atlantics, the only new main-line passenger engines with four-coupled wheels were the County class 4-4-0's of 1904, the Cities of 1903 and the Flowers of 1908. The second- and third-named were of the basic Dean type with inside cylinders and double frames. The smokebox saddle, incorporating the inside cylinders, and the boiler, as in the last engines built under Dean, were Churchward's work. There was a tank engine version of the County class, likewise a 2-6-2 tank approximating to the 2-6-0 mixed traffic engines. Heavy goods engines were 2-8-0, with tank versions again, and in 1919 there appeared the first of nine 2-8-0 mixed-traffic engines, which became the first eight-coupled locomotives in Great Britain to be used on fast passenger trains.

Then of course there was *The Great Bear*, a super-Star, in fact a Constellation, which appeared in 1908, with an enormous boiler having 3,400 sq. ft. of heating surface and a trailing axle to support the firebox end, making the engine the first Pacific-type in the country. She was a prodigy, and remained an isolated one. Attempts to use her on the Plymouth road led to trouble in respect of clearances, and she spent her life between Paddington and Bristol. Officially she ended by being converted to a 4-6-0 of the later Castle class, though not even her nameplates survived this operation, she becoming *Viscount Churchill*.

The formulae regarding what constituted rebuilding and what scrapping seemed to be something secret, written perhaps in a mysterious padlocked book at Swindon. For it was never admitted that *The Great Bear* was anything but rebuilt. On the other hand, a Great Western engine might be, and sometimes was officially scrapped after being in an accident, and then reappeared as a new engine with the same name and number. This happened to *King William III* which turned over in a collision near Shrivenham in

1936, and might have fared a great deal worse than was apparent. Noteworthy total losses were two Dean engines : 2-4-0 *Dart*, at Thingley Junction, and 4-4-0 *Mafeking* at Henley-in-Arden. Neither was " replaced ".

The early nineteen hundreds saw fierce competition between the Great Western and the London and South Western for the transatlantic traffic at Plymouth, and it was in 1904, in the course of this, that the 4-4-0 engine *City of Truro* (now preserved at York Railway Museum) and the Dean 7 ft. 8½ in. single *Duke of Connaught* made their famous joint record run between Plymouth and Paddington with the up mail train. *City of Truro* averaged 55·71 m.p.h. to Exeter, and 70·27 m.p.h. thence to Bristol. *Duke of Connaught's* average speeds were just over 70 m.p.h. to Swindon and over 77 m.p.h. on the gradually falling race-track from Swindon to Paddington.

An excellent run by *City of Bath*, non-stop to Plymouth with the royal train in 1903, emphasised the possibility of running the morning West of England express thus. In July, 1904, Plymouth was duly made the first stop for the leading section of the Cornishman. As a part of the ensuing publicity campaign, the train was ponderously renamed Cornish Riviera Limited Express. It was composed of standard clerestory corridor coaches, with a large clipper diner in the middle. Soon after, entirely new stock, similar to the dining car in contour, with no outside doors to the compartments, was specially built for the service. It was much admired, but was not so comfortable as some of the best Dean carriages. With the completion of the Hungerford route to the West, the non-stop running was of course shortened, but it still remained by far the longest in the world. The train left Paddington daily at 10.30 a.m., and reached Plymouth in 4 hours.

On August 17, 1903, the company opened a bus service, with two Milnes Daimler 22-seater 16 h.p. wagonettes, bought second-hand from Sir George Newnes, who had been running an experimental service in the Ilfracombe district. They plied now between Helston branch terminus and the Lizard. Such services expanded, as feeders to the railway, in many parts, though road passenger transport was not yet the basket of plums for which flash new operators were destined to scramble in the nineteen-twenties. Dusty white Wessex high-roads and deep Devon lanes resounded to the palsied progress of those early motors ; the rival London and South Western Railway invested in some Clarkson steam buses, and the two railways competed snappishly for the favours of rail-less Chagford. By 1927 the Great Western had 300 motor buses and coaches on the roads. By the end of the nineteen-twenties, however, the company had adopted a policy of holding substantial interests in the larger and more respectable bus undertakings, and finally ceased to be a direct operator in 1933.

The war of 1914-8 was naturally disastrous for spectacular train services, but the nineteen-twenties saw another strong bid for public esteem. The company awoke fully to the fact that quite a large number of people liked railways for their own sake, especially if they were good railways, and a new kind of publicity blossomed, which, however much the highbrows might deride its specious heartiness, achieved a great measure of its object. Public admiration for the Great Western rose, among the more fanatical, to positive adulation. No railway, not even the North Western in its prime, enjoyed such fervent hosannas. Nice little books about the Great Western, *for boys of all ages*, poured off the press with a speed which one now recalls wistfully ; posters appeared showing Great Western trains, as well as sunsets in the Golden West. In one of them a florid retired colonel was shown wringing a Great Western driver's hand, and booming: " Splendid run ! Thank you ! "

The Great Western was peculiarly favoured, not only by the merits of its road and equipment, but by the fact that it was the only large British railway to keep its individuality in 1923. Many people regarded it as a familiar old friend in a changed world. But deeds had to be done as well as flourishes sounded. What was needed was a really fast train, and thus was born the Cheltenham Flyer. This (forgive me, Paddington !) was a first-rate stunt, helped by Brunel's magnificently graded road between Swindon and Paddington, with no suburban congestion, Churchward's still splendid locomotives, and ably supported by some high-powered salesmanship. Given these, the traffic department had simply to furnish an express normally lightly loaded and make it into, successively, the fastest train in Great Britain, and, once more on the Great Western, the *Fastest Train in the World.* So, in 1923, the 3.40 afternoon up Cheltenham Spa Express, having loafed through Gloucester and Stroud to Swindon, was timed to cover the 77·3 miles thence to Paddington in 75 minutes, or at an average speed of 61·8 m.p.h. Churchward's *Saint Bartholomew* made the initial run with ease, and the public loved it. Part of the charm of the train was that it looked a perfectly ordinary Great Western express; some of the carriages were ancient, and the engine was a fair veteran.

Following the retirement of Mr. Churchward, his successor, C. B. Collett, produced in that same year of 1923 a new express engine, the very magnificent *Caerphilly Castle*, accompanied by the customary fanfare. She had the usual 6 ft. 8½ in. coupled wheels and the same 225 lb. pressure as the Star class. Star cylinders had increased in diameter to 15 in. with *Prince of Wales* in 1913; in the new Castle class, the four cylinders were 16 by 26 in. The boiler was larger, and with a tractive effort of 31,625 lb., these were the most powerful express engines in the country. They have also been one of the most successful classes ever built, and have been turned out at intervals over some 27 years. Several of the Star class were rebuilt as Castles, and the country was combed for suitable names, *Tintagel Castle* and *Corfe Castle* being triumphantly captured from Southern territory.

It was with the Castle class that the Cheltenham Spa Express became officially the Flyer. After going into hibernation for nine months of 1928-9, the train burgeoned as the fastest in the world, with a seventy-minute schedule between Swindon and Paddington, approximately 66·25 m.p.h. start-to-stop. It had outstripped such ancient records as the fast Caledonian bookings between Forfar and Perth and that of the North Eastern between Darlington and York. Competition became a matter now of national prestige, and with the the world's railways. For the Canadian National and Canadian Pacific Railways were at it over the water, and the C.P.R. produced a booked average of 68·9 m.p.h. between Smith's Falls and Montreal West, 124 miles. The Great Western had to go one better, so the Swindon-London average was pushed up to 69·2 m.p.h. On September 12, 1932, the time was cut to 65 minutes, making the average speed 71·4 m.p.h. Previously, on June 6, *Tregenna Castle* had made the run in less than 57 minutes, with six coaches weighing 195 tons full. More significantly, on the same day, the 5 p.m. *down* train, 210 tons headed by *Manorbier Castle*, reached Swindon in 60 minutes.

Particularly for the heavy West of England trains, C. B. Collett brought out his larger 4-6-0 King class, beginning with *King George V* in 1927. The previous year, the Southern Railway had produced *Lord Nelson*, a more powerful engine than the Great Western Castles. The new King, in most respects an enlarged Castle, recovered the " most powerful " distinction for the Great Western. With 16¼ by 28 in. cylinders, 6 ft. 6 in. coupled wheels, and a large boiler working at 250 lb. pressure, the engine exerted a tractive effort of 40,300 lb. The front end arrangement revived some of the problems associated with the old Dean bogie engines, clearances necessitating the bogie having outside frames and bearings at the leading end. The trailing end of the bogie, coming under the outside cylinders, was subject to like restrictions in reverse, so the frame had to be narrowed amidships and the trailing axle-boxes put inside. The original engine, *King George V*, was sent to the centennial celebrations of the Baltimore and Ohio Railroad in the United States, and returned, after running several demonstration trips on the B. and O., with a trophy in the shape of a large American engine bell, mounted on the front platform.

Following the appearance of the King class, several classes of light 4-6-0 engine were introduced, including the very successful two-cylinder mixed-traffic Hall class, which had originated with the conversion, in 1925, of Churchward's old *St. Martin* to a 6 ft. engine. In their time, the Halls have worked nearly every type of passenger and goods train on the Great Western main line. The job of naming them seemed to exhaust every eligible country house in England and Wales, for latterly the locomotive department was unearthing such titles as *Marble Hall* and *Caxton Hall*, and one half expected *Tammany Hall* and *Dotheboys Hall*.

Through the nineteen-twenties, the Plymouth non-stop run of the Cornish Riviera Limited was a summer prodigy. In 1935, it was fully restored, with Plymouth being reached in 4 hours and Penzance in 6 hours 25 minutes. New steel-panelled coaches, with end doors only and very comfortable seating, were built for the service. At the same time, the relief train leaving Paddington at 10.25 a.m. assumed the ancient and honourable name of Cornishman. Throughout this phase in history, the Great Western company stuck faithfully to the use of slip carriages, while they dwindled and vanished from other lines. The Limited and other trains, by this means, furnished fast services to intermediate places, and the company gave the slips the advantage of such conveniences as steam heat in winter, when elsewhere they were being discontinued owing to their apparently necessary reliance on the primeval foot-warmer. Acetate of soda heating was employed in a modified form, however, and lasted until the early nineteen-twenties even, on Great Western slip carriages.

Once again war came to the Great Western; Paddington was battered, and there was the devil to pay in Plymouth, where, amid dreadful destruction, Brunel's glorious bridge deflected a direct hit harmlessly into the Tamar before it could damage. Among locomotives, *Bowden Hall* was a total loss. But before all this, your author had good reason to remember Plymouth in the war; he was landed there in July, 1940, and found great comfort in the solidity and changelessness of the Great Western Railway.

The last of the great race of Swindon 4-6-0 locomotives formed the second County class, beginning with No. 1000, *County of Middlesex*, turned out by F. W. Hawksworth, successor to Collett, and the company's last C.M.E., in 1945. She had 6 ft. 3 in. coupled wheels, the same cylinder dimensions as a Saint, but a pressure of 280 lb. The superheating surface was kept decently down, faithful to the last, at 254 sq. ft. There was a redoubtable double chimney, massively bound by a bright copper cap as of yore. Great Western tradition was still safe. The last Great Western essay in express locomotive development was a Brown-Boveri gas-turbine engine, the first for a British Railway. It was built in Switzerland, and delivered to British Railways, Western Region, in February, 1950.

The old Great Western Railway came, at the end of 1947, to the end of its long years of sovereign independence. We, who knew it, can never forget it. For us, it belonged to the England of Jefferies and of Quiller-Couch, of Elgar and Vaughan Williams. Men who served other railways influenced them. The Great Western bent its servants to its own lore. And while the Many admired its spectacular side, there were those also who loved its byways. If these were of a sort to inspire Mr. Emett's Saturday Slow (to work between St. Torpids and Stuffworthy Junction), indeed, why not? The untroubled saunter of the Fairford branch train was a seemly prelude to visiting the venerable May Morris; to have gone to Kelmscott on the old Levis two-stroke would have been sacrilege. Grandly heroic was the progress of *King Henry V*, superb the thunder of *Pendennis Castle!* Yet how pleasantly thereafter might one dally with *Fair Rosamund*, or wander through western meadows with the languorous *Guinevere!*

PART FOUR

CHAPTER THIRTEEN

Parsons and Prawns

NOT once, but many times in the August sunshine, a little boy of two years sat on the grass below a great double hedge of hawthorn, at the top of a sloping meadow. To left of him, the Nadder meandered through its vivid water-meadows, and, nobly remote, the Downs stood against the sky. Beside him, his Scots nurse of the imperious blue eyes darned socks and mended rents. To right of him gleamed the rails of the London and South Western main line. At that immature age, he knew many of the engines: the gracious Drummond T 9's, the Adams bogies with their voluptuous curves and piquant chimneys, the veteran goods engines, dark bottle green with bright brass-edged splashers, double frames, and outside cranks that could be seen from a great distance, pounding up and down like toiling elbows. Most beautiful, the trains rushed by with shouts of joy.

Because of these things, for the baby beside the line was your author, it is difficult not to show partiality. Yet no favour is needed for the eulogy of this, the last of our four main lines. Although the shortest, it is unexcelled. The East Coast carries you a long way before you reach the hills of the Border Ballads and the severe magnificence of the Scottish North-east Coast. Over the flat lands of Huntingdon and Lincolnshire, the skies may wax superb, or low evening sun turn the birch boles into something magical and rare, but the same places can oppress, at other times, by their desolate void. Not always can you see the Backbone of England, nobly strong, beyond the Plain of York. The Great Western traverses grand country in North Wessex and South Devon, but with these alternate the Thames Valley flats, birthplace of jam, emulsion of fish-oil, gramophones and biscuits, and those marshes of Athelney, themselves sometimes beautiful, where King Alfred held the Danes and the ague at bay together.

On the West Coast are more alternations : The green places of the Trent Valley with the yellow grass and forlorn distances about Warrington ; the mirk of Lancashire towns with the magnificence of the fells ; the noble hills of Annandale and Clydesdale with the black frown of Coatbridge or the hag's leer of the Gorbals. I do not decry these things; they make up the flavour of each journey, and by night Coatbridge can be transformed from a dour wife into a fire queen. But the South Western main line takes you through a part of England that is wanton in its loveliness.

Beauty is restrained at first, as it should be. The old Basingstoke Canal wanders with a senile demureness on its way; the heath and pines where Surrey marches with Hampshire have a note of the sombre in their features. Then you come through the rolling downland to Salisbury Plain, a region so old in the history of men that it has the quality of eternal youth. Soldiers exercise on it, tanks scramble on its grey-green slopes, aeroplanes roar overhead, a helicopter may touch the short grass with its light phantastick toe before motor-borne sightseers, but these things cannot break the serenity of the Plain. It knows more than we about the history of Man and his transport. It has seen wagon succeed pack-horse, and coach come after wagon. It has seen Bulleid Pacifics go wailing on their way where once screamed Beattie's Patents. It saw the first automatic signalling installation in Great Britain, between Andover Junction and Grateley in April, 1902. It has seen mechanised armies on the move where once ran a solitary Daimler staff car. It has seen jet succeed airscrew where once His Majesty's Airship *Beta* pushed her yellow fish body laboriously into a light summer breeze. And the Ghosts of the Plain smile at all these, and leave us still guessing as to how the Stones were brought from Pembroke.

The great spire of Sarum beckons the train in from beyond Laverstock Down (and Salisbury appeared as *Sarum* in the working time-tables of the 'sixties). After Wilton, the gracious Wilton of George Herbert and of Edith Olivier, one is in the country of the water-meadows. To the north are the Groveley oak woods; up on the hills yonder, Jude Fawley and Sue Bridehead got lost on their walk from a place on the South Western to one on the Great Western, and lodged the night in a shepherd's cot, causing a memorable row in a college for young ladies.* There is Dinton, lately with a hideous dump inflicted on it, but a mile beyond it is the first crossing of the Nadder below Black Furlong wood with the great Ridge Wood beyond, and just before that (forgive me, Reader!) is Teffont Mill Crossing. The double hedge has gone now, and the little meadow has been thrown into a greater one, but two of the larger hawthorns still stand.

Less spectacular to strangers than the valleys of Devon, it is a most gracious country, this of Mid-Wessex. There is Shaftesbury

---

* Hardy's *Jude the Obscure*.

on its rock, and the ancient kingdom rolls on like a great garden from the Avon to the Exe. Exonia hides her tragic scars and still tries to put on a severe face towards the South Western line, but even the red brows of the County Gaol, bent over the Central Station, perversely remind one of the background to an ancient photograph of a Beattie locomotive. From the level meadows of Newton St. Cyres the line follows a frontier. Always to the right, the rich country of North Devon rolls out like a carpet towards the Atlantic Coast. Always to the left, the great hills of Dartmoor rise to meet the blue, or the rolling mist, or the flying clouds.

Emergence of the train on Meldon Viaduct has a surprise quality for which one may seek far in railway travel, and surprises follow all the way to Plymouth, as with the first view down to Calstock, with its viaduct, from a noble curve on top of the ridge between Tavy and Tamar, as with the first view clear down to Saltash, and Brunel's bridge. The Royal Albert Bridge belongs, as a bridge, to the Great Western line; as scenery it belongs, perhaps more than equally, to the South Western. Yes, it is a great line ! Who, by daylight, would need to read in the train between Weybridge and St. Budeaux ?

Yet, after all, it was not at first intended for the London and South Western to march through Wessex to Devon and to North Cornwall. The railway began as the London and Southampton, the conclusion of several schemes, in part strategic, and originating with a plan for a canal during the Napoleonic wars. So one can argue on the question of which *was* the London and South Western main line. At first, it was undoubtedly the Southampton line, but when expansion brought the direct route to Salisbury, and the Salisbury and Yeovil, and the Yeovil and Exeter, and the extension of these farther west, one could scarcely regard their whole as just another branch. The Portsmouth Direct was indeed another matter, and does not this time enter our story. But the South Western, like the Great Western, developed into something quite different from such inter-city lines as the great West Coast and East Coast Routes. It became a tree of many branches and must be considered as such, even though we arbitrarily lop off the Portsmouth limb.

Southampton was not much of a place in the early nineteenth century. It was not quite so dead a seaport as Rye or Sandwich, for one could still get in and out of it on a ship, but it was quite five streets away from Bristol and Liverpool, being an old town on the edge of a salt-marsh full of rotting hulks. But the magnificent land-locked harbour of Southampton Water had obvious possibilities, and in 1831 a Southampton Committee was forming what was provisionally called the Southampton, London and Branch Railway and Dock Company. It was a modest undertaking, save that it estimated a ten per cent. return, for it considered that two locomotives, making two daily trips, would suffice for passenger traffic, and three more for goods. Even so, the infant company was a seedy child, and Francis Giles, its first engineer, had very little to do. It had still ambition in the midst of its weakness, sufficient to envisage a branch from Basingstoke to Bristol. The day of the Great Western was not yet. At the end of 1833, a transfusion of Lancashire capital put life into the enterprise. After a tough Parliamentary fight, with violent opposition from the Lords and a very jolly time for the lawyers, the London and Southampton Railway Company was incorporated on July 25, 1834.

The next obstacle was inside the company. Giles was a poor tool, and nothing much was done until the exasperated Board politely intimated that if he cared to resign his onerous duties, they would quite understand. When Joseph Locke was appointed his successor, the value of London and Southampton shares rose with quite rude abruptness. The Grand Junction Railway was by then practically complete, and Locke's position as Chief Engineer was rather that of " Engineer, New Works ".

The Southampton line was a very different proposition from the gentle Grand Junction, having the high chalk Downs to cross and penetrate between Basingstoke and the valley of the Itchen by Winchester. The Stephensons would have tunnelled and tunnelled again. Locke disliked tunnels and preferred to trouble his new undertaking as little as possible in this respect, at the expense of very heavy surface earthworks. The great cuttings and 90 ft. embankments, punctuated by three apologetic little tunnels, and one somewhat longer (Waller's Ash), are his monument. Though the more eastern sections were fairly reasonable through the Thames Valley, the cutting by Wandsworth gave trouble owing to springs, and to this day one may see, on the up side between Clapham Junction and Earlsfield, the wooden tower of the old wind-pump which in early days kept the water down.

A long embankment stretched from near Merton towards Malden and Coombe, and another heavy cutting followed before " Kingston upon Railway ", as Surbiton was at first called, with the line level from Wimbledon for most of the way. From a point between the present stations of Weybridge and Byfleet, Locke allowed a long easy rise to a summit beyond Pirbright, and another, with considerable level breathing spaces, from near Farnborough to beyond

Basingstoke. The summit of the line was at Litchfield Tunnel, whence it fell practically continuously to just north of St. Denys. There was but one tiny stretch of level track near Swaythling; the gradient averaged about 1 in 250 for 17 miles to Milepost 73, just north of Bishopstoke (now Eastleigh). Altogether, considering that he had taken his line right over the Southern chalk, with no real tunnels, Locke had behaved reasonably kindly towards the engines that would have to work it.

The best of the original Southampton engines were probably those built by Sharp Roberts—2-2-2 for passenger and 0-4-2 for goods, and Rothwell's 2-2-2 passenger engines. Others were built in London by J. and G. Rennie, and a few of the oldest, including the company's first engine, *Lark*, were of the Bury four-wheel type, and were probably not much more useful than steam wheel-barrows. But the others, though small, were very much better than those of the only other main line railways out of London at the end of the 'thirties. The South Western fortunately did not suffer from engineering freaks, whether in engines or permanent way, as did the Great Western, and although Joseph Woods, the first locomotive engineer, scarcely earned an immortal name, he was not such a liability as Bury on the London and Birmingham. The original main line was laid with 75 lb. malleable iron rails. A contemporary observer commented on the steadiness of travel, compared with the Great Western, which of course was still wrestling with its original, frightful permanent way on piles.

I like the story of W. J. Chaplin, the great carrier and stage proprietor. At first a fierce enemy of steam conveyance, and a pillar of the Anti Rail-Road League, he suddenly disappeared from the English scene and shut himself away in Switzerland. After some time of deep meditation among the high Alps, he emerged, and this time plunged into the first wave of railway speculation. He was chairman of the London and South Western Railway from 1843 to 1852, and again from 1854 to 1858.

But this is looking ahead. The original London terminus was placed at Nine Elms, Vauxhall. Its rather pleasing Georgian stucco facade is still there, forming the front of the present great goods station, having survived unscathed the heavy bombing of Nine Elms in the early nineteen-forties. In its passenger days, it was an out-of-the-way place, in one of those regions of swamps, pollard willows and decrepit windmills that Dickens liked to choose for his more macabre scenes. Thence, after some initial trial trips, the Southampton company started running its first regular train service, as far as Woking Common, on May 21, 1838.

Thence, too, some eight years later, Robert Browning eloped to the Continent with Elizabeth Barrett. But the old station's first excitement came very shortly after opening. The company having advertised that some special trains would be put on to convey Derby Day traffic as far as the Ewell road near Kingston, a vast mob descended on the railway at an early hour, took the station by storm, and had to be broken up by the police.*

Nine Elms was linked to civilisation by buses and by Thames steamers. The original wayside stations were Wandsworth (adjoining the Freemasons School and Hotel, west of the present Clapham Junction), Wimbledon, " Kingston ", Ditton Marsh (now Esher), Walton and Weybridge. At this Kingston-upon-Railway, a select suburb immediately sprang up, not at first associated by name with the adjoining hamlet of Surbiton. It was one of the very first of the suburban dormitories made possible by railway transport, and was always kindly regarded by the Southampton company and its successors. Of South Western locomotive men, William George Beattie and Dugald Drummond lived there in after years. In 1877, W. G. Beattie had for a near neighbour the exiled Richard Jeffries, whom the workmen's train used to wake on the chill March mornings. The original Kingston station was near the Ewell road bridge. It was moved further west, out of the cutting, in 1845, but was not renamed Surbiton until the opening of the Twickenham-Kingston branch on July 1, 1863.† Though the successive old stations have long vanished, an unspoilt link with the past survives in the name and the handsome Georgian building of the London and Southampton Hotel.

Even before the main line to Southampton was complete, the company changed its name. There were two proposals to give railway communication to Portsmouth. One was by a branch from the Southampton line near Bishopstoke to Gosport, and the other a formidable rival in the shape of a proposed Portsmouth Direct Railway. The latter found much favour with the Pompeians, who at the same time objected very strongly to being fobbed off with a branch from a line so offensively named as London and Southampton. They were pacified by a clause in the Act of June 4, 1839, authorising the Gosport branch, which formally changed the name of the company to London and South Western Railway.

On September 24 of the previous year, the line had been extended to " Winchfield and Hartley Row ", on the site of the

* A longer and more picturesque account will be found in the present author's romance *Dandy Hart*.
† New Malden and Kingston were not linked until 1869.

INSET THREE

48. One of the
nvertibles running
n the broad gauge
ough Flax Bourton,
G.W.R.

WESTWARD HO
heading an up
opping train near
Dawlish

WORCESTER
ith high-pitched
iler and Belpaire
irebox, passing
hampton with an
West of England
express

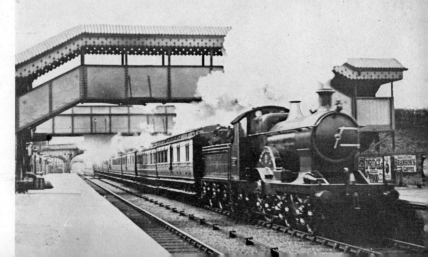

*(All from
omotive and General
ilway Photographs)*

51. Up Bristolian
Goring Troughs,
Great Western
Railway,
Castle class 4-6-0
engine
SIR DANIEL
GOOCH

(*Photograph by
Maurice W. Earley*)

52. Up Cornish
Riviera Limited,
Great Western
Railway,
composed of 1935
end-door carriage
and headed by
KING
RICHARD II

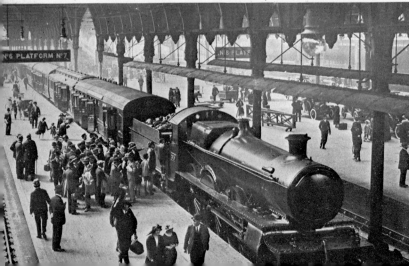

53. Paddington in
1924, after the
first run of the
accelerated
afternoon up
Cheltenham express
engine
SAINT
BARTHOLOMEW

(*British Railways
Photograph*)

54. Waterloo at the time of Mafeking
(*From an old coloured print " Farewell "*)

55. Waterloo at the time of Falaise Gap
(*From a poster by Helen McKie*)

56. Cowley Bridge Junction, Exeter Waterloo-Plymouth line on left Plymouth-Paddington line on right the observer is looking down the S.W. and up the G.W. main lines respectively

(Locomotive and General Railway Photographs)

57. Crediton in mixed-gauge days; old Beattie tank engine heading a train for the North Devon line; left, a South Western passenger brake of the fifties

(Locomotive and General Railway Photographs)

58. Meldon Viaduct near Okehampton Rebuilt Drummond class T9 engine crossing, with up North Cornwall local train

(British Railways Photograph)

Yeovil, about 1880,
showing L.S.W.R.
cross-sleepered sidings
and Beyer Peacock
goods engine in
foreground, shed on
extreme right;
L.S.W.R. "baulk road"
through passenger
station and second-class
carriage in bay

*(Locomotive and General
Railway Photographs)*

60. The present
station at
Templecombe

*(Locomotive and
General Railway
Photographs)*

61. Bournemouth
Central,
London and South
Western Railway,
about 1910;
steam car No. 3 at
down platform

*(W. H. Smith and Sons
Photograph)*

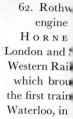

62. Rothw
engine
HORNE
London and S
Western Rai
which brou
the first train
Waterloo, in

(*From an oil pa*
by the Autho
the collection
John Pelha
Maitland, E
by permissic

63. The
METEO
a Gooch sing
the London
South West
Railway

(*From an o*
photograph in
collection of Ca
Rixon Buckn

64. The 10.15
Exeter-Wate
train near Te
Crossing, Dir
in the earl
'eighties;
L.S.W.R. Be
6 ft. 2-4-0 en
REINDEE

(*From an oil pa*
by the Autho

55. Adams's first design
4-4-0 express engine
No. 142
at Bournemouth West,
London and South
Western Railway,
in the early
nineteen hundreds

(Photograph by W. G. Head)

56. L.S.W.R.
Plymouth-Waterloo
express coming in
Lipson Junction,
Plymouth, G.W.R.,
headed by
Adams 4-4-0 engine
No. 660.
As at Exeter
up and down
directions of the
railways were
contrary

(Locomotive and
General Railway
Photographs)

57. Up special
Bournemouth
express near
Earlsfield,
London and South
Western Railway,
headed by
Drummond class
9 engine with
watertube firebox

(Locomotive
Publishing Co.
Limited)

68. A war casualty
Drummond
four-cylinder 4-6-0
engine No. 458
here shown on a
down South Western
train to Exeter
about 1920.
She was destroyed
by bombing at
Nine Elms in 19..

(*Locomotive and
General Railway
Photographs*)

69. Up Atlantic
Coast Express,
Southern Railway,
engine SIR KAY

70. Waterloo-
Bournemouth express,
British Railways,
near Farnborough,
engine LORD ANSON;
The coaches are
painted in an
experimental livery
officially termed
"plum and spilt milk"
and unofficially
"whale-meat and
snoek"

(*Photograph by
Edward Griffith*)

present Winchfield station, crossing the peat bogs and an arm of the great pond of Fleet, and having an intermediate station at Farnborough. On June 10, 1839, Basingstoke was reached from London, and Winchester from Southampton. Having linked the prawns with the parsons,* the company speedily got into trouble with the latter for running Sunday trains. Some of the correspondence was published in a very valuable series of articles on *Early Days of the L.S.W.R.* by G. F. Quartermaine in *The Railway Magazine* during the second half of 1936. The company was not in such sympathy with the Chapter of Winchester as was the Scottish Central with the Kirk Sessions, and there were some stately exchanges.

On May 11, 1840, the line was complete from Nine Elms to Southampton. The Gosport branch was troublesome through subsidence—it has been so since those days—and there was a bad collapse in the Fareham tunnel. It was opened on November 29, 1841, but had to be closed again during the winter and was not reopened until February 7, 1842. Practically all of this original London and South Western Railway had been engineered by Locke and carried out by the famous contractor Thomas Brassey. These two same giants were responsible, successively, for the Paris-Rouen Railway and the Rouen-Havre Railway, and thus carried out between them the first all-steam route between London and Paris. Brassey undertook to maintain the South Western main line in repair for a term of ten years for an annual sum of £24,000.

In spite of the original title of the proposed company, the new Southampton Docks began as a separate undertaking, incorporated in 1836, in which year also it acquired a large acreage near the old Town Quay. On August 30, 1842, while the first dock was still unfinished, two P. and O. steamers berthed there, and on the official opening day nearly a year later (July 1, 1843), the arrival of the P. and O. ship *Pacha* from Gibraltar inaugurated regular traffic. It was yet a far call to the day when the fastest transatlantic liners would be diverted hither from Liverpool.

Had the London and South Western Railway had its way in its earliest years, it is quite possible that it would have secured a monopoly of all south-western England and the Duchy of Cornwall. In those years it carried the Exeter mails as far as Basingstoke, whence they were taken on by coach. In the summer of 1844, it secured authorisation of a branch from Bishopstoke to Salisbury via Romsey, and it already had plans for a cut-off between the

* At the time of its promotion, the London and Southampton was derisively named the " Parsons and Prawns Railway " by sceptics.

main line and this branch, though this would have been scarcely direct, as planned, for it was to diverge from the main line at Hook Pit, near Winchester, instead of the obvious junction point of Worting. At the same time, plans were being considered for an extension from Salisbury to Sherborne and Yeovil, for a flank attack on the Great Western by a branch from Basingstoke, through Didcot, to Swindon, and for more outflanking moves in Devon and Cornwall and the securing of those parts against broad-gauge penetration. At the beginning of 1846, approval was given to construction of a direct line through Whitchurch to Salisbury, and its extension thence to Exeter via Yeovil, and on to Falmouth and Penzance. So far, Falmouth had little cause to thank the South Western, the original main line having caused the diversion of a good slice of its commerce to Southampton. As we shall see, the South Western's aspirations in South and West Cornwall were never realised. The Cornwall and Devon Central Railway Bill was withdrawn under Standing Orders and east of Exeter the company's thrust at Great Western territory was defeated in the Lords. The circuitous Salisbury branch was opened on January 27, 1847, for goods, and on March 1 for passenger traffic, to a terminus at Milford, a mile away from the site of the present station. This was still the South Western's outpost in mid-Wessex nine years later, when the Great Western branch from Westbury to Salisbury was opened. The two companies glared at each other from their opposite sides of the city, which became a sort of Hindu Kush, with the Great Western acting the Russian part. The Brighton-Cardiff through trains of later years, using both these lines, were then unthinkable, and neither company gave the Sarumites a direct railway route to London. Not until May 1, 1857, was the Whitchurch cut-off opened between Worting Junction and Salisbury. To this day the solitary up night train from the West of England to Waterloo makes its weary way from Salisbury to Basingstoke via Eastleigh. It is a very different sort of train from the equally solitary, but admirable 1.25 a.m. down express, which makes some of the very best running on the South Western main line of today, and people seldom regard the up train seriously unless they are accompanying horses, or pedigree bulls, or doing something equally heroic.

While Salisbury remained on a branch line, the South Western system was pushed on westwards by the opening, on June 7, 1847, of " Castleman's Snake ", the circuitous railway from Northam, Southampton, to Dorchester, via Ringwood and Wimborne. Traffic was worked at first from Blechynden. There had been slight subsidence in the tunnel west of Northam. Engines and carriages were hurriedly taken through the streets to Blechynden, and a twice-daily service began on June 1. Five trains daily were run as from June 7. Following repair to the tunnel, the first through train from Dorchester to Nine Elms ran on July 29. As we have seen in the G.W. story, the Southampton and Dorchester Railway (its nickname was derived from its shape and from the prominent Wimborne solicitor who was its principal sponsor) was originally promoted as a broad-gauge line, and its capture by the South Western was an important counter-offensive move. Moreover, at that stage in history the South Western regarded it as a step in the direction of the West Country. Powers were obtained in 1845 for an extension from Dorchester, through Bridport to Axminster and thence to Exeter. As a route to Devon, Castleman's Snake was going to outserpent itself, swallowing all sorts of prey, but the powers were allowed to lapse because the South Western Board renewed its interest in direct access to Exeter via Salisbury and Yeovil, this route being authorised on July 22, 1848. But even today, the S.W. station at Dorchester is at right-angles to the G.W. line to Weymouth, reminding us that the latter place was scarcely in the thoughts of the South Western a century ago, and up Weymouth trains by way of Bournemouth have to run past Dorchester station and back into it, after the classic style of Limerick Junction.

It was not likely that the South Western company would be long content with its Nine Elms terminus. The Metropolitan Extension, as it was called, was authorised in 1845, and construction of a four-track line through Vauxhall to a terminal site to the south of Waterloo Bridge, then occupied by " lay-stalls, cow-yards, dung heaps and other nuisances ", was begun in the summer of 1846. Locke was the engineer, and Tite was in charge of the architectural details, for what they were worth. All the line had to be on viaduct. East of Vauxhall it took a turn to avoid disturbing Vauxhall Gardens, and there were more curves to dodge the old Lambeth Gasworks and the grounds of Lambeth Palace. The new terminus had three platforms under an all-over roof, a locomotive shed and an inclined cab drive. Thither came, in the summer dawn of July 13, 1848, the elegant Rothwell locomotive *Hornet* with the night mail from Southampton and the forty passengers who were the first to use Waterloo.*

* There are some legends about this occasion. One, that the engine was called *Horton*, was probably due to a compositor setting *Hornet* as *Horten* and a bright sub-editor " correcting " the spelling of the latter. Another account, apparently dating from the 'eighties, describes *Hornet* as a Crewe-type engine. She was an inside cylinder 2-2-2 with sandwich frames, and so far no evidence has suggested that by 1848 J. V. Gooch had rebuilt her, though such things did happen.

So entered the London scene what was to become the city's largest railway station, indeed, the largest in Great Britain. Through what vicissitudes and changes has Waterloo passed ! The name of the station remained unsettled for years. It was variously known in early days as York Road and Waterloo Bridge. The latter became official, and there was an increasing tendency to drop the " Bridge ", though this continued to appear until 1886. A strange place was the Waterloo of early Victorian years. There stood the train under its barn-like roof, the morning express to Southampton with its slender red locomotive—*Snake*, *Meteor* or maybe *Sappho*—its six or seven four-wheel carriages, painted dark brown, each first class with the coat of arms lovingly painted by hand on the middle door and dragon wings, gloriously guled, on the other doors; here and there a brakesman's box sticking up above the nearly flat roof at the end, for in this respect the oldest South Western carriages followed Continental practice. Five minutes before starting time the gates were shut, the passengers were in, tall hats safely bestowed in the ceiling cords, massive petticoats tucked out of harm's way as the doors were shut, and a policeman in a chocolate swallowtail coat and a leather-crowned tall hat walked along respectfully requesting all travellers to hold tight until the train be well started. Another policeman out on the tracks, all solitary, signalled *line clear*, the guard in his scarlet-faced coat put away his turnip watch, whistled and waved his flag, and with a mighty jerk and a long shudder the train was out and away on its three-hour rumble to Old Clausentum.

No less prodigious was the arrival of an up train. First it would pull up at a narrow wooden platform on the country side of West-minster Bridge Road, and there tickets were collected and the passengers treated to a good sniff at the candle factory. An agile brakesman passed a rope round the coupling between tender and leading coach and perched himself on the front step. Restarting, the engine gave her train a good heave, then paused, and in the instant while the coupling was slack, the brakesmen twitched up the rope and the coupling with it, the released engine put on a spurt and ran to a side track, in her wake the points snapped over like scissors and the carriages slowly rumbled into the station, alone, under the control of the guard in his box or brake van. This was the practice in the 'sixties if not before; it went on until about 1878 for all trains, and was perpetuated for empty trains being worked in from the Clapham Junction carriage sidings until 1895.

Clapham Junction ! There was no such station in 1860, though the Thames Valley line had diverged at this bleak outpost of

Battersea since 1846, finally reaching Windsor at the end of 1849. In 1860, the London, Brighton and South Coast Railway was opened to Victoria, and in its course bumped into the South Western at the junction, but the companies did not know each other, and the South Western continued to stop its trains outside the *Freemasons*, where the passengers were safe from contamination by the company next door. Yet long ago the South Western had purchased the ancient Surrey Iron Railway, with a view to converting it to a modern line and affording thereby western access for the Brighton company to London by a junction on the present site of Earlsfield. The Brighton and the South Western then quarrelled, as on many later occasions, and the Surrey line fell into decay.

In 1863, the West London Extension Railway was opened to the junction from Addison Road, Kensington, and as both the Brighton and the South Western were parties to this, and ran their trains on it, there had to be twin stations where the lines converged. It was not, mind you, a joint station. The Brighton installed a stationmaster to look after their buildings and traffic, and the South Western, latterly, went one better with a station superintendent. A remote recollection of mine concerns changing at Clapham Junction in order to travel by successive South Western trains to Ravenscourt Park via Addison Road. The station had just been repainted on the South Western side, and much in evidence was a superb personage in silk hat, frock-coat and mighty gold watch-chain, looking to me exactly like King Edward VII. This, I long afterwards discovered, must have been the famous Mr. R. W. Goodden, a most eminent official who took charge of Cis-Alpine Clapham Junction in 1903. He was a noteworthy photographer, among other parts, and took many of the South Western's official pictures.

Of course the great thing about Clapham Junction, apart from its size and traffic, is the fact that it is not in Clapham, nor yet very near it. The name was probably due to the South Western having called its Freemasons station Clapham Common, as being more toney than Wandsworth Common, on the edge of which it actually stood. When the junction was turned into a station, it took over the name as well as the goodwill of the old place.

So far we have seen the South Western as a lopsided Y, with possibilities of either extremity being continued into the West of England. For, in spite of the imperial progress of the Great Western and its allies, the South Western was determined to get a finger in the Cornish pasty, and other things as well. Part of its method was to gain in the far west a sort of Falkland Islands Dependency, in the shape of the Bodmin and Wadebridge Railway. This had been incorporated in 1832 and opened on July 4, 1834 (branches to Wenford and Ruthern Bridge on September 30, 1834), an entirely isolated steam railway carrying both passenger and goods traffic. In 1845, a year after the Bristol and Exeter Railway had reached Exeter, the South Western took a lease of the Bodmin and Wadebridge, then about 200 miles from the nearest point on its own system. The local consequence of this was that the Bodmin and Wadebridge, for more than half a century, remained a perfect example of a very early railway, with light iron rails on stone sleepers, and incredibly ancient rolling stock, whereof the solitary first-class compartment was about the size of a growler cab and had its narrow seats and straight backs stuffed with hay. In the middle years, one of the original London and Southampton engines, the Sharp Roberts 0-4-2 goods *Pluto*, was shipped out to the west to work the Bodmin and Wadebridge. Later this was succeeded by a little Fletcher Jennings saddle tank called *Bodmin*. In 1886, the South Western bought the line outright, though it was still isolated. Latterly, before connection was made with the main system, the Great Western Railway was permitted to work it, through a connection to its own main line at Bodmin Road, and some Great Western trains continued to run to Wadebridge as long as company ownership endured. Not until June 1, 1895, did the South Western main line reach Wadebridge, and not until six months later was the partly parallel Bodmin branch physically connected with it. The ancient carriages were then brought up to London, where they were received with wonder and reverence. The old composite for many years adorned the concourse of the present Waterloo Station.

The direct route to Salisbury from Worting Junction, near Basingstoke, was opened by stages. It reached Andover in 1854, and Salisbury on May 1, 1857, turning that city into a backwater as far as the Great Western was concerned. Also during the 'fifties, there was some more sharp diplomacy in the interests of securing an enviable slice of Devon, and ultimately Cornwall, with railways ready-made, at such time as the main line should reach Exeter. During the late 'forties, the broad-gauge Great Western and Bristol and Exeter companies were not on such good terms as allies ought to be, on account of a proposed line called the Exeter Great Western, which was to provide a southern broad-gauge route to Exeter via Yeovil, Axminster, Honiton, Ottery and Stoke Canon. It was energetically opposed in Parliament by the Bristol and Exeter and the South Western. There was indeed a free-for-all fight between the conflicting interests for the railway occupation of East and North Devon; lines were authorised; Bills were thrown out; the investing public had the final word by refusing to be drawn after its experiences in the late Railway Mania, and powers obtained had to lapse.

But the South Western, during the 'fifties, got a controlling interest in the Exeter and Crediton Railway, a separately-owned broad-gauge appendage of the Bristol and Exeter Railway, by indirect purchase of shares. The Exeter and Crediton gave end-on connection with the Taw Vale, later North Devon Railway, also broad gauge. The North Devon Railway reached Barnstaple on July 12, 1854, and Bideford (old station) on November 12, 1855.

Having landed its commando in Crediton, the South Western then proceeded to invade from the east. Its own powers to build a Salisbury-Exeter line having lapsed, it was induced to support the Salisbury and Yeovil Railway (authorised 1854). I say induced, for the South Western shareholders were violently divided in their favour of this or the Dorchester route to Exeter, and two general meetings had been so noisy that hard-headed directors were rising from the Board and fleeing with their hands over their ears. During the 'fifties, confidence increased, and the Salisbury and Yeovil, as originally planned, was extended to reach Exeter via Crewkerne, Axminster and Honiton, largely coinciding with the projected route of the abortive Exeter Great Western. Yeovil itself was put on a branch, and could be bypassed by through traffic.

Unfortunately, the local company got into difficulties through lack of confidence, and nearly two years passed between the passing of its Act and the cutting of the first sod, which was performed at Gillingham, Dorset, on April 3, 1856. At Salisbury, the tunnel was completed and a new South Western station opened next door to that of the Great Western, on the west side of Fisherton Street. Thence, the Salisbury and Yeovil was opened to Gillingham on May 1, 1859; to Sherborne on May 7, 1860; to Yeovil on June 1, and the L.S.W.R. extended thence to Exeter Queen Street on July 19, 1860. Goods traffic to Exeter came later, on September 1, a curious inversion of the usual order of public opening. After all the initial fears for the S. and Y., it was a roaring financial success. By 1877 it was paying 12½ per cent.

A very different line was this from the old main line of the South Western to Southampton. In some twenty years, the power and efficiency of locomotives had increased, successively under John Gooch and Joseph Beattie, and the new line had an undulating character which drivers of the old Rothwell and Rennie single-wheelers would have viewed with alarm and dismay. Yet, to a remarkable extent, its gradients compensated one another; this line of the struggling Yeovil company was perfectly planned and superbly built. The two largest stations, Yeovil and Exeter Queen Street, had a remarkable affinity; each had a pair of peaked overall roofs, joined together but staggered, for up and down traffic. Exeter Queen Street has gone now, replaced by the present Exeter Central on the same site in 1932, but though Yeovil, too, has lost its all-over roofs, its pretentious Victorian-Tudor building survives.

Starting from Worting Junction, the line is generally falling, though with three short rises, nearly to Andover, which has a three-mile approach at 1 in 178 down. Between Andover and Salisbury, approximately 17 miles, it rises to and falls from a summit at Milepost 73¼, west of Grateley, with ruling grades of 1 in 165 (westbound) and 1 in 140 (eastbound). Out of Salisbury there is a short, sharp rise, and the line continues to make an undulating rise to Semley, 101¼ miles from Waterloo, and culminating in a climb at 1 in 145. Thereafter comes a tremendous switchback: down to Gillingham, up to Buckhorn Weston Tunnel, down again and up through Templecombe to Milepost 113½, with repeated stretches in both directions at 1 in 100. West of a point about midway between Milborne Port and Sherborne the ruling gradient drops at 1 in 80, followed by an almost unbroken climb at this inclination for nearly 3 miles through Crewkerne to Hewish Summit (Milepost 133¼). Thence follows a 13-mile fall, almost continuous, to Milepost 146¼ between Axminster and Seaton Junction.

Now comes the big climb, much of it at 1 in 80, but including half a mile at 1 in 70, and easing up to 1 in 132 through Honiton Tunnel at the top. The rise begins at Milepost 146¼ and ends just short of 153½. Thence to Exeter, just under 172 miles from Waterloo, starting with a mile at 1 in 90 before Honiton station, there are successive downhill stretches at 1 in 100 and a mile at 1 in 90 between Honiton Tunnel and Station, though the fall is seasoned by several brief uphill humps near and beyond Sidmouth Junction and through Pinhoe to Exmouth Junction.

For over seventy years there was little change about Exeter Queen Street, save that a big depot at Exmouth Junction came to succeed the old running shed and turntable that were situated almost in the station itself, where once *Herod* and *Vulture*, *Argus* and *Styx* had been posed for their photographs. The Exmouth branch was the first offshoot to be opened, excluding, of course, the Yeovil branch, which was technically an appendix of the main line. Early in the present century, an attempt was made to provide an inner suburban service, with halts served by the Exmouth branch trains. For a good many years it provided a mild sort of competition with Exeter's electric trams, but at the end the motor bus that super-seded the trams did for the local railway traffic also. Alas for Lion's Holt Halt !

To return to the mid-nineteenth century. In 1862 the South Western line at Exeter was produced down the hill, on a very stiff short incline at 1 in 37, to the Bristol and Exeter station at St. Davids, to which it was opened on February 1. Even before its arrival, the South Western had softened up the position by getting running powers granted over the Bristol and Exeter to Cowley Bridge Junction, to link up with its fifth column,* the Exeter and Crediton. But there was a bigger fifth column than that in the broad-gauge camp, namely, the North Devon itself. It was a typical broad-gauge railway, to be regarded naturally as a party to the Paddington-Bristol-Exeter alliance. It worked its own traffic with a rather odd collection of locomotives, including a seven-foot-gauge variety of Allan's Crewe-type goods and some queer 2-2-2 " express " locomotives having domed fireboxes and inside bearings to all the wheels, tender included. The carriages were of the usual broad-gauge cigar-box type, nearly flat-roofed and much wider than they were high. In the eyes of Paddington and Bristol, it must have looked quite an innocent sort of railway. Yet in 1862, it leased itself out to the London and South Western. Thus in three slick moves, the latter company was through the broad-gauge lines and occupying the rich province of North Devon. For as long as the old broad-gauge engines and vehicles lasted, the South Western continued to work them, though it mixed the gauges in 1863 for through running. There was already mixed gauge on the Exeter and Crediton, and in 1862 the daily service over the latter line consisted of five South Western trains daily in each direction, plus a Friday's only train and a through goods, all standard gauge; three North Devon trains running through to Barnstaple, and one Bristol and Exeter goods, all broad gauge. The 5.55 p.m. down train from Queen Street to the Crediton line ran in connection with the South Western down express leaving Waterloo at one o'clock and reaching Exeter Queen Street at 5.45. It took 27 minutes to reach Crediton, calling at Exeter St. Davids and Exeter St. Cyres† by the way. In 1865 the North Devon Railway was finally absorbed by the South Western, which extended it to the present station at Bideford, and to Torrington, on July 18, 1872.

---

* The old nickname of the Exeter and Crediton was Vicar of Bray Railway.
† Later renamed Newton St. Cyres.

It was the end of a campaign, but not the end of the war. The rising and very picturesque seaside town of Ilfracombe was wanting a railway with a very great want, but things moved slowly, partly by reason of its mountainous approaches. Three companies had their eyes on it; the South Western, the broad-gauge Devon and Somerset, and the London and North Western. The latter thought in terms of steamers from Swansea, though it was locally believed at one time that the North Western really contemplated some sort of a line in Devonshire. The long and laborious exertions of Ilfracombe in getting railway service were well described by Frank Box in *The Railway Magazine* (Volumes XLV and XLVI, 1919-20). It must suffice to say here that once again the broad-gauge interests were left standing. While the latter's Devon and Somerset Railway was making slow and painful progress from Norton Fitzwarren to Barnstaple, the South Western was giving active support to a local company for a line from Barnstaple to Ilfracombe via Braunton, to be built as a light railway under provisions of the Regulation of Railways Act, 1868, and to have end-on connection with our old friend the North Devon at Barnstaple. The Barnstaple and Ilfracombe Railway Bill went before Parliament in 1870. Those behind it were quite a family party. One of the directors was Joseph Hamilton Beattie, mechanical engineer of the South Western; his son, William George Beattie, as an expert witness produced drawings of a special locomotive which Papa had designed for this railway; J. E. McConnell, formerly of the North Western's Southern Division and before that of the Birmingham and Gloucester Railway with its Lickey Incline, also gave expert evidence, confirming that the Beattie family locomotive would manage quite well on a ruling gradient of 1 in 37; Archibald Scott and W. R. Galbraith, traffic manager and engineer, respectively, of the London and South Western, were also in the distinguished party of expert witnesses. The district's more eminent citizens were almost solidly behind the scheme, and the Barnstaple and Ilfracombe Railway Act received the Royal Assent on July 4, 1870.

It was a deuce of a line. Its violently curved 1 in 36 section was on the northern side of the summit, involving the ascent out of a terminus itself perched on a ledge above Ilfracombe, and extended for some 2 miles continuously to a point near Mortehoe. In the down direction there was a long climb for over 6 miles from a point between Wrafton and Braunton, more than half of it at 1 in 40-41. It remains the toughest of the ex S.R. lines over which express trains are run. The journey from Crediton to Ilfracombe remains to this day in full harmony with the beautiful main line west of Salisbury. It gently falls from near Copplestone, running down the green Taw Vale. There are Eggesford, South Molton Road, Portsmouth Arms and Umberleigh, situations as lovely as one could desire from some unkind sojourn. Then, north of Braunton, there is that superb climb up the narrow valley, past the *Foxhunters*, and on to the high tops by Mortehoe; whence from the train, in clear weather, one can look out to Lundy and the hills of South Wales, lying magically on the sea like a vision of St. Brendan's Isle and Tir na'n Og.

A funny thing happened about the special Beattie locomotives designed for the Ilfracombe line, for, after all the fuss, they were never built. Before the line was opened to Ilfracombe (on July 20, 1874), old Mr. Beattie had died. Young Mr. Beattie seems to have taken a lingering look at the design, which was for an outside cylinder 0-6-0 rather like a French Bourbonnais goods, then rolled up the drawings and requested Beyer, Peacock and Company kindly to oblige with some of their standard light goods engines, such as they were building for Sweden and other places. These, then, became the special " Ilfracombe Goods ".

At first, the Ilfracombe line was single track. It was doubled, in three stages, between 1889 and 1891, in which last year the section down to Ilfracombe terminus, with its twin tunnels, was thus completed. The North Devon line remains single track from Copplestone to Umberleigh, though many years ago the road-bed was widened and the bridges doubled for the additional track that has never been needed. The wide space between the platforms at intermediate stations reminds one of the old North Devon company that began with the broad gauge, then suffered its line to be leased and mixed, and finally sold out to the standard-gauge South Western.

Not on the mere laurels of a conquest in North Devon would the South Western company rest. There it had elbowed out the broad-gauge party, who had admittedly shown very little dash. The South Western aimed at a flank attack on Plymouth, the great broad-gauge fortress of the west; also, it never forgot that remote protectorate of its own, the Bodmin and Wadebridge. The route from Crediton to Plymouth, while fortunately not involving anything like the incline out of Ilfracombe, would have to scale the shoulder of Dartmoor on the northern side, with a summit level of 950 ft. near Meldon, approached by an almost continuous climb from the Exe Valley and successive stretches at 1 in 77. Divergence was made from the old North Devon line at Coleford Junction, north-west of Yeoford. From the summit came a sharp descent to join the Plymouth-Launceston branch of the broad-gauge South Devon Railway, completed in 1865. This would be altered to mixed gauge, and thus, by tactics already familiar, the South Western would get access to its friends' establishment by running powers.

Observe how the Locke tradition continued ! Go up and round, and avoid tunnels ! Robert Stephenson would probably have bored several miles of tunnels through the thickest part of Dartmoor. So drove to the West the old, despised Parsons and Prawns Railway, in whose remote ancestry had been a scheme for a ship canal from Southampton to London to cut out Napoleon's blockade of the Straits of Dover. By stages it reached Okehampton Road, near the present Sampford Courtenay, on January 8, 1867, and Okehampton, to which it was opened on August 29, 1871. This formerly isolated town on the edge of Dartmoor received the London and South Western Railway with great rejoicings, and a huge, sticky, gloriously greedy, Devonshire cream tea was consumed in the High Street by the local Old and Young. A photograph of the feasting has fortunately survived.

Can we recapture the spirit of those railway celebrations of last century, when decorous old towns went almost wild with delight at the advent of the first train ? Not easily ! The coming of the railway meant for them the end of an age-long isolation, often stagnant, such as we know no longer in these islands, save, perhaps, in the coming of the aeroplane to the Hebrides. But our grandparents and great grandparents, headed by mayor and macebearer, fêted their first trains as the bringers of untold social improvement and unbounded commercial expansion. It was Progress, and they believed in Progress. The train rolled in from the East with the promise of a glorious dawn, and the Vicar invoked a blessing on it.

On November 2, 1874, the South Western Railway reached Lydford, thus providing that pleasant place and its visitors with much more direct access from London than it had hitherto enjoyed by the still circuitous broad-gauge route via Bristol and Plymouth. Below Brentor, and about Lydford Gorge, exuberantly blossomed the villa-architecture of the 'seventies. It was not, however, until eighteen months had passed that the South Western succeeded in gaining access to Plymouth by mixed gauge on the S.D.R. branch line, the through service beginning on May 17, 1876. Plymouth North Road station, a couple of characteristic Great Western barns, was built to handle the traffic of both lines.

Once again, there was a case of William George Beattie ordering special locomotives, not of the company's standard type, for the new line, just as he had done at Ilfracombe. Beyer, Peacock and Company duly accommodated him with half a dozen 4-4-0 tank engines, Nos. 318-323, one of which is portrayed in my picture of an early Plymouth express. The design was a slight modification of one previously carried out for the German Rhenish Railway, which in its turn was a development of the standard Metropolitan type of 1864. The Plymouth Tanks, as they were called, were much more powerful than any existing South Western passenger engines, and if only they had been provided with tenders instead of side tanks and bunkers, as were some similar engines for New South Wales, they should have done very well on the hills of Dartmoor. They were built in 1875 in readiness for the new service to Plymouth, but while engaged on this they suffered badly from insufficient water and fuel capacity. After a while they were replaced on the Plymouth expresses by ordinary Beattie tender engines.

A West Country correspondent, who was a boy at Plymouth in the 'seventies, once described to me his delighted admiration on seeing the first London and South Western trains there. Hitherto, the boys and other people of those parts had in many cases never seen a standard-gauge train, and had the liveliest curiosity as to what it would be like. The noble Gooch eight-footers of the Great Western did not travel so far west, and the ordinary South Devon train was no oil painting. Even the Flying Dutchman, by the time it reached Plymouth, loafed in behind an ungainly 4-4-0 saddle-tank engine. The new South Western expresses were startlers. Both young Mr. Beattie and Mr. H. L. Lange of Beyer, Peacock and Company were artists when it came to locomotives. Graciously tapered chimneys, dazzling brass domes, and a rich chocolate livery stole the hearts of the youth of Plymouth when the " narrow-gauge " invaders came spanking down through Tavistock and Yelverton. Twenty years later, things were somewhat reversed, for Adams's South Western engines, though nicely balanced in their proportions, were severe-looking things beside William Dean's glittering Dukes.

That mixed-gauge back-way into Plymouth served the South Western trains for some fourteen years, though it was not altogether a happy arrangement. In 1885 there was an accident to a down South Western train near Yelverton, due at least in part to a degree of super-elevation on a curve which was insufficient for a standard-gauge train. Independent access, save that the South Western trains continued to use Plymouth North Road station and the line thence to Lipson Junction, was provided by the Plymouth,

Devonport and South Western Junction Railway, extending from a new terminus at Plymouth Friary, up the valleys of Tamar and Tavy to the existing South Western line at Lydford. It was opened on June 1, 1890, with a handsome new station at Devonport. At North Road, as at Exeter St. Davids, the South Western trains up and down now ran in directions contrary to those of the Great Western. The P.D. and S.W.J.R. was worked by the South Western from the first, though in the early nineteen hundreds it built a branch from Bere Alston, across the Tamar on a fine viaduct at Calstock, to join up with the reconstructed East Cornwall Railway to Callington, and on this it worked a service of its own with three tank engines and some odd carriages and wagons.

The final push for the possession of North Cornwall began at the end of the 'seventies. On January 30, 1879, a branch was opened from Meldon Junction, just west of the great viaduct across the Okement Valley, to Holesworthy, which became the railhead for Stratton and Bude. It was not completed to the last-mentioned until the late summer of 1898. During the intervening twenty years, the South Western doubtless felt that it had got Bude in its pocket anyway. From Halwill, on this branch, the North Cornwall Railway, worked by the South Western, was extended to Launceston (July 21, 1886), Tresmeer (July 28, 1892), Camelford (August 14, 1893), and to Delabole on October 18. On June 1, 1894, London and South Western trains reached Wadebridge and the isolated Bodmin line which it had supported for so long, though, as we have seen, it was not until November 1 that the ancient branch was physically connected to the main line. On March 27, 1899, the final section of the main line was opened at Padstow. The South Western company had captured the Atlantic Coast from Exmoor to Trevose Head, after a cold war of forty-nine years.

There remains the later history of the old main line, originally formed by the London and Southampton and by Castleman's Snake. In the early days, Bournemouth was an unheard-of place, a tiny village in the heath between Poole and Christchurch, supporting a handful of fishermen and a pub. Anyone eccentric enough to want to visit it travelled by Castleman's Snake to Hamworthy, opposite Poole, and thence confided himself and his belongings to Mr. Axford's daily omnibus.* In 1862, a branch line was built from Ringwood on the " Snake " to Christchurch, in which town someone invested in another omnibus, considerably damaging Mr. Axford's traffic returns. The South Western company pushed on from Christchurch to Bournemouth, giving a nasty jar to the Christ-

---

* Known in the vernacular as " Oxford ".

church bus in its turn, on March 14, 1870, and two years later extended this to Bournemouth West. At Bournemouth Central (originally named East), a very splendid station was built, and the history of the town as a major pleasure and health resort was truly begun. A branch was opened to Poole proper in 1872, and extended to meet the Bournemouth line in 1874. On March 5, 1888, a direct line was opened from Christchurch to Brockenhurst via Sway, the new fast service being inaugurated by William Adams's magnificent gold-medal engine No. 526 and a train of superior bogie carriages. The route to Dorchester and Weymouth was shortened on June 1, 1893, by the Holes Bay curve, cutting out reversal at Broadstone Junction, and the old Hamworthy branch, now moribund, was closed to passenger traffic.

In the previous year, a very important transaction took place. The London and South Western Railway took over Southampton Docks. Thereafter this company, and the Southern Railway after it, proceeded to turn Southampton into one of the greatest ocean ports in the world, culminating in the great new docks extension across the head of Southampton Water in the nineteen-thirties. And so the original South Western main line became, at last, part of the main land and sea route from London to the Americas, the Cape and the Antipodes.

CHAPTER FOURTEEN

Waterloo and the Rest

NO ! On the whole, and certainly in the older cases, stations were not the strongest point of the South Western main line in days past ! There were those barrack-like buildings in pale mud-coloured brick, like Andover Junction; there were the stark Dutch barns, already mentioned, of Exeter and Yeovil; there were such rambling and frowzy places as the old station at Wimbledon. Scenery and accessories were often peculiar—there were the tall, square telegraph posts, painted pinkish-brown like the carriages and the station awnings; there were odd little huts covering semi-autonomous locking frames about sidings, bearing such abrupt titles as " West Points ", and " Ground Frame East ".

In the 'eighties and 'nineties there was certainly some reform, but most of the stations built at this time were replacements of buildings so awful that even the South Western conscience could no longer abide them. Bournemouth Central has already received honourable mention, and I had rather a liking for Southampton West. When this was rebuilt as Southampton Central in the nineteen-thirties, I was glad that the old red-brick building survived on the up side, with its complacent leaden-domed clock-tower; moreover, when the German Luftwaffe attended to Southampton, I was perversely glad that the old building with its clock tower remained whole, even though new and admirable concrete buildings on the down side were battered.

Beyond Exeter the stations improved, as they ought, being newer. Bridestowe had some marvels of topiary, such as still survive at Ropley. Devonport has a good John Bullish sort of name, and its grey granite South Western station is in keeping, though it lost its massive roof after being damaged by bombs. But of course the prodigy of all South Western stations, nay, perhaps among all British and Irish stations, was Waterloo. Now, there are inexplicable affinities between certain railway stations as with other buildings. One may, when drowsy, mistake Lichfield (Trent Valley) for Tamworth on a dim evening; there are certain resemblances between York and Newcastle-upon-Tyne; there is an

Victorian Glory: Up Plymouth express between Bridestowe and Meldon, London and South Western Railway, in the late 'seventies; Beyer Peacock "Plymouth Tank" engine No. 320

extraordinary one between the Southern station at Blackfriars (old St. Paul's) in London and Westland Row in Dublin. But there never was anything like the old Waterloo, nor is there another British station resembling the present one.

In the previous chapter, we left Waterloo as a shabby caravan-serai with four approach roads and three platforms. Although it formed the terminus of the South Western's " metropolitan exten-sion ", it was not intended to remain so; the company proposed extending that extension, and to have its main London station at London Bridge. But, thanks to financial uneasiness, the chance was missed, never to return. A very early addition was the first of the Necropolis stations, just outside. Thereafter, for about ninety years, the South Western and the Southern carried the London Necropolis Company's funeral traffic to Brookwood. Once there was a daily funeral express, down and back, but in more recent years the motor hearse came and grew in favour until there was but a bi-weekly Necropolitan train service. It was finished by a parachute mine coming down on the private station outside Waterloo in 1941. The fathers and grandfathers of boys who watch trains today knew the Necropolis specials well. The engines were adorned with evergreens in our day, and for the trains we had a very coarse and unkind name.

On the opening of the original station in 1848, the chairman, Mr. Chaplin, proudly claimed that its three platforms would be ample for South Western traffic, and that of such companies that might " come and hire ". This was a friendly hint to the London, Brighton and South Coast Railway.

In 1860, as we have seen, the opening of the West of England main line added greatly to South Western traffic. The old Waterloo had another chunk added, haphazard, and called the North station, providing four more badly needed platforms. Four years later, the South Eastern Railway was opened to Charing Cross. As this company and the South Western were nowhere in com-petition, relations between them were cordial, and the South Western put in a single track connection to join those of its dis-reputable new neighbours. For a while, suburban trains were worked through, by means of a sort of valley bisecting the main line circulating area, but it was not a very remunerative traffic, and latterly the junction served only milk vans, and an occasional saloon or horsebox. The bridge which carried the connecting line across the Waterloo Road is yet there, with a remnant of platform and awning in the best South Eastern style. The northern wall of the old North station also survives still, tucked away beside the

" Village ", the block of offices standing between the present platforms 15 and 16.

Waterloo's first signal-box was the famous Crowsnest, a precarious-looking broody-coop perched atop a couple of poles against the gable-ends of the old roof. It remained there until the great rebuilding of the station in the present century. In 1867, the first Waterloo A Box was built on a gantry across the four approach tracks. It contained 47 levers, and from the gantry there soared high into the windy air, two great masts, each carrying three pairs of back-to-back semaphores, each pair on a common pivot in the ancient, classic Gregorian style.

In 1874, a new A Box, with 109 levers, replaced the original, and four years later there was completed the New (later the South) Station, a gaunt abomination containing an island platform, and offices and refreshment rooms quite separate from the older part of Waterloo. The old outfit was getting lumpy, like a diseased potato. Still, the New Station was welcomed as providing relief to some of the growing congestion, and as the Colonial Office had lately added Cyprus to its liabilities, it seemed good to the station staff so to call the New Station. This Cyprus had an entrance up a dreary stair from the Waterloo Road; its one village-terminal island platform served all the suburban trains to Epsom and Leatherhead, Hampton Court, and to Kingston via Norbiton. No intelligent foreigner could have been blamed for supposing that two or three different railways terminated at Waterloo, and that none had any connection with the establishment next door. But there was more to follow. The Windsor and Reading lines of the South Western always had a certain individuality and it was scarcely to be expected that they would not need something separate in the way of a terminus. In 1884, they were surely endowed with a " Windsor Station " beyond the party wall of the old North station, and to this was added some more in the following year. The place was known variously as " Abyssinia " and " Khartoum ". By 1885 Waterloo, with 15 platforms and 18 roads, was one of the largest stations in the world. It was probably the most frightful, though the old Waverley cum Canal Street at Edinburgh ran it close.

There was really little of exaggeration in the flounderings of Jerome K. Jerome's boating heroes in their search for the 11.5 to Kingston. (*To put an end to the matter, we went upstairs, and asked the traffic superintendent, and he told us that he had just met a man who said he had seen it at No. 3 platform.*) Needless to add, he hadn't. For a country gaffer, homeward-bound, or a nervous lady, the place was a nightmare indeed. I met one lady, who, as a timid girl, wanted to travel to Farnborough, and after going round in several circles finally wandered into Waterloo Junction. Finding a booking office there, she bought a ticket, and to Farnborough the South Eastern Railway kindly conveyed her, via New Cross, Croydon, Redhill, Dorking and Guildford. By the end of the 'eighties, the station, or conglomerate of stations, was handling 700 trains and about 100,000 passengers daily. In 1888 there was another reconstruction of A Box, which in its new form had 229 levers. This was still insufficient, as was the bottleneck at the rail entrance to the station over Westminster Bridge Road. Early in 1892, the approach was widened to take six tracks, and the signalling necessarily reconstructed. For three life-shortening days, May 15-17, trains were signalled in and out of the station by flags and lamps.

On July 11, 1898, the long-projected city extension, in the form of the Waterloo and City electric tube line, was opened by the Duke of Cambridge, with the public service following on August 8. The former occasion took place fifty years to the week after *Hornet* had brought the first night mail (and the first train ever) into Waterloo Station. Other sources of access to the Waterloo of 1898 included the long-lived ha'penny horse bus across Waterloo Bridge and the horse trams along the Waterloo Road, equipages immortalised, together with the Waterloo Junction bridge, by a once-famous steel engraving called *Popularity*, showing the vaudeville stars of the period. Mr. George Robey appears in it as a modest young man wearing a boater, well in the background, though Charlie Coborn already looks ancient.

At the end of the 'nineties, it having been felt for long that something really must be done about Waterloo, the first steps were taken, by the acquisition of land, towards its complete reconstruction. The plans were for a vast new station, *in one piece*, having what in railway clericalese were termed " twenty-three commodious platforms ". A plan of the station, as thus schemed, closely agrees with the new station as it was built. The important differences are at the Windsor end. Platforms 12-23 were to have gone in an even line from the central great cab drive to near the present site of the Victory Arch. As it turned out, the proposed site of platforms 16-17 was taken up by a parcel of temporary offices called " the Cottages ", and these in turn gave place to the permanent offices still known as " the Village ". On the Windsor side of the Village, old Khartoum was reprieved, and today contains platforms 16-21. Beyond it are sidings and the car-lift to the Waterloo and City line, down which the old Drummond tank engine No. 672 turned a back-somersault some time ago.

For some years, very little was to be seen of the metamorphosis of Waterloo. The work went on below ground, and the foundations for the great new terminus were complete on the south side by 1905. Thereafter, something new and vast began to loom where the South station had been. In 1909, suburban trains began to serve the new platforms one and two. Along the back of what was to be an enormous concourse area appeared the first sections of new offices.

As a railway station, which, after all, was its primary being, it became one of the best arranged in the world. Between 1911 and the outbreak of war in 1914, the old terminus of 1848 was swept away, and the range of new platforms increased, stage by stage, to 11. Between 1914 and 1919, little could be done, but by 1922, the last year of the old London and South Western company, the job was finished, with about 15,000 ft. of platform-face, and the grand entrance at the north-western extremity was dedicated as a war memorial. Queen Mary opened the new station on March 21, 1922. Goodness knows how posterity will describe the style of Waterloo Station, so let us leave it to posterity, Victory Arch and all.

Various refinements appeared during the ensuing twenty-five years of ownership by the Southern Railway. A well-known pharmacy opened a branch on the station, and so did a famous bank. In 1932, a public address system was installed for dealing with football crowds by loudspeaker, and a news cinema, adjoining platform 1, was opened in 1934.

The great A Box, straddling the tracks, underwent various modifications from 1892 onwards. Its original equipment included that tremendous array of bracket-post signals that used to vie with the Shot Towers and the Lion Brewery in adorning the south-ward prospect from the Savoy. The number of levers increased from 236 to 248, and then to 266, while the portentous signal skyline dwindled with the introduction of route indicators. In 1936 came upheaval. Since the previous year, preliminary work had been proceeding on a great change-over to electric point operation and colour-light signalling. With it was combined a grand rearrangement of approaches, with a flyover for the up slow road on the main line near Wimbledon. During seven hours of the night May 16-17, 1936, a thousand workmen carried out the great operation on the Waterloo approach roads. Autumn brought completion of the re-signalling programme, whereby six boxes, including the last of the South Western's " A Box " dynasty, gave place to a single all-electric box. This was in the small hours of

October 8. The last train to be signalled out by A Box was the 12-35 a.m. to Hampton Court. Fifty-five minutes later, the newspaper express pulled out, signalled by electric colour-lights.

Then there was war, and fire came to the city and to Waterloo. One retains odd, abrupt memories. A patient queue stands in the monstrous blacked-out station for the 1.25 a.m. train to the West. An American boy rhythmically chews under a blue lamp. Or it is high noon, when a flying bomb cuts out right overhead, and in the eerie hush an Irish barmaid stares at her beer engines and says, over and over again: " It's stopped ! Jesus ! It's stopped ! "

That one came down by the City Railway car-hoist. It was a bloody business, but the grim yellow-brick wall of old Khartoum stood firm. Waterloo might have fared worse. It was bombed again and again. The old South Western offices burned and tottered into rubble, but the main offices were saved. At the last, the great station still stretched its steel fan unbroken among the ruins of Lambeth.

With the beginning of 1948, company ownership came to an end for Waterloo, as for the rest of the British railways. But Waterloo celebrated its centenary with an exhibition, and a magnificent pair of Centenary posters was executed by Helen McKie, who had already commemorated many of the station's war-time scenes, and a delightful commemorative booklet was published.* On the first day, too, the exhibits included the old Adams express engine No. 563, and one of Surrey Warner's handsome tricomposite coaches, both restored to the aspect which they wore in the great days of the L.S.W.R.†

So there stands Waterloo, far-flung over the spot where *Hornet* brought in the night mail on that summer morning of 1848. The following figures belong to a daily census in its centennial year: Trains arriving and departing in 24 hours, 1,185; passengers using them, 190,678; trains arriving between 7 a.m. and 10 a.m., 132; trains departing between 4 p.m. and 7 p.m., 137. To the 21 platforms in the main station are added four in the eastern station, the old Waterloo Junction, and six underground platforms serving the City, Northern and Bakerloo lines. The electric signal-box has 309 levers, 16 train describers, and 153 track circuits.

* Written by Mr. H. G. Davies.
† A love-labour by Mr. A. B. Macleod.

CHAPTER FIFTEEN

Heyday of Nine Elms

THE first locomotive of the London and South Western Railway was the *Lark*, a 2-2-0 Bury engine bought from the contractor. There followed a few like her, then no more, which was just as well. Fortunately, too, the company did not, as did the Great Western, make Brunelian stipulations about large wheels and low piston speeds, gearing and so forth, consequently there were no monstrosities. Of the oldest engines, those built by Rothwell and Company seem to have been highly satisfactory, for during the middle 'forties, when John Viret Gooch was locomotive engineer, he continued to order standard Rothwell engines at the same time as building his own designs.

The Rothwell engine *Hornet*, which brought the first train into Waterloo Station in 1848, was, like the others, a 2-2-2 with sandwich frames, inside cylinders, and a big dome on the first ring of the boiler barrel. This dome was covered with a very ornate casing, square-based, fluted and bell-mouthed. All the engines had names and no numbers until the 'fifties, much the same naming conventions being followed as on the Great Western. For there was the usual spate of classical antiquities—gods and goddesses and Greek worthies—celestial phenomena, birds, mammals, reptiles and insects, both real and legendary. Perhaps the best-known insect, after *Hornet*, was the original *Firefly*, a little Rothwell single which was later converted to a tank engine with two domes, and worked on the Chard branch in the 'sixties. Among the others was *Sam Slick* (a Tayleur engine), which had a good, racy, Epsom Downs sort of sound.

J. V. Gooch was the first locomotive superintendent to design and build South Western engines at Nine Elms. He laid out the original works there, and turned out his first locomotive, the single express *Eagle*, in 1843. Gooch's passenger engines were variants of Alexander Allan's Crewe type, with double frames, inside bearings to the driving wheels, inclined outside cylinders, and in most cases domeless boilers. One numerous series, however, had the Rothwell type of boiler with a big dome at the front. All the passenger engines were of the 2-2-2 type. They are believed to have been painted Venetian or Indian red from the first, which colour was perpetuated by Joseph Beattie during the 'fifties.

A very famous engine of the Gooch period was the *Elk*, one of five Fairbairn 5 ft. 6 in. singles named after horned big game, and built in 1843. The *Elk* (driver David Markham) made a famous run in 1846 with a light special train from Southampton to Nine Elms, 78 miles, in 93 minutes. In view of this it is unsatisfactory to remark that little trace seems to have survived to show what *Elk* and the rest of the herd were really like in their prime. The late C. F. Dendy Marshall inclined to believe that they had inside cylinders. In T. H. Shields' paper on *The Evolution of Locomotive Valve Gears*, presented to the Institution of Locomotive Engineers in 1943, there is reproduced an old drawing of an inside cylinder 2-2-2 engine by Fairbairn for the London and South Western Railway. It appears to be identical with the standard Rothwell type. But the Elk class were recorded as having been (presumably when new) the first London and South Western engines to have Gooch expansive link motion, and the engine in Mr. Shields' paper has gab gear. One of the class as rebuilt, heading a local train, is illustrated in my *Nineteenth Century Railway Carriages*, and there shown as resembling a small version of an early Beattie express engine.

The largest and finest of J. V. Gooch's express engines were eight seven-footers—the Vulcan class—built at Nine Elms in 1849-50, and for some years unparalleled in the South of England. Of these, *Etna*, which was in a smash at Raynes Park early in 1861, and *Stromboli*, lasted until 1880. They were characteristic of the Crewe type, sub-family *Goochidae*. J. Beattie, who completed the class, gave them his own design of boiler with double firebox, feed-water heater, and large dome at the rear.

This Joseph Hamilton Beattie, an ingenious and fiery Irishman, succeeded Gooch in 1850. His first engines were sandwich-framed inside cylinder 2-4-0's, like nothing else on the L.S.W.R. before or after. They may have been at least partly Gooch's work. Thereafter the only standard South Western engines with inside cylinders, until 1887, were several varieties of 5 ft. six-coupled goods, some of Beattie design and others by Beyer, Peacock and Company. I have given the Beattie engines a chapter to themselves in another book, so here, like many others, they must be treated to a sketch only.

During the 'fifties, Beattie's express engines were 6 ft. 6 in. singles, with a somewhat inadequate adhesive factor. One of them, *Ironsides*, built in 1855, was soon after converted to a 2-4-0, and

J. Beattie made this his standard express engine thereafter. The last London and South Western single express engine (*Victoria*) was built in 1859, and in the same year the first new passenger 2-4-0's came out in readiness for the Exeter expresses. They were in two varieties, and generally those with 7 ft. driving wheels were employed between Waterloo and Salisbury, while those with 6 ft. 6 in. worked over the heavier road into Devon. Also in 1859 came out the first of numerous 6 ft. 2-4-0 engines for ordinary passenger trains, though later examples were not infrequently used on the expresses. The first Beattie goods engines, built in 1855, were also of the 2-4-0 type, with 5 ft. coupled wheels, though after 1863 the 0-6-0 type became standard. All the Beattie engines of this time seemed somewhat undersized, this being made more than usually apparent by their very low-pitched boilers. The usual pressure was 130 lb. In the St. George class of 1868, and many others, the cylinders were 17 by 22 in.

Yet these little, archaic-looking engines did surprisingly well on a main line which nobody could regard as a playground. Their fuel economics were unrivalled, thanks to the feed-water heaters which went with Joseph Beattie's patent double fireboxes. They were fast and free-running engines, and this virtue owed something to the excellent balanced slide-valves invented by William George Beattie, old Joseph's promising son and chief assistant. The younger Beattie's piston valves were another story. They were before their time, and caused endless trouble while they lasted.

Most of W. G. Beattie's locomotives, built during the 'seventies, were simply refinements of his father's standard types, more graceful of aspect than the earlier ones. They perpetuated the father's double firebox and the son's valves, and did very well while the old, light carriage stock lasted. In 1876, W. G. Beattie cut a caper. He designed and ordered from Sharp, Stewart and Company twenty new large 4-4-0 bogie express engines, with piston valves, and hopefully put them on to the West of England expresses. They were most unfortunate engines. Like several early 4-4-0 classes elsewhere, their boiler power was inadequate, and the valves were always smashing up. Their designer, in fact, spoilt his reputation with them. It was remarked that this was the only original design to be built by him; everything else was either based on his father's work or ready-made by Beyer, Peacock and Company. This was unfair to a man who undoubtedly knew a lot about valves and the art of making an engine *go*. Following the fiasco of the bogie engines, W. G. Beattie resigned from the London and South Western Railway, which his father had served in successive capacities since

the beginning, and William Adams succeeded him in 1878.
W. G. Beattie outlived both Adams and Dugald Drummond, who
came after.

The general reputation of the South Western in Victorian times
was that of a railway with rather slow trains, very heavy traffic,
and a difficult main line. But there were some good trains, even
outstanding ones. In 1841, the fastest trains took 2 hours 50 minutes
on the 78-mile journey between Nine Elms and Southampton.
In 1847, 105 minutes were allowed, and in the following year,
with the opening of the extension to Waterloo, making the London-
Southampton run one of 79 miles, the expresses took 110 minutes,
which was still excellent. J. Gooch's larger single express engines
were used. At over 43 m.p.h. average, they were unrivalled on
standard gauge. Later there was a sad deterioration on this, the
company's original main line, but things were better with the West
of England expresses, which competed with the broad-gauge Great
Western and Bristol and Exeter Railways.

Not that they were brilliant in the early 'sixties, when the line
was new. In 1862, the principal down express of the day was the
one o'clock out of Waterloo, which reached Exeter Queen Street
at 5.45 p.m., or at a fraction over 36 m.p.h. including stops.
Start-to-stop speeds included 40 m.p.h., Waterloo to Basingstoke;
and 29¼ m.p.h. Axminster to Honiton, up the long bank. The
engines were usually Joseph Beattie's Undine class 6 ft. 6 in. 2-4-0's
of 1859, with double firebox, combustion chamber and jet-condenser
feed-water heater.

In 1874, the down afternoon express left Waterloo at 2.10 p.m.
and reached Exeter Queen Street at 6.25. It was not a heavy
train, for it dropped a substantial portion at Basingstoke, whence
one of the two engines took this on to Weymouth. Average speeds
were 42·75 m.p.h. to Basingstoke; 42·9 m.p.h. thence to Salisbury;
38 m.p.h. Salisbury to Yeovil Junction; and 48·75 m.p.h. on to
Exeter. At the latter, a stop was made by the ticket platform just
outside, where the working arrival was 6.23 p.m., giving a start-to-
stop average, Yeovil Junction to Exeter, exceeding 50 m.p.h., an
excellent performance over such a road. There had been no
important change in the types of engine used since fourteen years
before. During the early 'seventies, the 2.10 was worked down to
Salisbury on alternate days by Joseph Beattie's 6 ft. 6 in. *Styx*
and W. G. Beattie's 6 ft. *Reindeer*. They were Yeovil engines, and
went forward from Salisbury on the following slow train. *Reindeer*
is illustrated on the 10.15 Exeter-Waterloo train at the beginning
of the 'eighties. The old 2.10 down was the South Western show

train in the ' seventies. It was named the Beeswing, like the Great Western's Dutchman after a celebrated racehorse.

Good coloured pictures of them are rare, and accurately painted models few, so it is not widely realised today what brilliant and graceful things were the old Beattie express engines of the London and South Western Railway, especially in the 'seventies, when they had much polished brass and had been restyled by the younger Beattie. They were more flamboyant, more Baroque, than most British engines; they had numerous complicated accessories, without at the same time achieving thereby the untidiness and clumsiness of contemporary French locomotives. An excellent F. Moore coloured plate of *Ariel*, as running in Joseph Beattie's time, was published in *The Locomotive* in 1912, and in one of the coloured plates of *Some Classic Locomotives* I have endeavoured to represent *St. George* in the days of W. G. Beattie.

Similar compliments cannot be paid to the general ruck of Beattie carriages. Up to the 'eighties, the South Western coaching stock was a collective prodigy. Though I doubt whether, by that time, it could muster quite such hoary antiques as those on the remoter broad-gauge branches of the Great Western, or quite such deplorable specimens as the South Eastern Railway was wont to inflict on its long-suffering third class, few railways could beat the South Western for the unspoilt medieval aspect of important long-distance trains. It was probably due to the fact that Joseph Beattie had been responsible for them from the beginning, through Gooch's time, that all the carriages took on the dignity of family heirlooms.

They were usually four-wheeled, occasionally six-wheeled, with three first-class compartments, or four second or third, an extra axle allowing for an extra compartment. Until 1876, when W. G. Beattie added a full and generous 12 in. at one glorious swoop, the standard distance between third-class partitions was 4 ft. 7 in. In these old thirds, the seat was a narrow board shelf, with the partition back stopping short at a sub-shoulder level. Pot lamps, sometimes sparsely disposed, emphasised the gloom of night travel. The painting now reproduced of one of the Beyer-Peacock tank engines on an up Plymouth train in the 'seventies shows a choice selection of Beattie coaches. The first and fifth are standard thirds, of which 93 were built between 1862 and 1866; the second coach, a first class of 1858; next, behind Aunt Marigold's head, is seen a second class as built between 1853 and 1860, possibly an ex-first, and after that a composite of 1873. The distantly seen van is also a survivor of the 'fifties. A close-up of a van occurs in the photograph of Crediton and in the old print called " Farewell ". In the latter original, this van is in two shades of dirty green, and the coaches are buff (possibly faded salmon). A more respectable assortment is shown in the picture of *Reindeer*. Here, the oldest carriage is second from the tender; it is a saloon of 1865 with a spacious lavatory—a regular audience chamber—at the leading end. The other carriages are of W. G. Beattie's types, beginning with a brake-third of 1876. Its liberal look-out arrangements for the guard were noteworthy, and of its period it was by no means a bad coach; also good was the second class following the saloon.

But there was no winter heating on that train, except by foot-warmers. My father handed down to me a superb memory of my grandfather arising in his wrath one frosty morning at Waterloo in 1881. The scene was one of those saloons, in which my grandmother was being packed off to Sidmouth to recover from something. The carriage was chilly as a morgue, but when the old lady finally rolled away to Devon, she was the better for about a score of footwarmers, sprawling all over the floor like reposing turtle in a tank.

Prominent in many old Beattie carriages were the " Müller's lights ", little portholes in the partitions, giving one a view of the people next door. They were put in after Franz Müller murdered Thomas Briggs in a North London train in 1864, and were still to be seen on country trains in the 'nineties. The different colours were also noteworthy. Joseph Beattie favoured varnished mahogany or teak as a variant to plain chocolate. In the 'seventies, several experiments seem to have been made, most memorably with greens and yellow-greens. The pinkish-brown, officially known as " salmon ", which was to survive until the nineteen-twenties on many carriages, has been recorded as appearing at the end of the 'seventies, though Mr. Wickham Legg, for many years a director of *The Railway Gazette*, told me that he saw at Winchester one of the first bogie carriages on the South Western, about 1880 or 1881, and that he rather believed that it was green. Mr. Frank Box recalls that later still, in the middle 'eighties, he saw a train of dark green coaches at Richmond.

Antique they may have been, but the Beattie carriages were undoubtedly well built. Two saloons belonging to the old royal train, which went to the Kent and East Sussex and the Shropshire and Montgomeryshire Railway, seemed to go on for ever, indeed, the S. and M. specimen, dating from 1844 or earlier, is still in use at the time of writing. The bodies of others served as sheds, notably outside Vauxhall and Waterloo, where for many years there was an ancient relic of the fifties. A six-wheel inspection car of 1877 remained in service as such when I saw it at Three Bridges, Southern Railway, in 1931, still painted in the old "salmon" colour.

Reverting to passengers' communication, "Müller's lights" were not liked by passengers. Old ladies were terrified when Tony Lumpkin grinned at them through the little hole; lovers, too, found that they gave the leering *voyeur* a stage-box position. Mr., afterwards Sir William Preece, when telegraph superintendent of the South Western company, made a trial of electric bells in the middle 'sixties, but a return was made to the old outside cord, which survived to the end of the century. They were all fallible. Even so, the southern railway companies showed more enterprise in this direction than their northern neighbours.

During the 'eighties and 'nineties, the London and South Western main-line trains rapidly assumed a much more modern appearance than that so long familiar. The old Beattie 2-4-0 engines gravitated to country services, though for quite a long time they continued to work expresses between Bournemouth and Weymouth, and some fast trains on the old main line to Waterloo. Nearly all the surviving single-wheelers were broken up at once, though *Victoria*, of 1859, knocked about until 1885.

William Adams perpetuated the Beattie practice of outside cylinders, though it was indeed his own, which he had employed previously on the North London and Great Eastern Railways. What was odd was that the younger Beattie, in his unfortunate bogie engines, had anticipated the Adams skyline. His plain chimney on these was, however, in one piece; that of Adams had a separate base. Early Adams domes, too, were small, with a lubricator on top.

The first three Adams classes were all 4-4-0. In 1879 appeared the "Steamrollers" and "Ironclads", tender and tank respectively, with 5 ft. 7 in. coupled wheels and very small solid bogie wheels. The former, weighing 47 tons without tender, were the heaviest and most powerful main-line engines yet seen on the South Western. People were impressed, also, by their sturdy simplicity. The old complications had vanished. Like the Beattie bogie engines, however, they had steam brakes. In their time they worked every sort of South Western train except the fastest expresses, and the last one, No. 0162, originally No. 388, ran until the end of 1925 from Exmouth Junction shed. The "Ironclads", so named on account of their massive side tanks covered with rivets, handled the heavier suburban trains, which were getting beyond the capacity of the little Beattie tank engines. Like the Plymouth tanks, they had insufficient water and coal capacity, on account of which they were rebuilt with longer frames at the rear, carrying an additional tank and enlarged bunker over a radial truck, making them 4-4-2's. One of them, No. 374, was in a very destructive accident at Clapham Junction in 1892. When hauling a down Windsor line train she overtook the fortunately empty carriages of a return Bournemouth excursion. Two were thrown on top of the engine, which ignited the gas escaping from the broken pipes. The glare from the burning train was visible for many miles around. This smash deserves recall in that it was the first on record in which a serious fire could be ascribed to the oil-gas lighting of trains. Like many other railways, the South Western had gone over from oil-pots to gas in the 'eighties.

Adams brought out his first express passenger locomotives in 1880, and one of these is now illustrated. They had 6 ft. 7 in. coupled wheels, 18 by 24 in. cylinders, 160 lb. pressure, and with a weight of 46¾ tons without tender, they were among the heaviest and most powerful express engines in Great Britain when they were new. Beyer, Peacock and Company built them, and such was the workmanship put into them that when they were broken up, over forty years after, most of the original rivets were still sound.

Like other early Adams locomotives, they were at first painted umber with black bands and green and orange lines. The famous light green did not come until the later 'eighties. Adams dropped engine naming, though he perpetuated most of the names on the surviving Beattie engines, even casting new brass plates for them. The only new engines to be named were the little 0-4-0 shunters in Southampton Docks, from the early 'nineties on, and a small 0-4-4 tank specially named *Alexandra* for the opening of the Bisley Camp branch in July 1890.

The first 4-4-0 express engines with 7 ft. 1 in. coupled wheels were built in 1883, and thereafter Adams followed the old Beattie practice of using seven-footers for certain of the expresses east of Salisbury. His designs increased somewhat in size in the early 'nineties, and his last express engines of both varieties, built during the early 'nineties, were very imposing indeed. Still more so would have been an eight-foot single which he designed but never built, maybe fortunately, for the South Western was never a line for single drivers, and was the first major railway in England to discard them.

Much of the work on these later designs was done by W. F. Pettigrew, later of the Furness Railway, for in old age William Adams, one of the most delightful and genial of engineers amongst a school of martinets, gradually lost his memory. For some years after his retirement in 1895 he was a familiar figure in Putney, where he lived, an inarticulate giant with an expression of vague benevolence, pottering about the quiet suburban avenues and on the Heath under the care of his faithful male nurse. Poor old Father Adams ! He was a great fellow in his day—a dashing engineer-commander in Victor Emmanuel's navy, excellent husband to his Isabella, and father to their numerous children, something more than an ordinary designer, and a sound locomotive man. When he left the South Western, the enginemen found his successor, Dugald Drummond, the devil to pay.

Adams's two most noteworthy contributions to locomotive design were his Vortex blastpipe and his bogie. The latter, with controlled sideplay to the central pin, came to be used all over the world. Of the remaining locomotives of his time on the London and South Western, the best remembered were the Jubilee 6 ft. 1 in. 0-4-2 mixed traffics, built from 1887 onwards, which were everywhere, and his 0-6-0 heavy goods, some of which survive after nearly seventy years. After 1887, passenger tank engines were of the inside cylinder 0-4-4 type instead of 4-4-2 with outside cylinders. Fifty of the goods engines went to the Balkans and the Middle East in the 1914-18 war, and never returned.

During the 'eighties, South Western passenger traffic grew very heavy; there was a certain deliberation about even the fastest trains, and their punctuality was not in quite the same street as that of the London and North Western. On the other hand, by then even the best trains carried third-class passengers, whom the Great Western still kept out of such lordly trains as the Flying Dutchman. The best L.S.W.R. down express in 1883 was the 2.30 p.m. from Waterloo, successor to the old Beeswing, which averaged 44·3 m.p.h. net speed from Waterloo to Exeter, or 41·2 m.p.h. gross, including stops at Basingstoke, Andover, Salisbury, Sherborne and Yeovil Junction. Its fastest run was the final stretch from Yeovil Junction to Exeter Ticket Platform, including the climb to Honiton Tunnel, which was made at just over 46 m.p.h. average, poorer running than a decade before. In the following year, the fastest booked run was one at 50⅓ m.p.h. from Basingstoke to Woking.

During this time, the carriages improved very greatly on the better services. Many bogie vehicles were built from 1881 onwards. The new third class of 1885 markedly resembled that of the Midland at the same time, and to younger generations be it explained that this is praise indeed. It must be admitted that this high quality on the South Western was confined to the express trains of the time. Gas lighting was a more questionable improvement. Lavatories were provided, but grudgingly at first. In the early 'nineties, W. Panter improved headroom by raising the cantrails and using a semi-elliptical roof, and some very sumptuous centre-corridor carriages (" Eagles ") were built for the American boat expresses. Local train stock was slower to improve; not until the turn of the century were modern suburban bogie sets introduced, though the despised and disreputable South Eastern had built a few right back in the early 'eighties.

Still, having reformed, the South Western did the thing thoroughly. By 1912, every regular passenger service on the L.S.W.R. was worked with bogie stock, from the best expresses to the Wadebridge market train. The four-wheel carriages had vanished; the surviving six-wheelers were marshalled into block sets for race and troop trains, and for a few workmen's trains. The latter loaded up to eighteen, in two sets of nine. Of other major railways, only the North Eastern and the Lancashire and Yorkshire made such extensive use of bogie carriages at that time.

During the 'nineties, tricomposite lavatory carriages were built in large numbers for the West of England expresses, to the great comfort and relief of mothers with large families going their several ways to Ilfracombe and Bude. With what curious affection could a little boy regard his own distorted reflection on a folding nickel-plate basin, or the Throne of Venus adorned with choice chrysan-themums ! At the turn of the century, the old centre-corridor boat-train carriages were gangwayed through to kitchen brake vans. For a while dining-car service co-existed with the older Pullman cars, introduced in the early 'eighties, but the latter were transferred finally to the Brighton line at the end of 1911.

To the Locomotive Department came Dugald Drummond, as rough a block of Scottish granite as ever rolled down the banks of Clyde, knocking chips and scraping moss from other rocks. The old order had indeed changed, and so it was with his work also. The new engines had little affinity with those of Adams. The first was an experimental four-cylinder simple, No. 720, with a leading bogie and two pairs of uncoupled driving wheels. This engine, the largest yet built for the South Western, was memorably hybrid. Boiler, frames, big-ends, bogie and cab belonged patently to the Drummond school established in Scotland, but the lack of coupling rods, and the outside cylinders with valves underneath, worked by Joy gear, shouted of Crewe and of Webb's three-cylinder com-pounds. No. 720 looked as if, in the unholy darkness of Carlisle Citadel, Drummond's *Waverley* had dallied with Webb's *Jeanie Deans* and had begotten monstrous offspring.

Five very similar engines were built later, and the original one eventually acquired a very large boiler, but more useful early additions by Drummond to the South Western locomotives were his 5 ft. goods engines (the " Black Motors ") and the first of his excellent 5 ft. 7 in. 0-4-4 tanks. The latter, which later on worked much of the suburban traffic, began by hauling Plymouth expresses west of Exeter. There, No. 252 was soon in an alarming derailment near Tavistock. About three years before, there had been the Doublebois accident on the Great Western (*q.v. ante*), and the use of 0-4-4 tank engines at high speed was liable to agitate the Board of Trade* when anything went wrong. So it was this time, although here the permanent way was at fault, and the new Drummond tanks were taken off the Plymouth expresses. All the same, and for many years after, both these and comparable engines of the Midland and the North Eastern companies ran steadily at high speeds elsewhere. All save two of the South Western series are still running at the time of writing. The two casualties have been No. 126, which was rebuilt and afterwards scrapped, and No. 672 which fell down the car hoist at Waterloo.

For express trains, Drummond standardised the 4-4-0 with inside cylinders and 6 ft. 7 in. driving wheels, similar to his Scottish designs, but larger, especially in the case of the T 9's built from 1899 onwards. Most noteworthy about these was the long coupled wheel-base, 10 ft., allowing for a generous grate area (24 sq. ft.) and, in later examples, the cross-tubes in the firebox which brought the total heating surface to 1,500 sq. ft. Cylinders were $18\frac{1}{2}$ by 26 in. and pressure 175 lb. The work of these beautiful engines belongs to the present century, surely, for even now as I write fifty years after, all sixty-six of them are still in existence.

Let us round off this chapter with a brief retrospect of the South Western train services of the 'nineties. In the summer of 1894, the afternoon express to the west of England ran to Basingstoke at a start-to-stop average of 48 m.p.h.; Basingstoke to Salisbury, 46·6; Salisbury to Sherborne, 47; Sherborne to Exeter Queen Street, 54 m.p.h. I love the way they knocked up the average by sprinting down from Honiton after the toil up ! This was surely the way Webb's L.N.W.R. No. 300 *Compound* failed when Adams gave her a fair trial on the South Western in 1884. This same train, running via St. Budeaux, reached Plymouth Friary in 121 minutes from Exeter Queen Street. The engines were usually Adams large 4-4-0's as far as Exeter. Thereafter, the engine might be an Adams 4-4-2 tank or one of the surviving Beattie 4-4-0's,

* The time of the Ministry of Transport was not yet.

The Honiton Climb: West of England express pulling away from Seaton Junction in 1945; Southern Railway engine No. 21C5, *Canadian Pacific*

rebuilt and considerably improved by Adams in the late 'eighties. Some tremendous running used to take place in the up direction on the steep drop from Okehampton to Yeoford.

At the end of the 'nineties, a most refreshing reform took place in speeds over the Bournemouth road, though the old Southampton terminus scarcely benefited from this. In 1899, there were two expresses timed to cover the 107½ miles non-stop to Bournemouth Central in 125 minutes, or at 51¾ m.p.h. West of Bournemouth there was some very good running over short stretches, and for a while the up Weymouth express was booked to run from Dorchester to Wareham, 15 miles, 5 chains, in 15 minutes. The actual working time was 17 minutes, but the drivers made it a point of honour to do it at the booked average of 60·2 m.p.h., and frequently did so.

CHAPTER SIXTEEN

From Drummond to Bulleid

THE early years of the present century saw on the South Western a continuation of the steady reform which had been begun by Adams and Panter, with Dugald Drummond firmly in charge of the locomotive department and, after a few years, Surrey Warner responsible for the carriages. Coach-building was carried out at Eastleigh, and there too, after the end of the first decade, locomotive construction began also. Eastleigh's first-born was the little 0-4-0 rail-motor tank engine No. 101 of class C 14, with outside Walschaerts gear, built in 1910. At one time she worked on the Bournemouth-Ringwood service via Hurn, and after serving the L.S.W.R. for seven years was sold to the Government. The old works at Nine Elms was swept away together with the old round running shed, into the limbo which was to engulf the old Waterloo Station.

Like the neighbouring Great Western, which had seemed to get up and shake itself after sloughing the broad gauge, the South Western showed increasing liveliness in its train services, and responded to the Great Western's thunderous bids for American traffic with spirit and dash, in spite of the much more difficult road to Plymouth via Salisbury. But in one respect the South Western never came into line with its neighbours, for to this day it has no water troughs. Early in the century there was talk about putting them down near Gillingham (Dorset) and waterscoops were fitted to the tenders of a few of Drummond's earlier 4-6-0 engines. But the troughs never came. It was published abroad that the undulating South Western profile gave no convenient levels for their installation. Let us do a little odious comparison of the Great Western and South Western lines between London and Exeter. Aldermaston troughs on the Great Western are 45-46 miles from Paddington; the same distance from Waterloo is an apparently eligible level between Newnham Siding and Barton Mill signalbox. Near Westbury, the Great Western line has troughs 97 miles from Paddington; the same distance from Waterloo is the level between Tisbury and Tisbury Gates. Between Cogload Junction and Creech

Junction on the Great Western are more troughs, 139 miles from Paddington; at like distance from Waterloo comes the level before Chard Junction. Of course, there is a plausible reason for the lack of South Western troughs—no water supply. What? No water in the lush rainy South-west? No water where water pours off the Downs and off Salisbury Plain? No water where the Nadder feeds its water-meadows and where the twin villages of Teffont Ewyas and Teffont Magna sit side by side on the vast fount that gives them their name? Well, well; it has long been the other official reason, so doubtless there is no water.

In spite of all this, the South Western boat expresses from Devonport managed to run at high speeds through the night to London, making one service stop, for changing engines, at Temple-combe. The Great Western, over which they had to pass between Cowley Bridge Junction and Exeter St. Davids, used to *exercise its right* to stop the South Western flyers there also. The engines were usually T 9 4-4-0's and the carriages were the old, gorgeous " Eagle Express " stock with gangways and kitchen-brakes added. Large bogie tenders made up for the lack of troughs to some extent. There was no doubt that the T 9's were fast, free-running engines, worthy rivals to the larger and more powerful Great Western " Cities ", which indeed they have outlasted by many years. Lightly loaded, hauled by the T 9's, or, after 1904, sometimes by the similar though larger boilered class L 12, the boat trains used to make some remarkable runs. In *The Trains We Loved* I tried to convey something of the enthusiasm and excitement of that un-official contest with the Great Western, but for the South Western it had a shocking end when, in the small hours of July 1, 1906 (the day the Great Western opened the Castle Cary–Langport cut-off, and got the advantage in distance), the South Western up boat express, headed by L 12 engine No. 421, was derailed and almost totally destroyed while rounding Salisbury's curves at most reckless speed.

The original idea on the South Western had been to rush the Transatlantic passengers to London in time to get to their hotels, leep off the journey, and wake for a late breakfast. It entailed going to bed round about four o'clock a.m. After the smash, the trains proceeded more sedately, and sleeping cars were put on, so that a properly complete night's rest could be passed on the London and South Western Railway. Surrey Warner's sleepers were very creditable cars, notable for having movable brass beds instead of bunks, but their South Western career was short. From 1910 on-wards, the South Western company endeavoured, most successfully, to concentrate all its American traffic on Southampton, with but a short railway run to London. The sleeping cars were sold to the Great Western, which, having lost two in a fire, used the remaining couple for many years.

In 1905, Dugald Drummond brought out No. 330, the first of his four-cylinder 4-6-0 engines, and at the time the largest passenger engine in Great Britain, with 6 ft. coupled wheels and an outsize in boilers to supply the four cylinders, but this and several succeeding varieties of 6 ft. 4-6-0 were scarcely brilliant as express engines, and spent most of their working lives on heavy South Wales coal trains between Salisbury and Southampton. Considerably better were the 6 ft. 7 in. 4-6-0's of the 443 class (1911), known variously as " Paddleboxes ", because of their great broad semi-continuous splashers, or as " Double-breasters ", owing to their broad flat fronts covering the smokebox and the outside piston valves above the platforms. They were much improved by the fitting of superheaters by Robert Urie, but still tended to run hot. This fault was rectified to a great extent by raising the platforms and cutting out the paddlebox splashers during 1930-1. All but one of the ten were then given Wakefield mechanical lubricators, an improvement suggested long ago to Dugald Drummond by a rash driver, who was all but hurled out of the window for it. Drummond's end, in 1912, was violent but perhaps fitting, for he was fatally injured by an explosion in Eastleigh Works.

Now Drummond's four-coupled express engines were more successful by far than his 4-6-0's, from the T 9's to the D 15's, the final big ones of 1912. In his 6 ft. 1 in. 4-4-0's of 1903, the S 11 class, built for the West Country lines, he perpetuated a tradition begun by Joseph Beattie as far back as 1859, when the hills of Devon had first loomed on the South Western horizon. The T 9's could certainly run, and one used to see these little engines walking off with quite astounding loads at holiday times. Charles Rous-Marten, and, later, Cecil J. Allen, dealt faithfully by them. The real fun was between 1903 and 1906. In the former year, the Great Western's fastest time to Exeter was 3 hours 35 minutes, and the South Western's, over the shorter but stiffer route, 3½ hours. On June 2, the South Western cut its best time by 15 minutes, and the drivers were tacitly encouraged to run ahead of time, with the result that there were instances of the old T 9's making Salisbury (83¾ miles with all its ups and downs and roundabouts) in 82 minutes. With one of the competing boat expresses, No. 336, one of the later T 9's, ran from Templecombe to Waterloo, 112·5 miles, in 104·5 minutes, average speed approximately 64·6 m.p.h. On the Southampton road, the only outstanding running at this time was with the boat trains, one of which (engine No. 708) on June 5, 1901, covered the 79½ miles from the dockside to Waterloo in 76 minutes. The load was light—three of the old " Eagle " carriages and a van, but the run was a fine one for all that, with necessarily slow start and finish. As already remarked, on the old main line Bournemouth was favoured by non-stop runs in 1899,* and with the introduction of the T 14 " Paddlebox " 4-6-0's in 1911, the time was cut from 2 hours 5 minutes to 2 hours for the 107·9 miles. In absence of troughs, it could be a very near thing in the matter of water, even with 4,500 gallon bogie tenders. The usual week-day load consisted of two four-coach lavatory sets, amounting to 208 tons tare. In 1914 there were two runs daily in each direction, non-stop between Waterloo and Bournemouth Central, but the 1914-18 war put an end to such running, which did not reappear until the summer of 1929. In 1914 the fastest time between Waterloo and Exeter was 3 hours 14 minutes, in both directions.

Robert Urie, who succeeded the late Drummond, had been with him as works manager at Eastleigh, and, years before, at St. Rollox on the Caledonian. Yet for all Drummond's possible influence, Urie's work was very different. He revived the use of two outside cylinders, favoured in the past by Gooch, the Beatties and Adams. He built unexceptionally large engines, outwardly distinguished by high platforms, outside Walschaerts gear and piston valves, and a general aspect which amateurs of the period regarded as " Continental ", accentuated in the later engines by very severe-looking chimneys with a narrow beading below a capuchon. Most of us boys were horrified at such monsters, and invented slanderous stories against them. I was one of the caddish exceptions. The first time I saw one of Urie's new express engines of 1918, at Salisbury in that same year, I returned thanks in a loud voice that my sanctified London and South Western should produce so superb a thing.

Bob Urie brought out his first big 4-6-0's, eleven six-foot mixed traffic engines, in 1914. Ten were quite new, and one, No. 335, was a very thorough rebuild of an odd Drummond four-cylinder engine of 1907. These, and some very similar engines which appeared immediately after formation of the Southern Railway, perpetuated the " mixed traffic " tradition of the South Western line, which Drummond had kept up in his time with large numbers of 5 ft. 7 in. 4-4-0's. Urie's practice continued the use of piston

* Sam Fay, then superintendent of the line, wanted a 115 minute timing, and even ran a trial train down in 110 minutes. Then the Chairman read him the Riot Act.

valves and Walschaerts gear, which Drummond had put on his later and larger engines, but put an end to the smokebox steam dryers and water-tube fireboxes. Urie also introduced super-heating, and eight of his first engines were so fitted, four with Schmidt superheaters and four with Robinson's type. Later, he superheated all new engines and many of Drummond's. His Eastleigh superheater contained a maximum of 24 elements, and raised the temperature of the steam from 380 degrees F. at the regulator (180 lb. pressure) to 650 degrees. An excellent drawing of this superheater occurred in his supplementary lectures to Drummond's *Lectures on the Locomotive.*

The original Urie 6 ft. 4-6-0's of 1914 worked right through the ensuing war years without a general repair, and surely proved themselves. They were not conspicuous in the public eye. Fast night goods and van trains were their chief concern; one was normally on the Tavy—the night express goods from Nine Elms to Plymouth, which they worked east of Exeter. In minor details they showed a quaint throwback to the old Beattie 6 ft. 2-4-0's, for the platform dropped in a shallow step behind the outside cylinders.

Urie, like Drummond, made great use of interchangeable com-ponents, common to two or more classes.* One boiler did for the 5 ft. 7 in. goods (S 15, 1920), the 6 ft. 7 in. N 15 express engines of 1918, and the later 6 ft. 4-6-0's of class H 15, turned out in 1924; the 4-6-2 and 4-8-0 tanks of 1921 had the same boiler, valve gear and bogie, and so on. The express engines, on their firs appearance, had 22 by 28 in. cylinders. The last years of old Bob Urie's career may have appeared frustrated. This reverend engineer—he strongly resembled a benevolent Presbyterian minister —came late to his professional majority. For most of the time that he held office, war was in full blast, and the more obvious type of locomotive heroics necessarily in abeyance. In 1923 the South Western was incorporated in the Southern Railway, Urie's last engines—the second series of H 15's—appeared in the following year, and with them the separate history of London and South Western locomotives came to its close.

Yet his influence was lasting under the Southern Company. Richard Maunsell of the South Eastern and Chatham succeeded, and for a standard express engine he took Urie's design of 1918, the N 15, gave it smaller (20½ in.) cylinders and 200 lb. pressure, improved the front end design, and thus produced one of the most

---

* Largely traceable to Stroudley's practice on the London, Brighton and South Coast Railway.

useful and reliable express passenger engines the country had yet known. He dealt similarly with Urie's S 15 goods class, and a distinguished authority has tersely described them as " best value for money ever built ".

Before leaving the old London and South Western Company, one may recall one half-forgotten campaign in the South Western-Great Western feud of the early nineteen-hundreds. It began when the Great Western started a service to St. Malo via Plymouth. Now, Brittany was on the London and South Western Railway, whose name was writ large on a prominent building in St. Malo docks. *St. Malo*, neatly inscribed in white on red, was as much a standard L.S.W.R. coach label as *Aldershot*, or *Padstow*, or that delightfully crowded one *Gosport via West Meon*. In 1908 the South Western counter-attacked by opening a service to Ireland via Southampton and Queenstown, with the benevolent co-operation of the White Star Line. The trip was weekly, lasted about 25 hours, cost £4 11s. first class or £3 7s. second class, and for a glorious day and night the passengers could (with reasonable luck) stuff themselves with everything the famous White Star *cuisine* had to offer. It was a luxurious way of going to Ireland, which Fishguard-Rosslare never has been, but a Wednesdays-only service had its drawbacks.

Maunsell's version of the N15's became a general-service express engine for all the Southern Railway, and they came much in the public eye through a quarrel, the curious history of which may some day be told. The thing broke surface with a series of violent and obviously inspired Press attacks on the new Southern Railway Company, a few of them mildly justifiable and most of them spiteful. The Southern's counter-offensive comprised a popularity hunt, including a grand scheme for stimulating public imagination by naming the engines. For years, named engines had been few in the South country. The practice had almost died out on the South Western with the passing of the Beattie engines; there were but few engine names on the Brighton, which once had named all its locomotives; *Snowdrop*, *Europa*, *Xanthus*, *Huz* and *Buz*, *Flirt*, and other highflyers of the London, Chatham and Dover were long forgotten, and in all its history the South Eastern had managed to produce only such seldom deer as *Folkstone (sic)*, *Flying Fox*, *Joan of Arc*, and for a few brief months *Onward*. On the Southern, the N 15's suddenly blossomed as the King Arthur class. *Excalibur*, the original engine of 1918, flashed, mysterious and brave, and the Knights thundered over the hills of Wessex.

The Southern trains at this time perpetuated the final London and South Western livery, for the engines were a yellowish-green, plainly lined out in black and white, while the carriages were sage green, lined-out in black and orange, with white roofs. This last style appeared on the first electric suburban trains of 1915, then, for no apparent reason, on the old first-class race sets, and in 1919 on some new steel-panelled corridor trains built by Warner for the Bournemouth expresses. It was generally introduced about 1921. The West of England expresses continued for some years with older corridor coaches and diners, many of which last had clerestory roofs and no side doors except to the central kitchens. The decorative schemes were respectably stuffy. At the end of the nineteen-twenties Mr. Maunsell made great improvements in seating by ordering, it is said, several varieties and, in a spirit of pure constructive criticism, sitting in each in turn. Certainly, thereafter, the Southern Railway achieved some of the most comfortable third-class carriages in the world.

In 1926 Maunsell produced his first entirely new express engine (that is in design) for the Southern Railway, the legended *Lord Nelson*, which, with her tractive effort of 33,500 lb. at 85 per cent. of 220 lb. per square inch was, briefly yet gloriously, the most powerful passenger engine in the country. A return was made to four-cylinder propulsion, following some experiments with the old Drummond 4-6-0 No. 0449.* The cranks of this engine were reset at 135 degrees to give eight impulses to each revolution, in order to produce a more even torque with a softer exhaust. Even those most cautious people, the British enginemen, agreed that it caused a wondrous transformation in an engine which they had never before expected to praise, and the new engine was made likewise. Sixteen Lord Nelsons were built, some differing slightly from others, all but the original one (No. 850) during 1928 and 1929. No. 852, *Sir Walter Raleigh*, was given a self-trimming tender, and also survived a direct hit in the bombing of London during September, 1940. Other Battle of Britain casualties included No. 458 (a " Paddlebox ") and No. 257, an Adams 0-6-0 tank. Only No. 458 had to be broken up. The *Raleigh*, hit at the firebox end, had new half-frames welded on.

All the Lord Nelsons had the usual 6 ft. 7 in. coupled wheels except No. 859, *Lord Hood*, which had 6 ft. 3 in. and all except No. 865, *Sir John Hawkins*, had the 135 degrees setting of the cranks. O. V. S. Bulleid improved the design by installing Lemaitre multiple blast-pipe nozzles and wide chimneys; the four $16\frac{1}{2}$ by

---

* The new No. 449 was *Sir Torre*, a King Arthur built in 1925; there were two " duplicates " at this time, the 0449 mentioned and No. 449, an Adams seven-footer built in 1883.

26 in. cylinders remained unchanged. The Nelsons have been noteworthy engines, if not quite such an outstanding investment as the King Arthurs. The design had a strong bearing on others, to wit the Royal Scots of the L.M.S.R.

On the West of England main line the King Arthurs held much of their own until the coming of the Bulleid Pacifics in the 'forties. Beyond Exeter the most powerful engines allowable over Meldon Viaduct were an imported design, the South Eastern and Chatham type 2-6-0's of Mr. Maunsell, and fast passenger trains continued to be handled by old Drummond 4-4-0 engines, albeit much rebuilt. The year 1930 saw the advent on the Southern of Maunsell's Schools class 4-4-0's, with three cylinders of similar dimensions to the Nelsons' four, and, for their size and type, very large and powerful boilers; with only two coupled axles, the adhesive weight was as high as 42 tons, but the balancing was excellent and the class could run wherever a King Arthur might. Pressure was the same as the Nelsons. While the Schools were to be best-known on the old South Eastern main line, and for a while on the difficult Portsmouth Direct line, they come within our survey on account of the excellent work which they have done on fast Bournemouth expresses, making the resuscitated non-stop run of what now came to be known as the Bournemouth Limited, with dashing regularity. No. 900 *Eton* was the first. When the names of the original batch were announced, someone remarked that there was no *Westminster*, a black injustice, seeing that Westminster's half-boarders and home-boarders suffered more than boys of any other foundation from the vagaries of the Southern Railway's suburban train service under conditions of fog, ice, snow and chronic congestion. So No. 908 became *Westminster*. *Floreat alma domus!*

The South Western Railway had been an early user of Pullman cars, more particularly on the Bournemouth line, though there was a short-lived Pullman working to Exeter in the 'eighties. Sherlock Holmes summed up the misadventures of Silver Blaze in a Pullman car on the South Western, returning from the Winchester races. Either Holmes momentarily forgot which line he was on, an unlikely hypothesis, or the faithful Doctor misreported him as saying, at Clapham Junction, that they would be at Victoria in ten minutes. Still, it was prophetic, for the last of the South Western Pullmans were transferred to the London, Brighton and South Coast in 1911.

More modern Pullman cars reappeared on the Southampton boat trains some years after the formation of the Southern Company. An all-Pullman train, the Bournemouth Belle, began running on

Sundays, then on week-days during the summer, and from the beginning of 1936 daily all the year. It was usually hauled by a Nelson. The Devon Belle is much more recent—1947. As remarked, 1929 saw the return of the Bournemouth two-hour non-stop expresses, in the shape of the Bournemouth Limited, normally loaded up to 360 tons. Cecil J. Allen has recorded a run with 4-4-0 *Malvern* and 415 tons behind the tender covering the 107·9 miles in 114·5 minutes, while *King's Wimbledon*, with 345 tons, made it in a minute fraction over even time.

The eleven o'clock portmanteau train from Waterloo to the West of England became the Atlantic Coast Express in the course of the Southern's popularity drive, previously mentioned, the name being selected by open competition among imaginative employees, and bestowed in 1927. Its coaches had nine different destinations, and in summer, with duplicate and triplicate running, it became more of a service than a train. The 1939 timings of the Atlantic Coast Express included, 86 minutes Waterloo to Salisbury; 83 minutes Salisbury to Sidmouth Junction (75·8 miles); and 14 minutes for the final 12·2 miles to Exeter Central.

The late war, like its predecessor, packed up the fast train services of the great days of yore. But in the midst of it came Mr. O. V. S. Bulleid's first original engines. Hitherto, all we had seen of his practice had been an outbreak of wide chimneys and multiple blast-pipe nozzles on the Nelsons, some of the Schools, and six of the King Arthurs. We had heard something about Pacifics and 4-8-0's which Mr. Maunsell had designed but not built, and we wondered whether the new chief was about to serve them up at last.

He was not. The prodigy that emerged from Eastleigh in 1941 bore not the remotest resemblance to anything else on British—or foreign rails. *Channel Packet*, first of the Merchant Navy class three-cylinder Pacifics, beat imagination with her great but invisible boiler carrying 280 lb. pressure, her mysterious chain-driven radial valve gear shut up in a box, her firebox thermic syphons, her extraordinary air-smoothed casing and tumble-home tender, her 6 ft. 3 in. solid boxpok wheels and electric lighting installation. Here at last was something more than usually original. Also, I thought, on seeing her for the first time, here was the most imposing new locomotive that had issued from Eastleigh since Urie's first express engine of 1918. Of course, her aspect aroused a howl of execration from traditionalists in both professional and amateur circles,* but those who had admired were unrepentant, and today I love to see these noble engines thundering westward where long

* So did Churchward's 4 - 6 - 0's on the Great Western forty years earlier.

ago the baby, that was I, had come to know and love the Drummond T 9's.

Later I was in the party attending a trial run from Waterloo to Exeter, with an enormous train that stretched far out of Waterloo at the start. We got away like the wind through the suburbs, but something began to happen in the neighbourhood of Winchfield. We smelt things, the speed dropped, I put away the borrowed stopwatch that formed my luggage, and stuck my head out of the window. Yes, the great engine had to come off at Basingstoke. Clouds of smoke seemed to be coming from the box of tricks underneath. People rushed round, looking grave and anxious—except Mr. Bulleid himself. May I be forgiven for recording now that he looked like a boy with a new and wondrous mechanical toy that had done just what he expected it might, and furnished an excuse for more tinkering. Rescued by two veterans of Basingstoke, we picked up another Pacific at Salisbury, which proceeded to show us how such an engine could take a huge train up to Semley against vacuum brakes that leaked on, and also a new way of climbing to, and accelerating through, Honiton Tunnel, from a dead stand at Seaton Junction. It was a memorable journey in all respects.

Well, the Merchant Navies have proved themselves, and so have the similar, rather smaller West Countries, built at Brighton during 1945-6, which are proof against the restrictions in force on Meldon Viaduct, and consequently rub shoulders with such ancients as the three old Beattie engines at Wadebridge. The year 1942 saw the construction of the first new 0-6-0 goods engines to appear on the South Western main line since 1897, that fantastic but most efficient Q 1 class (an old friend of mine called it the Toad class), which contrives to achieve a tractive effort of 30,000 lb. with two 19 by 26 in. cylinders and an all-up weight of $51\frac{1}{4}$ tons. Here indeed is a locomotive cleared for action, for with a boiler weighing 22 tons, engineering restrictions allowed only 30 tons for all the rest of the engine. Hence certain normal portions of locomotive anatomy are lacking, with results peculiar, and shocking, to the eye. I have heard, even, of the sudden appearance of a Q 1 shaking the equanimity of a visiting Russian.

This is not surprising. What else could one expect of a man accustomed at home, not only to big engines with real chimneys, but to engines with wide railed-in platforms all round, confronted suddenly with something having a frying-pan for a chimney, a saucepan-lid for a dome, and no provision at all for enginemen wishing to circumnavigate the boiler, without running aground.

Having thus hinted that Mr. Bulleid gave to the Southern Railway, and to the South Western line, the ugliest British locomotives since the early days of the Glasgow and Garnkirk Railway, let us, in parting, waste no further invective, but conclude with a note on coaching practice.   Mr. Maunsell had inherited from the L.S.W.R. a stock of uniformly middling-good carriages.   There was nothing magnificent, like the old London and North Western twelve-wheelers, nor yet anything memorably bad, like all the North London coaches.   But from 1930 onwards the Southern Railway built the most comfortably-seated ordinary third-class carriages of any British Railway, and for steam services it built corridor stock only.   Mr. C. Lynes, who was chief draughtsman of carriages and wagons under Mr. Maunsell, designed the Airstream ventilator, which spread to all British railways, and under Mr. Bulleid the good work went on.   With that we must leave the South Western main line, now a not inconsiderable feature of the map of British Railways, beautiful as it has always been, and never more so than from the rear windows of the Devon Belle.